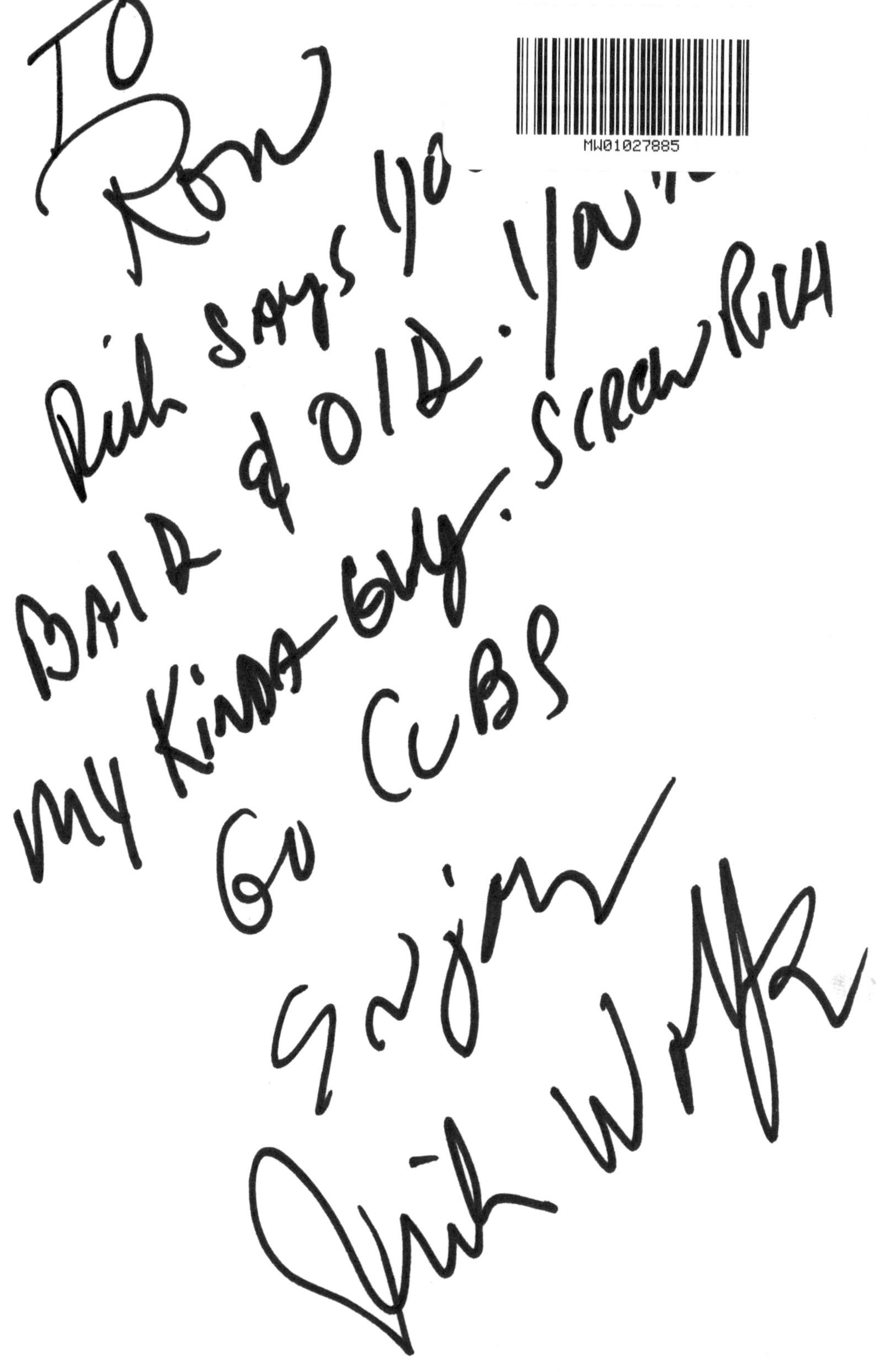

MW01027885
To Ron
Go Cubs
Enjoy

I Remember Harry Caray

---

by Rich Wolfe and George Castle

SPORTS PUBLISHING INC.
Champaign, IL 61820

Director of production, book design: Susan M. McKinney
Dustjacket design: Joe Buck

We have made every effort to trace ownership of copyrighted photos. If we have failed to give adequate credit, we will be pleased to make changes in future printings.

ISBN: 1-58261-002-9
Library of Congress Catalog Card Number: 98-86645

Sports Publishing Inc.
804 N. Neil
Champaign, IL 16820
www.SportsPublishingInc.com

Printed in the United States

For all the Cub fans growing up in the cheap seats of Wrigley Field,
waiting patiently, patiently, patiently . . .

—G.C.

To the Les Shepkers and Jack Marlows of the world—
Harry's type of guys.

—R.W.

"All right, everybody ... A one, A two, everybody ... A three ... Take me out to the ball game ... take me out to the crowd ... "

— ***The Sounds of Summer, from the Voice of Summer*** *(Photo courtesy of Steve Green).*

CONTENTS

"There goes Miss Chicago."

—***Harry Caray, any day*** *(Photo courtesy of Harry Caray's Restaurant).*

ACKNOWLEDGMENTS

Thanks have to go out to Dutchie and Chip Caray for being so gracious with their time and candid with their remarks in the midst of a tumultuous time in their lives. Thanks to Marty Cohn for his help on the project. More thanks must be given to the Chicago Cubs' front office staff and players for organizing their memories of Harry Caray. And thank you to everyone who shared their anecdotes.

Particular credit must be given to Hall of Famer Jack Brickhouse for authoring the foreword to this book. Brickhouse was recovering from surgery to remove a brain tumor and had a hoarse voice from a tube that had been placed in his throat during hospitalization. A pro's pro, just like Harry Caray, Brickhouse still was able to dictate the foreword in the great ad-libbed fashion that made him a Chicago broadcast legend. The stamina, endurance and positive attitudes that marked both Brickhouse and Caray are rarely duplicated anywhere else.

Yeoman's duties were performed by Craig DeVrieze. He spent many hours slaving away, transcribing many of the interviews from tape.

The editing of the manuscript couldn't have been accomplished without the computer skills of Laura Elizabeth Castle. Her old man is used to employing a 1980s vintage laptop computer. He had to wave in Laura from the bullpen. She's a maestro on the keyboard, moving files around like chess pieces. Welcome to the publishing business, Laura!

Thank you to Dreaming Dog Agency, as well as Peter Bannon, Mike Pearson, Susan McKinney, Joe Buck, Dave Kasel, Bret Kroencke and Amanda Romine from Sports Publishing Inc.

Rich Wolfe and George Castle
June 1998

"The Good Lord wants the Cubs to win."

— Harry Caray after the "immaculate deflection" bounced off Lee Smith's shoulder to start a game-ending double-play, August 2, 1984 *(Photo courtesy of Bill Wills).*

FOREWORD

Harry Caray and I were competitors, contemporaries, and most importantly, friends for more than 50 years. In that time, I met an unbelievable number of people who also knew Harry and had at least one story about him.

When we first met, Harry was broadcasting the Cardinals games and I was doing the Cubs and White Sox on TV in Chicago. Before either of us traveled regularly with our teams, I'd see him in the off-season when Harry would come to Chicago or I would go to St. Louis for one reason or another.

Harry and I were social friends as well as professional colleagues. I'm happy to say that I may have played a small role in Harry coming to Chicago, where he became bigger than ever.

After Harry left the Cardinals in 1969, he went to work for the Oakland Athletics and owner Charles O. Finley. Those of us who knew both Harry and Finley really didn't give this one much of a chance. Harry was his own man, and Finley wanted to control everybody, including his announcers. So after the 1970 season was over, I learned that the White Sox were looking for an announcer. Stu Holcomb was their general manager under owner John Allyn.

I called Harry to tip him to the opening. He said, "Yes, I know about it. I'm negotiating with them. We're not too close together on money." I said to him, "Harry, lower your sights and come on in. Ordinarily, I don't like your kind of competition. But Chicago is your kind of a town. Besides, if you come in, it could put 10 years on both of our lives. You'll be in the American League, I'll be in the National League, and we won't see that much of each other. We won't have that many chances to wipe out each other's health."

The White Sox and Harry got together, and the rest is Chicago sports broadcasting history that entered an even higher profile chapter when Jim Dowdle, head of Tribune Broadcasting, hired Harry to replace me after I voluntarily left the booth as Cubs announcer in 1981.

Ironically, one of my favorite Harry stories is not a baseball story. I related this one when I saw Chip Caray at a Broadcast Advertising Club luncheon that introduced him to Chicago on May 18, 1998. Going back three decades or so, Harry and I had both traveled to East Lansing, Michigan, to do a Big Ten football game involving Michigan State. We managed to get a ride to the airport after the game from a local friend. We turned on the radio; Harry had a request to listen to a football broadcast from another station. Why? Because the broadcaster was Harry's son, Skip. The pride in Harry's face as he listened to his son broadcasting that game was something else to witness. He literally was glowing.

Harry was lucky. He lived to not only see Skip, but also Skip's son, Chip, both become highly regarded, major-market sports broadcasters.

Another great story is that night Harry was struck by that car in St. Louis, breaking almost every bone in both legs. He spent the entire winter stretched out in bed, both legs in casts. The odds were against him ever walking again. But the next April, the Cubs opened in St. Louis. I was there in the clubhouse, getting ready for the broadcast. In walks Harry on two good legs. He said, "I told you I'd be ready for the season, and here I am."

Years later, my wife, Pat, and I visited Harry and his wife, Dutchie, in Palm Springs. We played tennis, and he ran my legs off. So much for a guy who was not supposed to walk again.

What was the secret to Harry's unbelievable appeal? He was a guaranteed audience builder. He was his own man. Harry never copied anybody. He was fearless when it came to criticism, when he felt it was required. A lot of broadcasters don't directed at the people signing their paychecks.

Harry was the beneficiary of a once-in-a-lifetime type of chemistry that involved personality, ability and a great broadcast outlet. He even managed to become that popular and important in people's lives without a great ball club to work with most of the time. Credit Bill Veeck's foresight in being able to grasp the ordinary working stiff's desire to have fun in the ballpark and have a regular guy like Harry leading them. He was one of the fans, and broadcast games with that in mind. He's was talking their language.

Even after his passing, I don't think Harry's appeal will go away. When a great personality leaves us, people mourn, but then the memory fades away. Normally, a year from the time that personality dies, people will say, "What was that guy's name?" But in Harry's case, a lot of things in the game and on the air will keep reminding fans of Harry, much more than anyone else anyone has met, outside maybe some of the great presidents and other civic and social leaders.

Arne Harris, who directed Harry and me on Cubs telecasts for almost 35 years, said, "Brickhouse was Sinatra, while

Harry Caray and Jack Brickhouse *(Photo courtesy of Harry Caray's Restaurant).*

Harry was Elvis Presley." I was on the spot where TV first needed to be sold. Years later, Harry employed TV in a manner that made the masses grateful for his presence.

I hope you'll enjoy the many dozens of memories contained in this book. I defy you, as you read this book, to remember anyone who touched as many different people and left them with stories about him as Harry was able to deliver.

Harry was truly unforgettable. There are plenty of stories left over for several sequels.

Jack Brickhouse
Legendary Hall of Fame Chicago Sports Announcer

PREFACE

Harry Caray won me over. It took the better part of two decades. But why shouldn't Harry do that? He always was an audience builder.

Caray was the enemy, the announcer for the two teams that most opposed the Chicago Cubs, my ancestral favorite (my grandfather, not long off the boat from Europe, rooted for Hack Wilson and Co. from the Wrigley Field bleachers). Harry was, after all, synonymous with the St. Louis Cardinals and later the Chicago White Sox. And I grew up with the voice-busting home run calls and other favorite catch-phrases of Jack Brickhouse, Mr. Enthusiasm himself, on the air while Ernie Banks, Billy Williams and Ron Santo authored "Cub Power." The combination of Brickhouse and the all-star players hooked for life another generation—me and scores of other Baby Boomers.

On hot August nights in 1969, I felt the euphoria of a Cubs team seemingly closing in on its first pennant in 24 years. The Cubs would win during the day, prompting Santo to click his heels in glee and Brickhouse to proclaim that the "merry men of Wrigley Field roll on and on." And here's the slightly static-filled signal of KMOX-Radio in St. Louis, booming 300 miles northeast through the Midwestern humidity, carrying Caray's defiant descriptions of a Cardinals club vainly trying to close a nine-game gap with the Cubs.

"The Cardinals are coming, tra-la, tra-la," Harry crowed in a Bud-soaked voice whenever the under performing Redbirds pulled one out. That enraged me. The audacity of this announcer, taunting the Cubs as the Cardinals existed on the periphery of the pennant race. And yet, while Caray raised your blood pressure, he kept you listening. You turned him on the next night, and the night after. Love me or hate me, but don't ignore me. He had the formula.

Two years later, Caray continued his showmanship, only this time it was right around the corner. And he now was a Pied Piper for revived, emboldened White Sox fans, who seemed to hate the Cubs far more than the Yankees, Athletics, Royals, any American League team that beat out the Pale Hose for first place in the post-World War II era. The Cubs never played the Sox, and yet many of the Sox fans I knew were just livid at the thought of the North Siders. How they handled the Cubs' three-game sweep of the Sox at Wrigley Field June 5-7, 1998, I'll never know. But during the middle of the Nixon Administration, the fans shadow-boxed the Cubs, and Harry was their spiritual leader.

Still, you listened. He was compelling, and set loose on Rush Street in a town featuring 4 a.m. bar closings, became even wilder and crazier than his St. Louis days. Many have marveled how Caray almost single-handedly doubled, then tripled, Sox attendance from 1970 to '72, causing the team to eventually void a $30,000 attendance bonus in his contract he had far exceeded. He did it in his first two seasons in 1971 and '72, crowing on a jerry-built network of suburban AM and FM stations. One signal, WEAW-FM, covered much of the market from a tower atop the John Hancock Center. But remember, these were the days when FM was a secondary radio medium, full of classical music, simulcasts of AM signals and the occasional "underground" rock music outlet. Caray's voice was virtually a natural transmitter; he didn't need non-directional nighttime patterns and 50,000-watt blowtorches. People found Caray's voice, and they were hooked. Even me, even with Sox fans lambasting a Cubs team they never faced on the field.

I remember sitting in old Comiskey Park's left-field grandstands on a Wednesday afternoon in August with the Yankees in town in 1972. By this time, Caray had earned renown for working day games, beer and fishnet in hand, from the centerfield bleachers. On this day, Sox strongman Dick Allen blasted a Lindy McDaniel pitch almost on a straight line toward Caray. The rocket hardly rose more than 20 feet across the ground. Caray left his seat and waved his fishnet. But he never got the ball, which finally smashed into some empty seats near him, 475 feet from its launching pad. Caray and Allen. What a combo. A mouth and a bat teaming up to save the Sox.

I really never met Caray during this period. And in his early Cubs days, I kind of kept a respectful distance. I was just starting to work as a sportswriter for a chain of weekly papers. Harry was just too big for little ol' me to approach and hobnob with. And did he ever get big when the Cubs finally finished first in 1984. My regret was that Brickhouse, who had left the booth and was replaced by Caray three years earlier, couldn't call the division clincher. At least Jack was in the booth to provide color that night for Harry, who would turn out to be the only play-by-play TV announcer ever to utter the magic words, "the Cubs are the champions!"

Caray's impact on Cubdom and the WGN-TV national cable audience was immeasurable. He simply was a larger-than-life character who represented baseball. Like Big Bird or some other favorite character, he was the cuddly grandpa on the games for kids. My daughter, Laura, gazed at a close-up of Steve Stone one day in 1986, just as she was mastering the language as a toddler. "There's Harry Caray!" Laura exclaimed. To her, anyone on TV associated with a Cubs game had to be a Harry Caray. He was that overwhelming.

Finally, as the 1980s waned and I felt more comfortable around the big stars, I started to talk to Caray during his rounds at Wrigley Field. His Hall of Fame induction in 1989 provided grist for one conversation. It was when he first addressed his mortality. "I want to go out with my boots on," he said at the time. He loved his work so much that retirement just didn't compute. A voracious reader, he saw my Hall of Fame piece. "That's good stuff," he said. "Why aren't you downtown (working for the Chicago Tribune or Sun-Times)?" I mumbled something about not having the right connections to be summoned to the Midwest's version of journalistic Olympus. "Hey, maybe you can talk to someone, Harry?" I meekly suggested. He never did, but that wasn't his obligation. Just the fact he read my story, liked it and let me know was ample pay back.

Mind you, Caray was no saint, and never pretended to be. He could be prickly. On several occasions, I'd say something in a conversation with which he would vehemently disagree. Any attempt to debate Harry was futile. He stood his ground and let you know in no uncertain terms. He might even upbraid you. Are you going to argue with a legend on his own turf? But, true to the many descriptions of him, he never carried over the disagreement to another day.

Almost every day in the Wrigley Field press box or down on the field, Harry would spot me and wave an enthusiastic greeting. He was the ultimate people person. If you were encountered on his daily routine, he'd make sure to say hello. Some of my favorite times were joining him for an inning or so in the Wrigley Field press box lunchroom, when he had the fourth, fifth and sixth innings off from TV duties in 1995 and '96. Harry sat there alone, watching the game, keeping his scorecard.

This was a time to hear Caray's off-the-cuff comments about the game and players, even stuff he couldn't put on the air. One day he railed against one Cubs player's seeming fascination with his gold chains over fundamental play. During these sessions, it was also "ask and ye shall receive." "When was the first time you were ever on TV?" I queried one day, knowing Caray was around to see the video medium's birth. His encyclopedic recall kicked in. "It was 1947, a sports-panel show," he responded. Amazing that he'd remember such a minute detail of his life from five decades back.

He also had his witty and even ribald side, a side so many folks remember. When Laura was around 5, I took her up to the press box for the first time—and her first meeting with Caray. Gazing upon her, Caray responded with a nearly standard comeback: "Save her for when she's 18, and I'll come calling." I got back a good one at the ol' ladies' man: "If you come calling then, Harry, you'll be looking at the wrong end of a shotgun. I know how you work." Laughs all around.

He loved being around anyone who appreciated baseball. And there was a time when he found his celebrity getting in the way of others' work. One day in spring training, he suggested to his wife Dutchie that the couple move to another area of the very accessible press box in the old HoHoKam press box in Mesa, Arizona. Why? Harry and Dutchie were sitting among the writers covering the Cubs, and fans constantly were leaning over, asking to talk to Harry. He didn't want the writers disturbed, so he moved a ways down. While Caray watched a game in the spring, he asked that fans not line up for autographs. But between innings, he signed nonstop as the lines snaked down the rows of seats.

By 1997, there was an eerie feeling that the Caray era was starting to wrap up. He was not scheduled to work the Cubs' season opener that season on the road at Pro Player Park in Florida. One month prior to that in spring training, I asked Harry about not going on the road while he and Dutchie watched a Cubs-Athletics game at Phoenix's Municipal Stadium. A look of terrible sadness enveloped his face. Harry Caray not working a Cubs season opener? Fate intervened, though. Announcer Josh Lewin got sick, and Caray was summoned to fill in, with the misfortune of watching the start of the Cubs' 14-game losing streak.

As the forgettable '97 season drew to a close, I asked Caray to contribute a couple of comments to my syndicated baseball radio show, "Diamond Gems," that offered a retrospective on Game 7 of the 1967 World Series between the Cardinals and Red Sox. Caray had broadcast that game with Pee Wee Reese for NBC-Radio. He told me to come into his WGN booth about an hour before the game. I put the mike up to his mouth, rolled the tape, and nothing happened. Harry couldn't clear his throat. His powerful spirit was so willing, but his flesh had grown weaker. Twenty minutes later, he stuck his head into the press box and called out to me to try it again. But we agreed to do it the next day, and Harry was able to provide the flashback. Still, the inability of Caray to summon his distinctive voice for two minutes of conversation was unsettling, even frightening.

I last saw Caray at the media party right before the 1998 Cubs Convention. I needed to gather material for some season-preview stories, so I had to flit about the room conducting interviews. Caray, of course, was busy elsewhere in the room being the center of attention. As the party drew to a close, I heard a familiar voice hail me from behind. "What's the matter, George, you're too big to talk to me anymore?" It was Harry. But before I could respond, he was hustled away to officiate at the convention's opening ceremonies.

There's some unfinished business at work here. I wish I had the chance to just make a minute of small talk with Caray when he greeted me. There was no proper closure, no good-bye and good luck, with his death a month later.

Now is the proper time and place: Thank you for your good wishes, Harry. And thank you for all the memories.

George Castle
June 1998

INTRODUCTION

It Was Just a Matter of Time . . .

Before I had to leave the first day of spring training at Scottsdale Stadium and head home to watch the funeral of my imaginary childhood friend on TV. We go back a long time; we met when he was finishing his first decade of announcing St. Louis Cardinals games and I was finishing my first decade on this planet. An intermediary named Philco introduced us one night in a granary on a farm in Iowa as I was practicing hoops—or basketball as we called it in those days. Once the chores were done, it was the same ritual every night:

Start way on the left side of the radio dial ...There was Earle Gillespie on WTMJ in Milwaukee describing Braves' action for the team that had just moved from Boston...

A little bit to the right was Detroit's WJR where young Ernie Harwell sang the praise of Goebel's Beer and told stories about being baptized in the Jordan River or being Margaret Mitchell's paper boy in his Georgia youth...

A slight twist of the dial towards the barn was WLW-700 AM—The Big One in Cincinnati—where the Reds' Waite Hoyt talked about the taste of Hudepol Beer...

A little farther south on the dial was WGN and if the Cubs were on the road you could listen to Jack Quinlan, the Cubs' talented new, young play-by-play man...

Skip past the middle of the dial where the White Sox announcers were boring...

A quarter twist more and you could listen to the Davenport Tigers in the Class B, Three I League. They were not as exciting as the previous year because their best player, Harvey Kuenn, and their only announcer, Milo Hamilton, had already gone all the way to the Big Leagues...

But just a smidgen farther on the dial—towards town—and there it was: Magic flowing through the air from KMOX-1120 in St. Louis, Missouri; excitement and enthusiasm from that guy named Harry Caray...Yep, that's the game to listen to tonight. It was gonna be fun. It always was.

In those days, when Elvis was the King, Little Richard was the Queen and Springsteen wasn't even in middle management, there were slide rules but no Major League team west of St. Louis, a rapid Robert Feller but no batting helmets, a bazillion Wayne Terwilliger and Tommy Glaviano baseball cards but no Frank Lejas or Mickey Mantles, the Cubs were in the 46th season of their first five-year plan, there were bums but few homeless, bomb shelters but no Mark McGwire, and there was Harry Caray and no one else.

He brought his friends with him. They had neat names like Jabbo and Rip and Slats and Country, Vinegar Bend and The Kitten, but it was clear his best friend was Stan the Man.

Who needed to watch the pictures on that new Stromberg-Carison thing my parents were watching in the farmhouse parlor when I could listen to a Picasso? It was Christmas morning every broadcast; hope sprung eternal every night, I was a perfect fan, Harry was 154-0 managing from the booth (although it seemed like he did better than that). We never won a pennant but sometimes we felt like World Champs...then it was just a matter of time before one of my parents would yell from the front porch to bring the radio back in to the house for their 10 o'clock news... But that was okay because we had The Kitten throwin' in Brooklyn tomorrow night...Eastern game, had to get the chores done earlier.

It was just a matter of time before I left the farm and my imaginary friend whom I had never met left St. Louis. I went to college in Indiana, he went to Oakland to work for a man from Indiana who owned the Oakland A's. He found out that Gertrude Stein did not lie: there was no *there* there. I went to work in New York City, he went to work in Chicago.

Harry developed his Caray-oke seventh-inning act during his decade plus on the south side of Chicago until he was driven out by junkyard dogs—not Leroy Brown's. He probably whistled as he passed the graveyard at 35th and Shields and headed for the corner of what and if.

And then the unthinkable happened. There are some enduring mysteries in life like George Hamilton, Dennis Rodman and Dan Quayle that cannot be easily explained...but Harry Caray going over to the Cubs? Absolutely impossible, had to be a misprint, Rock Hudson would play for the other team before that would happen. No way! What's next? Lights in Wrigley Field? Not the hated Cubs! Every Cardinal fan knew that Wrigley Field was the last refuge of scoundrels...say it ain't so, Harry.

To this day I have never gotten the memo saying it was a practical joke.

Pssst, pssst—pull this book a little closer right now and I'll tell you a secret: Harry Caray went to his grave a Cardinal fan, period, good-night, good-bye, so long, farewell, *adios*, school's out, eight ball corner pocket, set up the road blocks, close the airport, wake the kids, call the neighbors, book it, St. Peter. God knows that Cub fans are nothing but a bunch of people who can't afford World Series tickets.

It was just a matter of time before my imaginary friend came to life.

In the fall of 1987, three college mates of mine opened Harry Caray's restaurant in Chicago and were so kind to invite me to a private party the night before it opened. What a party! A guy hit me with a crack back block at the bar which is how I met a sportswriter named Bill Jauss. I had a nice chat with a guy named Rich Taylor about his days at Providence College until his wife informed me that their last name was Daley and then the magic moment...Forget the Pope, forget the Beatles, forget Ann Margaret...Okay, forget the Pope and forget the Beatles, there was my friend of 30 years...and he chatted with me as if he knew, well you know what I mean.

Harry Caray *(Photo courtesy of Ted Patterson).*

Some years later, we would have lunch and then dinner and have a blast swapping stories...and they were all true stories, give or take a lie or two. His favorite one of mine, which I'm sure he had heard a dozen times, involved two Americans caught in Mexico attempting to smuggle drugs, one was a Cub fan and the other a Cardinal fan. They were brought before the captain of the firing squad who informed them that he would grant each one a last wish providing that it was reasonable. The ugly Cub fan said he could die in peace if he could hear Harry Caray sing "Take Me Out to the Ball Game" one more time. The captain said, "This is your lucky day. We have cable in the palace, our head of security is a moron and a Cubs fan and he tapes every game." The captain turns to the Cardinal fan and asks if he has a reasonable last wish. The big, good-lookin' Cardinal fan replies, "I sure do, *señor*!" The captain says, "Well, what is it?" And the Cardinal fan says, "Shoot me first." Harry loved it or so it seemed.

I used to kid Harry by saying the only reason that the Cubs, since they installed lights in 1988, played night games on every day except Friday and Saturday was his agreement with the Cubs stated he had to get an early weekend start on Rush Street.

Chicago knows how to throw a funeral. Some cities know crime, some know music or cars, others know marathons, but if you're famous and passing on, Chicago is where you want to be. My late Irish father would have loved Harry Caray's funeral with Harry's friends Pete Vonachen, Mike Roarty and Jim Dowdle telling funny Harry Caray stories. I was laughing like a hyena...and then at the end when the casket holding my very best childhood friend came down the center aisle and "Take Me Out to the Ball Game" was being played slowly on bagpipes, I—if you dare tell anyone this, especially my kids, I'll call you a rotten liar—started to cry...and started to remember, "Hello again, everybody" and "The Cardinals are coming, tra la" and "Holy cow, look out East St. Louis, Duke Snider just hit another one" and—I'll deny it—cried some more...Then the casket disappeared from camera view and his phrase, "So long, everybody" hit me really hard and I was glad no one was around.

And then it came to me, just a few minutes before I was holding my sides while laughing—what I'll do is write a book with Harry's friends telling funny stories. Why cry when you can laugh? Someone would write the book, I knew it was just a matter of time.

The possible titles were rushing through my mind as I called my agent in Indianapolis; I hate agents by the way... "Wrigley Field Days, Rush Street Nights," "You can't go to Heaven unless you're a Cardinal fan," "Harry We Heartily Knew Ye," "Let me hear ya, now," "Hello again everybody," "So long everybody," etc.

My agent came through with a book contract and I embarked on the most fun six months any sports fan could hope for. I played hooky from life while I chatted with Stan Musial and Mike Ditka, shot the breeze with Jack Buck and Chick Hearn, got the inside scoop from Butch McGuire and Mike Roarty, laughed with Tim McCarver and Mike Veeck and had my coaching tips ignored by Dan Devine and Charlie Spoonhour. Luck, thy name is Rich!

But the best thing about writing this book was no bubbles were punctured, he was Damon Runyon, he was THE last of the Mohicans, he was even better than you wanted—wished—him to be. He was the real McCoy. He was a man's man and a fan's fan. He had what I knew he had when I was a kid. But few adults—aside from Bill Veeck, Mike Roarty and Jim Dowdle recognized—he had magic. I'm tellin' ya—write it down and underline it—the man had magic. Before Doug Henning had a rabbit, before Earvin Johnson had a moniker, and before David Copperfield was a model husband, Harry Caray had magic.

Where's Harry now? If the Lord's willin' and the creek don't rise, he's at a ball game...maybe even at that field that Don Lansing has just a few miles north of where Harry and I spent my youth. I can see it now: "Holy Cow, Kinsella. Is this Iowa?"...and Shoeless Joe breaks in and says, "No, Harry. This is Heaven."

Shoeless Joe switches his weight from one foot to the other, everyone knew Joe had heard—after all there were a lot of ears around—that Harry had left the South Side years before. Shoeless Joe smoothed a wrinkle on the olde English Sox lettering, turned, looked Caray right in the eye and said, "Say it ain't so, Harry." That was the day Shoeless Joe went to a higher level. In heaven, some say it was help from the cherubins and seraphims, but I know it was arranged by the Cardinals.

If that's where Harry is, I want to be there with him. Everyone wants to go to heaven but no one wants to die ... but we are all going to die someday. It is just a question of when. It is just a matter of time.

Thanks for the dance, Harry!

Rich Wolfe
June, 1998

PROLOGUE

Wouldn't a lot of us want to be like Harry Caray?

Wouldn't we all like to say what we think and not especially worry about the consequences? Wouldn't we all like to stay out late while still getting up early to put in a full day of work? Wouldn't we all like to engage in conspicuous consumption without paying the consequences, knowing we'd be on our feet, on the job we coveted and got 52 years previously, at age 83?

And most of all, wouldn't we all like the adoration of millions, to be even more popular than the entity that we describe on the job?

Maybe that's why we tuned into Harry Caray, from start to finish, and tuned in even more frequently as he lasted long after most entertainers were put out to pasture, their best works consigned to the late movies, oldies and nostalgia radio stations, and dusty tomes in the back of libraries.

The most popular sportscaster of all time, Harry Caray lived four lifetimes in one. He packed more living into one day than most of us could ever dream of in a month—or longer. He also had three careers as a baseball announcer: riveting verbal picture-painter with the St. Louis Cardinals, wild man on and off the air with the Chicago White Sox, and lovable grandfather-figure, more popular than the team, with the Chicago Cubs.

Most of us have to follow a structured 9-to-5 life, answering to people who we often don't like. Harry Caray expanded those parameters while scripting his own life as he went along.

"He was one of less than a handful of people I've ever met who have gone through their entire lives playing exclusively by their own rules," says John McDonough, the Cubs' vice president of marketing and broadcasting, and a close Caray associate for almost 15 years.

"Everyone would like to say, 'You know what? I stayed up last night until 2 in the morning. I got up at 5. I had a great day. I squeezed as much out of life as I possibly could.' And he actually did.

"If you look what happened to his life, he was divorced a couple of times, he was paying a couple of alimonies, he was hit by a cab. Probably for a portion of his life he drank to excess. He ate late all the time. He probably didn't exercise a lot. He violated every rule of nature, and lived larger than everyone else. He kind of looked conventional wisdom and life in the eye, and beat it."

There's a little, or maybe a lot, of Harry in all of us. Few get to act on those impulses or the leeway to actually act out those desires. So maybe Harry was carrying the torch for those of us who had to be left behind.

"The rest of us are concerned about fat grams and cholesterol and sodium and eating late," McDonough says. "You shouldn't drink too late because it will affect your sleeping. He didn't do that. He lived every minute and loved it.

"He didn't worry about the things you and I worry about. I doubt Harry every really worried about mortgage payments. How many lawns do you think Harry ever cut in his life, or how many sinks do you think he ever fixed? Probably none. Wouldn't we all like that?

"Harry's axiom was, 'Live it up. The meter's running.'"

That meter kept running for Harry Caray until February 18, 1998. Harry had been knocked down, emotionally and physically, several times in his life. He always got up, returning to his old self, bigger and better than ever. But on this day in Palm Springs, California, Caray couldn't defy the odds again. We were all surprised, even though we knew he already had beaten the actuarial tables by a country mile and was somewhere in his 80s. Caray had become virtually immortal. If anyone was going to live forever, signing on Cubs telecasts with his familiar, bravado greeting, throw in his requisite "Holy Cows" and sing off-key in the seventh inning, it was Caray.

He had a body chemistry that's for the books. Out almost all night most days, he never tired and never missed a baseball game due to illness until his 1987 stroke. He could seemingly drink to excess—the hard stuff, not his publicly favored Budweiser—and never get drunk. Any number of consumption sins should have finished him off a decade or two earlier. And here Harry Caray was on his feet at age 83, planning to show up for work as usual.

By the 1990s, Caray had long since ceased to be a technically competent broadcaster. Cataloguing his mistakes and mispronunciations with names became a cottage industry, yet his popularity continued to soar. He had trouble clearing his throat a lot, a drawback that wouldn't get any broadcaster in the front door. And yet, he was front and center, ahead of everybody else.

Through it all, Caray had become baseball's top entertainer and ambassador, admired by the average fan and top celebrity alike. Instead of being the exciting announcer of his Cardinals days and the booth bomb-tosser of his White Sox years, he now became . . . Harry Caray. He portrayed himself, a character straight out of a scriptwriter's pen. Truth was stranger than fiction.

In his lifetimes, Caray had earned the right to play, well, himself, in public as well as private.

"One thing that separated him from most," former Cubs manager and general manager Jim Frey says, "was that like some actors and musicians, in the last years of their life they become the image they created. Harry Caray was one of the few people who you see who have a long, long, long career, and become that person they have portrayed. He loved being Harry Caray."

McDonough was on the same wavelength.

"Harry became a caricature," he says. "Harry became somebody who was almost bigger than life. He was somebody who had that certain spirit where he was almost impenetrable, where he could get away with saying anything—by and large he could. He was bulletproof. Sometimes he would say things we would cringe at, but we would also laugh at. He was the only guy who could get away with it.

"Harry probably was the only broadcaster in the history of baseball who was a dual-purpose broadcaster. He brought people into the ballpark as well as being a human rating point or two. People tuned in because they might hear about his alimony payments, what bar he was in last night, or his disagreement with Steve Stone over something said on the air."

Say what you want, do what you want, be what you want. Harry Caray had more than made up for time lost as a kid.

All the biographies state that Harry Caray's birthday was March 1, 1920. But most folks knew better. He was older by anywhere from three to seven years. After his death, the *St. Louis Post-Dispatch* tracked down a birth certificate that confirmed Harry was born as Harry Carabina in 1914.

"He'd shave a couple of years off his age every time he'd go to a new city," his son, Skip Caray, said a few years ago. So how old was Harry, Skip was asked then. "That's family business."

But whatever the specific reason for the elder Caray fudging on his age later in life, no matter what his specific birth date, the fact remains he had to endure a deprived childhood in an unforgiving, less enlightened time in St. Louis. He was orphaned at a young age and lived in foster homes. Eventually, he went to live with his uncle, the brother of his mother, Daisy. But his uncle ran off and Caray lived in his teen-age years with his aunt, Doxie Argent.

Always a baseball fan who played some sandlot ball, Caray followed the Cardinals during their "Gashouse Gang" years. Listening to their broadcasts and the clipped, stilted announcers of the time, the brash young man believed he could do better. Even though he had responsibilities as a working stiff and young father in the early 1940s, he embarked on a career in radio, his brashness emboldening him to contact Merle

Jones, the general manager of St. Louis blowtorch KMOX-Radio, at his home.

Caray didn't make the cut at KMOX, but he was encouraged to farm himself out for more experience. He landed his first job in 1943 as an announcer at WCLS-Radio in Joliet, Illinois, where, prompted by the station manager, he shortened his name to its present form. The following year, he moved on to Kalamazoo, Mich. and WKZO-Radio, where a co-worker was another future broadcasting giant named Paul Harvey.

Soon he was back in St. Louis, hosting a nightly sports show. In 1945, he finally landed a play-by-play job announcing Cardinals games. His first game would link him with a team that would provide his greatest popularity. The Cubs beat the Cardinals, 3-2, on Don Johnson's single in the ninth inning.

Not long after, the Cardinals' broadcasts shifted to KMOX, and Caray's popularity built, helped by a network of more than 100 stations throughout the Midwest, South and Great Plains. Caray's tell-it-like-it-is style endeared him to millions. And his longtime association with Budweiser began when brewer August Busch, Jr. bought the Cardinals in 1953, saving them from a possible move to another city.

Caray spread the word of the exploits of Stan "The Man" Musial while wearing his heart on his sleeve, a fan given the privilege of working a microphone. If Kenny Boyer couldn't come through in the clutch, Harry let his widespread audience know that, pulling no punches. And if Boyer connected, Harry was ecstatic. He ran the gamut of emotions as any fan, but his 50,000-watt pulpit often got him into hot water with players. Always, he persevered.

Many announcers were statistic and analysis wonks. Not Harry.

"I'm not that much for statistics," he once said. "I'm for human interest. I deal in humor and entertainment and in human nature, the human side of the story."

His unique style was only part of the reason for his popularity in St. Louis. Long after TV had been established as the dominant broadcast medium, Cardinals owner Busch had strictly rationed the number of televised games to no more than 40 per season, all on the road. In contrast, in Chicago, all home Cubs games were televised, with the majority of road games added to the schedule in 1968. Thus, TV announcer Jack Brickhouse had the higher profile than his radio counterparts. Not in St. Louis. If you wanted to follow the Cardinals, you had to listen to Harry on the radio. He came through, painting one of the greatest word pictures with his enthusiasm. Vintage tapes of the era prove that no announcer of the era could touch his palette.

Ken Boyer and Harry Caray *(Photo courtesy of Ken Patterson).*

While Caray first described plenty of Cardinals foibles in the 1950s, then long-awaited pennants in 1964, '67 and '68, he also developed his bon vivant reputation. Night life became his sideline. Caray went through two marriages and five children.

The Busch family tired of Caray's off-the-field antics and abruptly fired him in 1969. However, Caray's departure from St. Louis turned out to be the best career move he ever could have experienced. It pointed him to the direction of Chicago—and superstardom.

Charlie Finley (Photo courtesy of Oakland A's).

Caray worked one season for Charlie Finley and the Oakland Athletics in 1970. The relationship of Caray and Finley, both their own men, wasn't fated to last. Still, Caray didn't feel his one season in Oakland was a lost one.

"As enthused as I had been over watching Stan Musial, Ken Boyer and Enos Slaughter, I found myself getting caught up in the developments of the young players on the A's—(Reggie) Jackson, (Sal) Bando, (Catfish) Hunter and (Bert) Campaneris," he said later. "It made me realize that it was the game of baseball and not necessarily the team which made me feel the way I did about broadcasting baseball."

Such a philosophy helped save the White Sox for Chicago when he moved back East in 1971. Hired to help a franchise that had lost a record 106 games in 1970, Caray was almost personally responsible for reviving attendance the next season for a team that had played some home games in Milwaukee in 1968 and '69. And Caray accomplished this feat without a 50,000-watt AM outlet. The Sox fortunes had dipped so low only a jerry-built network of suburban AM and FM outlets aired Sox broadcasts in 1971 and '72. Harry's loud-and-clear delivery landed them back on a big station for 1973.

Waving his fishnet from the booth to snare foul balls and broadcasting games from the centerfield bleachers at Comiskey Park, Caray first experienced the phenomenon of being more popular than the team itself. At the same time, he angered players and manager Chuck Tanner with his candid comments. Third baseman Bill Melton, now a Chicago broadcaster, still can't talk about Harry's barbs 25 years later. He declined specific comment for this book, although he admitted Caray was a great entertainer and overall good for the game. Tanner, though, has long buried the hatchet and has nothing but good to say about Caray.

The announcer became so controversial by 1975 that Chicago station WMAQ-Radio considered putting him on a seven-second delay, a first for a live baseball broadcast. Sox owner John Allyn tried to fire Caray during a live TV interview in late 1975. But Caray's job was saved when Bill Veeck rescued the nearly bankrupt team from Allyn for the 1976 season.

The first contract negotiation with Veeck was hilarious, loud and very public. Caray and Veeck were scheduled to meet at the Executive House hotel's restaurant in the winter of 1976. Hard of hearing, Veeck shouted to an approaching Caray and his attorney, Marty Cohn. "Hey, Harry, I want to make you an offer to work for me," bellowed Barnum Bill. Playfully mocking Veeck's loud tones, Caray shouted back, with the restaurant patrons suddenly taking notice, "That sounds great, Bill." Veeck then countered: "How 'bout $100,000 a year, Harry?" Caray's response came as Cohn couldn't get in a word edgewise: "That sounds great, Bill. When do I start?" The amazed diners applauded the exchange.

Teamed with the eccentric Jimmy Piersall in the booth, Caray really stepped up his guerrilla theater of the air in the late 1970s. Veeck also began Caray's trademark "Take Me Out to the Ball Game" sing-along in the seventh inning during this time.

But his Sox relationship did not outlast the change of ownership in 1981, when Veeck sold out to a group headed by Jerry Reinsdorf and Eddie Einhorn. Caray did not take to the new owners, who wanted to de-emphasize the appeal of the announcers, start a pay-TV operation, and clean up the image of old Comiskey Park as the "world's largest outdoor saloon." That acrimony never died down for Caray, who held few other grudges. Although he later patched things up with Einhorn, he couldn't speak well of Reinsdorf—all the way through to his last in-depth interview with the Chicago Tribune's Paul Sullivan a month prior to his death. Reinsdorf, asked for comment for this book, politely declined.

Behind-the-scenes talks landed Caray with the Cubs for 1982, angering incumbent announcer Milo Hamilton, who had earlier been promised the job vacated by Brickhouse at the time. But Caray helped revive the sagging Cubs in a way Hamilton never could. His personality and seventh-inning singing, conveyed nationally on WGN-TV's new cable signal, held the fort until the Cubs surged to win the National League East in 1984, prompting a quantum jump in team popularity.

Caray's own profile exploded. He simply sucked up popularity in front of the packed houses and via the satellite-borne exposure. He returned the love to the fans as the most accessible star. He rarely refused an autograph or an offered conversation, drawing more well-wishers than any individual player. Soon he was a commercial star, dancing with pretty girls in a Blues Brothers black suit and proclaiming himself a "Cub fan and Bud man."

He became the people's star.

"The uniqueness of Harry is if he met a guy on the street, he had the same interest and enthusiasm as if he knew you 100 years," Chicago radio sportscaster Bruce Levine says. "Every day he'd come to the ballpark was like the first day he came to the park. He was excited to see you. He'd say to me, 'I can't wait for the game to start, because no matter how many of these I've seen, this one is going to be different. We're going to see something today I've never seen before. And that's what keeps my enthusiasm going.'"

He made sure he gave the fans credit when he was finally inducted into the broadcasters' wing of the Baseball Hall of Fame in 1989.

"I think of the fans, and perhaps that's who I represent here today," Caray said in his rousing induction speech at Cooperstown. "You. The fans. We are all fans of the world's greatest game—baseball. I know it's the fans who are responsible for my being here. I've always tried in each and every broadcast to serve the fans to the best of my ability. In my mind, they are the unsung heroes of our games.

"The baseball players come and go, but the game goes on forever. The players, the writers, the broadcasters, no matter how great, all are temporary actors on the stage. It's the game, it's baseball, that moves ahead and reaches new heights all the time, generation after generation. And I'm very proud of being a part of this important piece of Americana."

Such beliefs merely increased his popularity. How big did Caray become with the Cubs? When he suffered his stroke in the winter of 1987, celebrities far and wide clamored to fill in for him during his broadcasts. And when he returned during the season, Caray received a congratulatory call on the air from none other than President Ronald Reagan. Some of the same folks, and other big names, jockeyed to try to sing "Take Me Out to the Ball Game" in his honor during the 1998 season. The Cubs had to turn down some celebrities; they had so many booked to lead the crowd in the seventh inning.

"With the exception of George Burns, he's probably the only mega-, superstar who ever got bigger as he got older," Cubs marketing chief McDonough says.

"Here was a guy, 83 years old, who was bigger than he was when he was 73, and bigger than he was at 63," Jay Blunk, the Cubs' director of advertising, says. "How many people 83 years old are on live TV every day? I don't know of anyone else."

Caray's appeal was unaffected even as his tried-and-true play-by-play skills began to fade due to age. His on-air mistakes grew. Andre Dawson became Andre Rodgers. Rafael Palmeiro became Rafael Palermo. Ryne Sandberg became Ryne Sanderson.

Caray usually took questions about his gaffes with good humor. "Hey, I broadcast the games Andre Rodgers played," he grinned, recalling the 1960s' Cubs and Giants infielder.

Chicago Sun-Times sportswriter Dan Cahill even penned a weekly feature of Caray's mistakes on names, dubbed the Harry-O-Meter. Some of the gaffes—with the real name in parentheses—are: Mark Gray (Grace), Hector Villanova (Villanueva), Sammy Cepeda, Sofa, and Segui (Sosa), Taffy (Tuffy) Rhodes, Galen (Glenallen) Hill, Eddie Murphy (Murray), Mel Salazar (Stottlemyre), Sid Hernandez (Fernandez), Hal Marsh (Morris), Lennie (Rick) Wilkins, Dennis (Derrick) May, Steve Booshay and Belcher (Buechele), Chet (Chico) Walker, Kevin Seltzer (Seitzer) and Steve Smith (Stone).

Cahill recalled that Caray, in Cincinnati, was speaking from "Three Rivers Stadium" instead of Riverfront Stadium. He also sang "Take Me Back to the Ball Game" instead of "out." And on a long drive by the Cubs' Kevin Roberson, Caray started his trademark call, "It might be ... It could be ... "Then he asked partner Steve Stone: "Did he catch it?" The ball actually left the park.

It didn't matter. Harry was so lovable, a gate attraction and advertising money-maker, that he had his job for life. He simply did not have to portray a verbally correct play-by-play man. He was doing TV, and the pictures displayed the action. Harry was the rest of the show, a geriatric superstar whose zest for life we wished we could have grabbed ahold of.

Caray knew he had less time ahead than behind him when he got emotional on the air after the final Cubs game of the 1995 season. The Cubs had just made a last, desperate dash for a wild-card playoff berth with an eight-game winning streak, and Caray was enthused.

"I have often gotten emotional at the end of a season," he told Fred Mitchell for an article in *Cubs Quarterly* magazine. "First of all, as you get older the realization hits that there is an end somewhere down the line. And when the curtain comes down on the season, you can't help but think, Who knows? This might be the last one. And that thought always is with me. I am not ashamed of it. It is a matter of fact. Nobody is immortal."

But Caray came close. He cast such a giant shadow at his workplace that many old Wrigley Field hands believe he'll simply show up one day.

"Even though he's been dead for a few months, it's hard to imagine he's not alive," sportscaster Levine says. "You still expect him to come right through the door (and be the center of attention)."

Caray broadcast two more seasons after that emotional farewell. He was on his feet, celebrating Valentine's Day, 1998 with his wife, Dutchie, when he collapsed. He never retired, never was shunted aside. His last day of work was in the job he loved. And he knew Chip Caray, his grandson, would join his broadcast team for 1998.

"He went out like a king," Levine says.

The fans treated his passing like royalty. A shrine of flowers, baseball memorabilia and beer bottles started growing outside Wrigley Field on the night of February 18.

"That night, I walked out around 6 p.m., and people were three or four deep around that little shrine," Blunk recalls. "There was silence. A guy walked up out of nowhere, turned on his boombox, and started singing 'Take Me Out to the Ball Game.' Everybody else joined in. I went home. I got my son, who was 2 1/2, and my wife and came back here. We had to see it. There was an even bigger crowd. So many people came up with things, with notes."

The nicer items were put into storage at Wrigley Field. Some were sent to Dutchie Caray and her family. The memories, though, can never go into mothballs. And neither can Harry Caray's giant shadow.

The Wrigley Field crowd roared like never before when Dutchie Caray filled in for her husband on Opening Day, 1998. The Cubs won eight of their first 10 games. Harry's name was invoked by many as watching over the team's turnaround. By June they had leapt into contention with a 10-game winning streak. One victory was fueled when a gap-splitting drive, hit by the White Sox's Magglio Ordonez, got stuck in the right-field ivy at Wrigley Field. That ground-rule double prevented the lead run—and possibly the winning run —from scoring from first base in the eighth inning.The Cubs went on to beat the White Sox in extra innings, extending the winning streak.

"Harry kicked that ball into the vines," Sox announcer John Rooney huffed.

"Harry was in the vines," Cubs shortstop Jeff Blauser mused later.

If Harry's overpowering personality carries any clout in an afterlife, the Cubs won't lose much longer. In the corporeal world, though, death does not do Harry Caray and his legion of fans part.The echoes of "Holy Cow" and "Cubs win!" will not fade as long as anyone's alive who heard his never duplicated voice and style on the air.

"They're all scampering for that souvenir out there ... Boy, I'd like to see him give somebody in those bleachers a souvenir ... Two balls, two strikes ... Stan waits ... Now the stretch, from the belt, here's the pitch ... Line drive! There it is! ... Into left field ... Hit number 3,000! A run has scored. Musial around first, on his way to second with a double ... Holy Cow, he came through ... Listen to the crowd."

— ***Harry Caray, May 13, 1958***
(Photo courtesy of Ted Patterson).

CHAPTER ONE

Family and Friends

Dutchie Caray

The same kind of persistence Harry Caray employed breaking into the broadcasting business was used to snare the woman who shared the roller-coaster ride of the last 23 years of his life.

If you think Caray had chutzpah in pestering KMOX-Radio general manager Merle Jones for his first job back in the early 1940s, what would you call his six-year chase of the former Dolores Goldmann of University City, Missouri?

Nicknamed "Dutchie" partly for her ethnic background, the third and last Mrs. Harry Caray hardly has a kiss-and-tell story to relate. Simple. She wasn't in the mood for kissing and certainly didn't want the process of telling everybody that she was going out with a celebrity.

"I didn't want to get married," Dutchie Caray says of fending off a determined Harry Caray starting in 1969. Almost up until the day the two were married in Chicago on May 19, 1975, a life with the Mayor of Rush Street was not something she was planning.

"I was divorced and trying to raise five kids," she says. "I didn't have a hell of a lot of time to do anything else other than cook, clean, iron, wash, and get the kids ready for school.

Trying to get her mind off domesticity as her 40th birthday (August 22, 1969) approached, Dutchie's friends Bill and

Dutchie and Harry Caray *(Photo courtesy of Steve Green).*

Flo Postal took her out to Brennan's, a restaurant in Ladue, Missouri, a St. Louis suburb. Who should come walking in at about the same time but Harry Caray, then in his 25th season as Cardinals announcer?

"Harry saw Flo, and he asked Pat Brennan (the proprietor) who that good-looking gal was," Dutchie Caray recalls. "Bill was off talking to some other people, and Harry thought she was alone. Harry was introduced to her, and it was suggested he meet one of her friends—me.

"The next couple of times I was in there, Harry happened to come in, and he talked to me. I really wasn't following him, because I didn't have time to do anything or listen to games. Harry sent a bottle of champagne to my table, but that didn't impress me. I had so many other things on my mind."

Caray kept asking Dutchie to dinner, but she turned him down. "I just wasn't interested," she says. He stepped up the campaign, calling her at home. Again, she told the announcer she was busy and worked late. No problem, we'll go out to dinner late in the evening, he responded. Eventually, reluctantly, Dutchie finally took him up on his offer, but first only in the company of the Postals.

Then Caray was abruptly fired from the Cardinals job after the 1969 season. He continued his pursuit of Dutchie long-distance from Oakland, where he worked on Athletics games in the 1970 season.

"He'd come back to St. Louis on days off," she says. "It got to the point where he would call me from Oakland and tell me when he'd be coming in."

Caray even enlisted good buddy Pete Vonachen in the wooing process. More folks got involved in the act when Caray migrated to Chicago to work for the White Sox in 1971 and greatly expanded his circle of cronies. Dutchie came up occasionally to go out with Caray, but expected nothing to come of the relationship. Caray started to have different ideas, though.

"He began asking me to marry him," Dutchie says. "That went on for three to four years. I kept saying no."

"No" was still the answer even after the couple obtained a marriage license. But Caray simply wore down his best gal. When he had finally overcome her last bit of resistance in 1975, he took no chances that she'd get cold feet. Friends summoned Judge Norman Barry to the Ambassador East Hotel, where Caray lived at the time. Harry's buddies, Ben Stein and Emmett O'Neill, quickly arrived to serve as witnesses, and the vows were exchanged at 4 p.m. on May 19.

"He really was persistent," Dutchie says in an understatement. "He got his way no matter what. He was just so adamant about getting married."

Did they quickly book a honeymoon? Nope. The couple immediately left for Comiskey Park, where Caray broadcast the White Sox game that night. The next day, Dutchie left for St. Louis to tell her children about the changes in her life.

"My kids were so mad at me," she says.

Eventually, the melded family settled into an entertainer's schedule. Dutchie's children went to Chicago to spend part of the summer, and the newlyweds soon bought a winter home in Palm Springs, California. Harry was here, there and everywhere, traveling for business. But in quieter moments, the couple often stole away for a day or two to Lake Geneva, Wisconsin, where they spent time with Caray's circle of close friends.

Caray continued his post-midnight circuit all over the big leagues. But always, always, he came back to Dutchie, and told her often how lucky he felt.

"He said he wished he could have met me when he was much younger," she says. "But I could not have survived (the marriage) if it had happened then. I feel it would have never worked earlier. Toward the end, he said so many times, 'I don't know what I would have done without you.' We had a great life. We went everywhere, did everything."

Caray helped keep the couple far younger than their years with his active schedule. He not only wanted to feel younger, but he wanted the record to show he had shaved years off his real age. By the time he ascended to true superstardom with the Cubs, Caray was listing March 1, 1920, as his birth date—six years later than the actual day. Even though a slew of archival articles had long disproved Harry's fib, he maintained the 1920 birthday to the end.

"In my opinion, he did that because he was afraid he wouldn't be able to work," Dutchie says. "He just wanted to broadcast baseball, and he feared they'd get rid of him if they knew how old he really was.

"He wouldn't have had anything to do besides baseball. He felt better when he had something to do. He wanted to get up and go to work each day. He just couldn't wait for baseball to start. We had our spring training plans all ready for this year ..."

A much mellower Caray became a doting step-grandfather in recent years. He was the softest touch for Dutchie's grandchildren, Brendan and Caitlin Newell.

"He just loved Brendan," Dutchie says. "He just thought the sun rose and set with him. I could not believe how much he loved that baby. He told me how lucky I'd be, that I'd be around when Brendan would grow up. And Caitlin just adored him. She was just starting to get to know Harry. She called him 'Pop.'"

Harry's presence was so powerful that oh-so-many folks expect him to walk in the door at Wrigley Field any day and light up the place. Dutchie Caray has some of the same feelings. He's gone, but he's not gone. He possessed such a powerful life force that even death can't erase his persona. Somehow, his spirit never left the Friendly Confines, evidenced so powerfully by the waves of emotion on Opening Day, when Dutchie filled in brilliantly as the maestro of "Take Me Out to the Ball Game."

"I had the weirdest dream that Harry was here," Dutchie says of one May night in 1998. "I gave his clothes away, but I had this feeling that he'd walk right in here."

Chip Caray

Chip Caray has not missed a beat in succeeding his grandfather as WGN-TV's top baseball announcer. There was no rough transition period, no problem in raising one's voice as Kerry Wood zeroed in on the 20-strikeout mark against the Astros, no missed cues for commentary when producer/director Arne Harris presented his staple crowd shots of hats and attractive women.

But as the latest in the line of Caray announcers settled in, there was still a sense of trying to change the family his-

Skip, Harry and Chip Caray *(Photo courtesy of Steve Green).*

tory. Harry Christopher Caray III may share a name with his famous forebear, but he vows he won't share a lifestyle. It was a sense of "better late than never" in getting to know his grandfather. The younger Caray does not want a repeat of family separations that kept grandson from really relating to grandfather until the last decade.

"I didn't see him much when he was with the White Sox," Caray, who grew up in St. Louis, says. "I didn't really catch on with him until the cable (WGN's signal) began penetrating St. Louis. I'd see him when he'd come down to Atlanta (where father Skip Caray worked) and I was out of high school. I'd go to games with my dad, hang out with my grandfather, and we'd have dinners after the ball games and stay out and all that kind of stuff. Those were the days when I really started talking with him about getting involved in the business."

The elder Caray, seeing his family scattered about due to two divorces, began to reel everyone back in when he expressed pride at his Hall of Fame induction speech in 1989 over having three generations of the same family handling pro sports broadcasts. Chip, two years out of the University of Georgia, had just been named the TV voice of the National Basketball Association's Orlando Magic. In 1991, Harry, Skip and Chip, who by then added Braves cablecasts to his resume, were finally reunited on the air during a Cubs-Braves telecast at Wrigley Field.

Harry Caray never used to celebrate Christmas with family, scarred by his memories of joyless holidays as an orphan in St. Louis in the 1920s. But in the last decade of his life, he softened and began holding Christmas gatherings of the far-flung Caray clan. Chip Caray missed all but one due to conflicts with his Magic schedule.

"Everyone wants to have a Norman Rockwell-esque-like Christmas celebration," he says. "But later on in his life, and largely in part because of Dutchie, he was able to understand the importance of family, maybe not so much for him, but for everybody else to be able to spend time with him at that most important of holidays.

"The one time I was able to go, almost the entire family was there. It was great to see everybody for the first time, sit down and have dinner, shoot the breeze, and get to know your relatives, see your cousins and second cousins. It was one of the happy memories I had, and I'll always cherish it.

"It may have repaired (feelings) for him, but it was still painful for a lot of members of the family, and still for me, too, that so many things were missed, were forgotten, and were put on the back burner. This business takes a great toll on you, and you miss things that are important, maybe not to you, but to other people. Later on in my grandfather's life, he did start to understand that he was important to us, not because of who he was as a broadcaster, but who he was as a person. We were sad and disappointed that we didn't have more of an opportunity to have him understand the role he played as a patriarch, not just a professional announcer."

Harry Caray, of course, looked forward to pairing up with Chip on Cubs broadcasts in 1998. But his death not only thwarted that dream-teaming, but also prevented him from meeting his first great-grandchild, Summerlyn, infant daughter of Chip and Susan Caray. Dutchie Caray accompanied Susan and Summerlyn Caray to games at Wrigley Field early in the season when the latter pair came up from their year-round Orlando-area home. Chip Caray feels a further sense of loss that his grandfather could not meet the first of yet another generation in his family.

"There's always going to be this terrible void that he didn't meet his great-granddaughter," he says. "He at least got to see a picture of her. He was really looking forward to meeting her. It came five or six weeks shy of happening. It's a great lesson to anyone to take advantage of every day, because you don't know what will happen. You have to appreciate your family.

"Mind you, I'm not at all bitter or angry. It's just one of those situations where what this business gives you, it also takes away. I made a promise to myself and my family that baseball is going to be very important in my life. But when baseball is not going, my family is going to be the love of my life. Some of the sacrifices my father and my grandfather have made, taught me both by what they've done and what they haven't done that you have to put your kids and your family first sometimes. That's what you should do in any event. Hopefully, I won't make the same mistakes that my predecessors have made, but hopefully, I'll follow the successes they've had as well."

Chip Caray is thrilled that his grandfather was able to find stability and love in his 22-year marriage to Dutchie.

"She's not my grandmother, but I am grateful for the things she was able to do," he says. "She was with him through his illnesses. Think of how Don Drysdale passed away. He was by himself in a hotel room. That would be the most horrible way to go. To know that he was around loved ones and friends, in the environment he was in, I'm sure makes everybody in the family feel good. I am grateful that he had someone who gave him happiness."

In the end, Chip Caray concedes that baseball gave his grandfather the grounding he always desired after a rough childhood. And he agrees with Dutchie Caray that Harry's love of the game kept him going into his dotage.

"This is a sport and a business where the bug really bites you," he says. "Once it gets into your system, it's a virus you never really get rid of. My grandfather loved the game, loved being around it, and it kept him alive. He could not have functioned without baseball, without Opening Day, without the joy and love of the game. They kept him going.

"As he got older, he said, 'I've got to hang in there. These people need me.' That's a great tribute to him and a greater tribute to the fans.

"He was the prototypical walking, living example of the American Dream. To go from being an orphan to a member of the Hall of Fame, maybe one of the most beloved people in this city's (Chicago) history, we would all take that deal right now if we could have it."

Pete Vonachen

If it wasn't enough hearing Harry Caray's baseball stories for more than three decades, then buying a baseball team for yourself absolutely quenched your thirst for the game.

With Caray's encouragement, longtime buddy Pete Vonachen of Peoria, Illinois, took the plunge into ownership and a place as one of Caray's off-the-air characters he always mentioned during Cubs broadcasts. Vonachen was one of Caray's closest friends, and ended up as one of three eulogists at his funeral, getting off some funny lines Caray himself would have loved.

"Since I became close to Harry in 1950, I really got interested in the game," Vonachen says. "In 1983, they had a team in Peoria called the Peoria Suns in the Midwest League. It was the California Angels' Class A affiliate. The guy who owned it was just there one year and didn't do very good. It was obvious he had to leave town.

"A couple of sportswriters grabbed me two or three times and took me out for drinks. Everybody in Peoria knows you

Pete Vonachen *(Photo courtesy of the* Peoria Journal Star*).*

get a couple shots of V.O. in me, I might do anything. So they talked me into buying the ball club.

"I kept telling Harry 'They want me to buy this team down here.' He said, 'Oh, you got to do it. You got to do it.'

"I'd never been around a baseball team. I didn't know. Plus, I was getting ready to retire. I'd had two or three businesses and I didn't know whether I wanted to take on a baseball team. I know baseball, but operating a team is all together different. I had no experience whatsoever, but they kept talking and said, 'We've got to have professional baseball in Peoria.' That's how I got into it.

"I was trying to figure out whether to buy this thing. And Harry was saying, 'You'd have a ball.' Then I ran the team (as the Cubs' Class A farm club) until 1988."

Vonachen's relationship with Caray actually began with a basketball connection. Baseball came later.

"In February of 1950, Bradley (University) was going to play St. Louis University," he says. "And back in those days, Bradley, Cincinnati, St. Louis, those teams were all in the Top 50 in the country. In fact, in 1950, Bradley was rated No. 1 a lot throughout the season. They played in the finals of the NIT against CCNY and got beat and they played in the finals of the NCAA—you could do that back in those days—and played CCNY and lost again.

"Harry was doing St. Louis basketball. He'd do Cardinals baseball and then University of Missouri football and then he'd go right into St. Louis University basketball.

"Back in those days, I was operating the concessions at the old Robertson Field House. That was my job. I had just graduated from Bradley in 1949. This was the first job I'd ever had. The school gave me the contract. It was a brand new field house that seated 8,000 people.

"So a guy by the name of Dave Meister, who was sports information director at Bradley, came to the field house on a Friday afternoon—the game was on Saturday night — and he said, 'Did you ever meet Harry Caray?' I said no. He said, 'Do you want to meet him? I've got to go out to the airport and pick him up.'

"We went out and got him and we were driving from the airport to the Pierre Marquette Hotel. He says, 'What is there to do in this town?' I said, 'We'll pick you up at 6:30 right here.'

"It took us from 6:30 that night until 4:30 in the morning to show him what there was to do in Peoria. We pull up at the Pierre Marquette and he said, 'What's this?' I said, 'Harry, it's after 4 in the morning. Everything's closed.' I knew of a couple of after-hour places, but I had to work the next day.

"The next day I went to work, ran the concessions and we had a jammed house. After the game I said, 'I think I'll wait until Harry gets off the air and I'll go up there and say goodbye to him.'

"He got off the air and I went up and shook hands and said, 'Harry, it's nice meeting you. Hope we can get together again sometime.' And he said, 'Whoa, wait. Where are you going?' I thought, 'Man, I'm beat.' He said, 'I've got an 8 o'clock flight in the morning. Let's you and I have a short night. Just a couple of drinks.'

"At 4:30 in the morning, we pulled up in front of the Pierre Marquette. During the night, I had said, 'Don't worry about getting a cab. I'll take you to the airport in the morning.' T here was no way I was going to go home and sleep and get up, so I went up, took a pillow and blanket and slept at the foot of his bed so I could take him to the airport in the morning.

"So that's how I met Harry Caray. Boy, we had a hell of a time."

Caray and Vonachen hit it off despite their different backgrounds.

"You know, when you look at it, from a professional standpoint he and I had nothing in common," Vonachen says. "It's just that we had the right kind of chemistry. I don't know. We just seemed to hit it off.

"One thing. A lot of people liked to argue with Harry and he loved it when people argued with him. In fact, he'd have some guy going real good, he'd look at me and wink and he'd keep it going. Dutchie would be going nuts because he was baiting him.

"But I didn't do that. If Harry said this is what we're going to do and this is what I think ... We'd have disagreements, but we wouldn't argue about it.

"Our friendship was so personal. It had nothing to do with his job or my job. It was just that we were two guys who hit it off, got along. We'd spend time together, laugh and have fun.

"A lot of times, we would go out and not even talk baseball. We'd just go to a couple of bars on Rush Street or whatever, sit around and shoot the breeze. If he wanted to talk baseball, we'd talk baseball. If he didn't, we'd talk about something else."

Vonachen witnessed how Caray was a voracious reader. If you wrote something about him, he'd see it. World events, politics, business. Harry read it and then could argue about it.

"Harry read three, probably four newspapers every day from cover to cover," he says. "He was very, very well versed on most anything. There weren't a lot of things in this world that Harry couldn't talk very intelligently on. And I don't think a lot of people realized that."

Vonachen also survived some hair-raising rides with Caray. As with his brushes with health problems and being hit with a cab, he was virtually indestructible.

"He was a driver's education dropout," Vonachen says. "He was absolutely the worst driver. When we would ride with Harry do you know what we would say? 'Our Father who art in heaven ...'

"I mean this guy, if he was in the left-hand lane and wanted to go to the right-hand lane, he went. I don't care if there were 16 semis there. He was going to go. And God always protected him.

"There are two Avanti Restaurants in the Phoenix area. One on Scottsdale Road and one on Thomas. We always went to the one on Scottsdale. So one night Harry decided we were going to go to the one on Thomas. We'd never been over there.

"I said I'd drive. And Harry said, 'No. No. I'll drive.' I said OK. It's raining like a son of a gun. So we start out there and he's bumping close to the curve and I said, 'Geez, Harry, move over.' He moved over.

"We've got cars turning left, one right. (Don) Niestrom's hiding in the back, I'm riding in the death seat. Finally, we said, 'Harry, you're driving in the turn lane.' He said, 'Boy. You got to watch how some guys drive around here.'"

Caray's eccentric motoring skills did land him in the hoosegow once.

"He was out in Indian Wells (near Palm Springs) visiting some people," Vonachen says. "He started home and he had his bright lights on and he didn't realize it. So the cops pulled him over, and of course Harry had had a few drinks. And he says, 'I'm Harry Caray' and the cop said, 'So what?' They gave him a sobriety test. Walk the straight line. That sort of thing.

"Harry said 'Wait, I've had two broken legs. I can't do that.' They threw the cuffs on him and he spent the night in the Indio jail until they bailed him out the next day. I don't know what the rules were then. Anyway, they felt he was suspect enough to put him in jail.

"Hell, I got pulled over twice with Harry and we never got a ticket. I remember once going to Lake Geneva. A Wisconsin state trooper pulled us over and Harry said, 'You stay in the car. Let me take care of this.' He walked back and the trooper was coming up with his pad. I was sitting in the car, looking through the rear view mirror. I couldn't hear, but I could see. All of a sudden this cop looked up and got the biggest grin on his face.

"Well, they shook hands and then Harry was talking to him, patting him on the shoulder. The guy got a pencil out, giving Harry his name, his son's and daughter's names. They shook hands again. The trooper got in his car. Harry came back to ours. He sat down and said, 'I got to send them a shirt and a couple of autographs.' He said the trooper told him, 'Tell your buddy to take it easy,' and that was the end of it."

The fans would re-energize Caray even though he wanted to call it a day—a phenomenon so many who have dealt with him witnessed.

"Especially the last few years, we'd leave the booth and start down the ramp and he'd say 'Man, am I tired,'" Vonachen says. "And I know he was bushed, because he put everything into the game.

"We'd get to the bottom of the steps and there would be a lot of people waiting. He'd say, 'Get me out of here. I'm tired.'

"I said, 'C'mon Harry, we got an appointment.' And he'd say 'Yeah. Yeah.' We'd get down to the car he'd just say, 'How can I turn down those little kids?' He'd go back and sign autographs for everyone. And that's the best example of what really made Harry tick."

Vonachen recalls a visit with Harry in St. Louis when Harry still was married to his second wife, Marian.

"There's a place called McQuary's. We whizzed down there after a Cardinals game and grabbed some ribs and went right home. He said, 'I was out a little late last night and Marian's not too happy with me.' It was a nice apartment. We went up there and Marian's still got a big burr under her. He brings me along because he figures she's not going to say too much. So he drags me into it.

"She wasn't too happy with us. In the apartment, if you went through the bedroom window, there was a roof on the apartment below. So Harry and I crawled out on the roof and ate the ribs out there, so Marian wouldn't be giving us hell all the time. I'll never forget that night."

Once Harry really chided Vonachen for a couple of episodes involving his ownership of the Peoria team.

"I'm not proud of something that happened in 1988. I just hate to lose. We had lost nine straight and now we're losing again. Our manager, Jim Tracy, had just been tossed out. The umpire was having a bad night, the poor guy. And everybody was on him to the extent where our manager and three of our players had gotten tossed.

"Now the fans are on the ump and I'm after him, too. We'd lost nine straight and I was just about going crazy. I felt myself losing control and I said, 'I'm going to do something awful stupid if I don't get out of here.'

"So I started to walk to the clubhouse, got just about to the bullpen and somebody hit a pop fly. The umpire called it fair and I'm going to tell you, it was a foot foul. Boy, I went bonkers. I went nuts.

"I'm on the field and I'm giving this umpire hell and he's saying, 'Get out of here, Pete. This crowd's going nuts.' They had to go back to the archives to find out what you do with an owner who runs out on the field.

"So he says, 'Get out of here. You've got this crowd going nuts.' I said, 'It's not me. It's your lousy calls.' So I got on my knees and begged him to throw me out. By that time, Rick Kranitz, our pitching coach, had grabbed me by the collar and said, 'Listen you SOB, get out of here or they're going to throw you out of baseball.' And he's dragging me by the collar to get me out of there.

"Now, as I'm leaving the field, I see the bats, the balls, the catching gear, all of it, in the dugout. So I said, 'Wait a minute. I've seen this on TV.' So I threw everything on the field. Everything.

"I got suspended for 12 games and fined $1,000. I said to the league president, George Spelius, 'You know, our clubhouse is outside the fence. Can I sit on top of the clubhouse and watch the game?' And he said, 'Yeah. That's outside the fence. You've got to be off the field an hour before the game and you can't go back on the field until an hour after.'

"The first night, I got a lawn chair, stretched over the gable there with an umbrella and the crowd was loving it. Loving it. I'll never forget I had a cell phone there and I called Greg Maddux to tell him what I was doing.

"After that first night, we went on a two-day road trip, and radio station WMBD got into it and started a contest. Any person with the best limerick, a poem or a song that had WMBD, Pete Vonachen and the Peoria Chiefs in it got to sit up there with me. Meantime, I had a carpenter go up and I had this big platform built up there.

"We had two people every night sitting up there. I had a charcoal grill. I cooked hot dogs and hamburgers and I had beer for them. The first night back with all this clamor, we had 7,000 people, the biggest crowd that's ever been in the ball park. We had to rope off the warning tracks. The next night we broke the record again.

"The first night, I had a wireless microphone and our announcer says, 'From the owner's sky box'—which was this folding chair sitting on a roof—'Pete Vonachen will now lead us in 'Take Me Out to the Ball Game.'

"The other story occurred in 1984. We had an organist by the name of Rocks Buckland and he was listening to my tirades about the umpires and said, 'Should I play "Three Blind Mice?"' I said, 'Yeah.'

"That umpire's mask went 100 feet in the air. I went running down there and said, 'What's the matter with you?' He said, 'You can't play that song. It's disrespectful to us. That organist is out of here.'

"I said, 'I want to tell you. If you throw that organist out, you'd better throw the organ out too, because I've got another guy who can play it.'

"Harry always got very upset at me when things like this occurred. Well, you tell me one time when Harry got on an umpire. He might have said it's a bad call, but he was very respectful to umpires. He was right. I will never condone what I did.

"He said, 'It's not your job to be out there doing those sort of things. All you do is make yourself look bad.' He was right. I always respected what Harry said. He would get on me about it."

Sometimes Harry went to Peoria to watch games.

"He was there in 1985 when we switched from the Angels to the Cubs and our opening day pitcher was Greg Maddux. Harry came down to kick off the start of the Cubs' relationship with the Peoria Chiefs, and he brought Shawon Dunston with him. He was down again when we dedicated the stadium in '92 and then he was down the year of the strike in '94. It was hard for him to get here. The two times he came other than the strike years, we sent a charter flight to pick him up and flew him back right afterwards."

That essence of Harry, and all of Vonachen's decades with his friend enabled him to put both heartfelt emotion and humor into his eulogy at Caray's funeral.

"I was lucky," he says. "I had the good Lord on my side. I'm not that good. It just kind of rolled out and it just came from the heart. That's the best way to describe it. It came from the heart. I read some of it because I wanted to make sure I didn't pass over some things, but a lot of it was ad lib."

Grant DePorter with Harry Caray *(Photo courtesy of Harry Caray's Restaurant).*

Grant DePorter

Grant DePorter didn't have to go out on the town with Harry Caray. Ol' Holy Cow himself would arrive in his company frequently, once the ultra-popular Harry Caray's restaurant got started in November 1987 at the corner of Kinzie and Dearborn in Chicago.

Now managing partner of Harry Caray's, DePorter can offer any kind of memory you want of his friend.

"Around the same time Chip decided to join the Cubs, Harry's spirit got totally re-energized," DePorter says. "He'd never been happier that I had ever seen. For like four months, he was just whatever he could do. Mr. Nice Guy.

"He called me up and said, 'Grant, you're probably getting lots of fan mail and stuff. I said, 'Yeah, Harry.' He said, 'Why don't I come by, we'll have lunch and I'll just sign it all.' I said, 'Well, I don't think you want to sign it all. It's a lot.'

"So we sat down, and Dutchie was with us, and had three hours of lunch. As he's signing, to kill time he started telling me his life story. We went through a three-hour lunch and only made a small dent. Then he came back the next day, we had like a three- or four-hour dinner and this is just another dent.

"Then we did another dinner—this was in January before the Cubs convention—and then he said at the end, 'Oh, my gosh.' But he would have killed me if I had left out one letter. He wanted to respond. So he had me UPS the rest to Palm Springs. Within a week, I had it all back. I was just amazed."

Of course, DePorter could always tap into Caray's wellspring of life stories.

"During that time, he told me about his first meetings with Elvis Presley. Harry was in Memphis, gets a call from somebody on the phone. A voice goes, 'Hello, Harry, this is Elvis Presley.' And Harry goes, 'Yeah. Yeah. Right.' He doesn't believe it.

"The voice goes, 'I am Elvis. I'll prove it to you. Look out your window in a minute.' Harry looks out and all of a sudden he sees this pink

Elvis Presley

Cadillac driving up toward the hotel and Harry goes,'It might be. It could be. It is. It's Elvis Presley.'

"So Harry and Elvis talked for a while. Harry's saying,'Hey, Elvis, why don't you join me at the game?' Elvis said,'I'd love to, but if I went there, they'd tear the place apart, but why don't I hook up with you after the game?' So Harry says,'Yeah. That's nice.' He doesn't believe it."

"After the game, someone approaches him and says Mr. Presley sent his Rolls Royce for you. Took him off to Graceland, and it's Harry and Elvis and some other people out at Graceland. They're sitting, talking for a long time. And Elvis says to Harry,'Oh, my God, I'm so rude. You probably haven't eaten all day, have you? Do you like ribs?' The next thing you know, Elvis called his favorite rib restaurant and when Elvis called, I guess the whole place comes over.

"Harry said they brought barrels full of ribs, and they sat, talked and ate ribs until 4 a.m. Drank Budweiser and ate ribs.

"Several years later, Harry was in Vegas and there's Elvis' name up in lights. Harry paid some guy $20 to get a note to Elvis. Elvis got the note and Harry said Elvis ran out of the dressing room, grabbed him, brought him into the dressing room and basically played another whole night with him."

After Caray collapsed on Valentine's Day in 1998, DePorter began playing his famous partner's favorite song at a specific time each night.

"We heard it all on the news on Sunday and on Monday we started playing a tape of him singing 'Take Me Out to the Ball Game.' We did it at 7:30, that being 7 1/2 like 7-and-a-half innings.

"The whole crowd, everybody in the place sings along with Harry every night. That's our ongoing tribute. We're going to do that forever. People love it. Sometimes they get up on the bar and yell,'Let me hear you. A-one, a-two ...' We have a 120-inch big screen TV we installed in January that we show it on.

"We've had in Nancy Faust, the original (White Sox) organist who played with Harry. We had the video with the Cubs' organist, so we had to sync it up since she was used to Harry kind of leading her with his mike. But her back was to Harry. So it was really hard to play and look over her shoulder and see where Harry was. But we got it down.

"We actually gave the big Harry glasses to everybody in the bar while Harry was in the hospital. We were trying to sing so loud that Harry could hear us."

Harry's voice was so distinctive you didn't have to see him to appreciate him.

"I get a call from someone asking if we let dogs in the restaurant," he says. "I said we only do it for guide dogs with blind people. The guy says, 'Well, I'm blind.' So I say fine.

"So he comes in and he's very nice. The dog's out there. I went out to talk to him and the guy is very nice. I had no clue who this guy was, and I was curious that he was by himself and doing all right. He said he loved baseball, and I recognized after a little bit that I had seen him on 'Primetime Live' two nights before.

"He told me about Mike Veeck and how he felt he had to go to Harry Caray's, because Harry had been close with Bill Veeck. Mike had mentioned Harry Caray's and he had to make his pilgrimage there.

"It was kind of weird talking to him because the whole place is visual with Harry's life on the wall. We had to describe it to him, what's actually there. Harry with Pete Rose. Harry with Stan Musial. And what they're doing."

Harry Caray's restaurant became a magnet for celebrities from virtually Day One.

"This was in the first two months the restaurant was open," DePorter says. "Harry was here with Stan Musial and Tanya Tucker walks in. Tanya Tucker and Harry start talking. They like each other. And Harry says, 'Hey, you wanna sing with me?' She says sure. So shortly thereafter, they're both in the bar, singing 'Take Me Out to the Ball Game,' and Stan Musial whips out his harmonica and starts playing backup. The whole bar was singing along."

DePorter says Caray maintained his good cheer despite having booze banned in his life by his physicians.

Harry Caray serving 45-cent beers at his restaurant
(Photo courtesy of Harry Caray's Restaurant).

"He hadn't had a drink since he fell in Miami (in 1994)," DePorter says."He would drink O'Doul's or nonalcoholic wine. Being the consummate Bud man, he would put a Bud bottle in front of him, but the glass was filled with O'Doul's. He was going to support Budweiser to the end."

But never, ever did Caray—Cub fan, Bud man—ever object to anyone else enjoying libation. And, in fact, he helped his legion of rooters get through the worst losing streak in Cubs history, the wild-and-crazy 14-gamer that opened the 1997 season. Beers were virtually on Harry at his joint for nearly two weeks.

"We did 45 cent draught beers until the Cubs won their first game," DePorter says. Forty-five cents was based on 1945—the last year the Cubs won the pennant and the first year Caray broadcast major-league baseball.

"We started after they lost the first six," DePorter says. "And it just went nuts. Harry and us, we were getting so many

Harry Caray Restaurant, 33 West Kinzie, Chicago, Illinois *(Photo courtesy of Harry Caray's Restaurant and Bart Harris Photography, Inc.).*

phone calls. Harry was getting calls around the clock. We got so many calls here, we could have five or six radio stations on the phone at one time and we ran out of managers. I would be handing phones to customers. Someone told me we were even on the MGM Grand's tote board. People were betting how many beers we would serve before the Cubs finally won a game.

"We were in every paper in the country, on every radio station. We were the lead story on ESPN every day, where they would do updates on how many beers. We went to 50,000 beers sold. We actually had Harry behind the bar serving beer and that was an unreal sight. We actually had people lined up around the building. You couldn't get people in the building.

"When he had that Budweiser in his hand trying to hand it out, it looked like God reaching to Adam.

"When the Mets finally lost to the Cubs, a headline in the *New York Times* read, 'Mets raise the price of beer in Chicago.'

Like others close to Caray, DePorter was amazed the former kept his Chicago home phone number listed, considering his popularity and controversy he generated—not to mention all the tipsy folks who drowned themselves in low-cost brews in April 1997.

No one ever thinks to even look in such an obvious place," DePorter says of the phone book. "They don't call 411 and ask for Harry Caray. So he didn't get a lot of calls, but he did get calls.

"Dutchie, it drove her nuts, because fans would call and try to talk to him for hours, express their opinion. 'Harry, the Cubs suck. What are we going to do about them?' Harry just wanted to always be in touch with the fans. He wanted to make them feel like they could always get ahold of him.

"That's why his seat in the restaurant, table 70, was the closest to the door. So every single person who came in would have contact with him. Also his seat in the bar was closest to the door.

"People would call me up and ask, 'What were his hobbies?' Beyond baseball, it was just socializing. He wanted to be with people. I couldn't see that he did anything beyond that. He liked to hang out and talk with people.

"He came into this restaurant every other day, from April to November. Sometimes, he'd come in for lunch and dinner and just talk to people.

"He could even be in the bathroom and people would want his autograph. He would never turn anyone down, though. Ever. He was always very nice about it. He had to sign an autograph for everybody.

"I've heard stories about every other celebrity in the city. At some point, they're just rude. Harry was always thankful."

DePorter said money never was that important to Harry.

But didn't Harry have a tab at the restaurant? Was there any limit on the tab?

"No," DePorter replies. "He worked the room. He worked about a million times harder than anyone could have asked. He worked this place. He loved it. He loved people. So it was perfect. He was the Bud Man. What better restaurant celebrity could you have? A guy who'd been around for almost 54 seasons, was the spokesman for Anheuser-Busch.

"I sponsor the fifth-inning scoreboard at Wrigley Field, and I wanted to do Harry Caray trivia. So I wanted to come up with all these questions, I didn't want any boring stuff. The Cubs came up with, 'What year did Harry start with the Cubs?' That was fine.

"But 'How many Budweisers did Harry drink in his life?' I thought was better. Plus or minus 5,000 or 10,000. I calculated 73,000 Budweisers and 300,000 alcoholic drinks, based on information he had told me. That is a lot of liquor.

"That's the kind of stuff I was trying to get up on the board, but they wouldn't do it. Dutchie and Harry and I figured that's what it was."

Pete Stazzone

***Pete Stazzone** (Photo courtesy of Kate Oelerich Photography).*

Now a Scottsdale, Arizona, businessman, Pete Stazzone was a co-founder of Harry Caray's Restaurant. Stazzone traces how the idea to name the restaurant came about.

"We were in the process of developing the hotel on Congress and Dearborn, which is now called the Hyatt on Printer's Row," he says.

"We needed to put a restaurant in there, as well as room service. The building was a historic building called the Morton Building. So we called it the Morton Hotel. Of course, the natural was to go to Arnie Morton and put in a Morton's Restaurant.

"So we were negotiating with Arnie. At the same time, we were purchasing the building which is now Harry Caray's Restaurant. At the time it was Miller's Steakhouse. It was boarded up. We were going to buy that property and put a 20-story high rise on that site, because it had been announced some Canadian firm was going to build the Illinois World Trade Center across the street. Something like that. So it was a real estate play."

Stazzone and Co. had to bring in an expert in the business.

"We hadn't been in restaurants," he says, "so we were talking to Rich Melman and all the big restaurant people in Chicago to put a restaurant on that site, because it already had proven to be a pretty successful steak house. We felt we would at least have a tenant for the first floor.

"During the middle of this, Arnie Morton withdrew from the hotel project and some of the big restaurant people were booked and couldn't get to us for nine or 12 months. And they wanted an exorbitant price.

"We hired a guy named Dan Rosenthal, who happened to be chief operating officer for Morton Restaurants. Morton's Steakhouse hadn't gone nationally at that point. Arnie said he had this great guy who was going to be leaving. So it was perfect. We started a restaurant company called Chicago Dining Authority and hired Dan Rosenthal to head it up. We said here are these two places.

"When we hired Dan, Harry had just had a stroke and it was unknown if he would be returning to the booth and what shape he would be in. So at that time, Jimmy Rittenberg had opened Ditka's and it was wildly successful, in terms of gross revenues at least. And Dan Rosenthal said there was an article in some paper that quoted Jimmy Rittenberg saying the only celebrities that he would consider opening a restaurant with were Mike Ditka and Harry Caray.

"Our understanding was, that's probably true. Let's see if we can get Harry Caray. One of Harry's best friends we knew was Ben Stein, who happened to be an investor in our Morton Hotel project. So we decided maybe we can approach Harry via Ben Stein. Ben knew us. That's how it all came about."

"I attempted to put a Harry Caray's out here. We got it all together, got the approval of Harry and Grant DePorter. Then the building got sold in the process. The new owners doubled the rent, gouged us and made the numbers a little more difficult."

Once Caray got involved, he even provided his own design ideas for the restaurant.

"Harry definitely didn't want a sports bar," Stazzone says. "He wanted something like Gallaghers in New York. Upscale fine dining. He didn't want to be associated with just some saloon.

"So we built that restaurant and in fact, when we opened it, we didn't even put TVs in there because we didn't want people going in there thinking it was a place to hang out, drink beer and watch baseball.

"But the people who came in came from all walks of life. From people with tuxedos to the construction worker right of the job. And, of course, they came in to see Harry. And Harry is synonymous with the Cubs and baseball. We had to put TVs in.

"I remember the original projections. The merchandise part just blew by what we had projected. As well as the projected revenues just from the restaurant."

Mike Roarty

As marketing chief of Anheuser-Busch Co., Mike Roarty couldn't have dreamed up a better spokesman and beer salesman than Harry Caray.

"We did a series of commercials where we had Harry doing the boogie, dressed like one of the Blues Brothers, dancing with showgirls and so on," Roarty says. "And he's singing, 'I'm a Cubs fan, and I'm a Bud man.'

"And you know Harry, he really put a lot of enthusiasm and energy into it. So it was just a classic spot. And everybody in Chicago loved it.

"So I just told the story that people often asked and still do: How did you ever get Harry to do that commercial? I said, 'It was easy. We just followed him home one night with a cameraman.'"

But the fact that Caray returned in the 1980s to peddle Bud after being dismissed by the brewery as Cardinals announcer in 1969 wasn't as automatic as you'd believe.

"A lot of people didn't think so," Roarty says of Caray's comeback. "They thought I was crazy, but it couldn't have worked out better.

"There were people that knew he didn't leave Anheuser-Busch in good graces. There were hard feelings, mostly on his part. He was the Busch guy in St. Louis and he was well known for that. He was such a great salesman, just like he was in Chicago.

"But if anybody ever found a natural home, Harry found it in Chicago with the Cubs. It couldn't have been made for him better.

"I felt at the time that Harry would do what we needed him to do. We had a disastrous strike in 1976 and we had no beer in Chicago for awhile. Well, the strike lasted for three months, but the damage lasted for about six by the time you filled the pipelines, got back on your feet and got everybody going. And a lot of retailers in Chicago were mad at us because they weren't getting product.

"And so there were a lot of hard feelings to overcome. We had been the No. 1 beer in Chicago and we lost that. We dropped to No. 3 or 4.

"During that period of time, we needed something to give us a shot in the arm. And there was Harry. We talked to him and told him we were going to sponsor the Cubs. We wanted him to be our spokesman. And he had to do a lot of thinking, too.

"But he came to the conclusion, as I did, that it would be fun."

Roarty first met Caray at an Anheuser-Busch company function.

"Harry was one of those people who would talk to anybody and he talked to everybody," he says. "And he made himself available and accessible. He was just like a fellow you've known all your life. It kind of started there.

"Then as time went by, we got closer, especially with the association of the Cubs.

"In '87, he came in for a Cardinals-Cubs game, and he and Dutchie and my wife and I and Jack and Carol Buck went out to dinner at Tony's restaurant here in St. Louis, which is a premier Italian restaurant and one of Harry's favorite places.

"Tony's is a very pricey place, but it's also the finest Italian restaurant, I think, certainly, in the Midwest and maybe the country. They do it right with the tuxedos and all that kind of stuff. But it's not the kind of restaurant where people come over and hassle you.

"So we had a great evening and we're having dinner. Other than a nod of recognition or a brief hello, people left us alone. Harry and Jack were reminiscing and the stories were just hilarious.

"We had a great evening and when we stood up to leave, somebody in the back of this dining room said, 'Welcome home, Harry.' And you have to appreciate he's just had the stroke, he was coming back, but he was still struggling with it a little bit. And here this guy in St. Louis said, 'Welcome home, Harry.'

"And at that point, instantaneously, the whole room stood up and gave him a rousing standing ovation. We all got misty eyed. Jack shed a tear, all of us were just stricken by this.

"And Harry, he's the only one who took it in stride. 'Thank you very much, thank you.' Waving like some guy campaigning. It didn't faze him one damn bit and we were all crying."

Like everyone else, Roarty drew great amusement from Caray's verbal malapropisms. Big, obvious names were not immune.

"Jim Dowdle gave a great eulogy and in it he talked about how Harry had a way of mispronouncing names and sometimes forgetting them," he says. "It didn't faze him, just one of his idiosyncrasies, especially after the stroke.

"Michael Jordan was at a game and they asked him if he would go upstairs and be interviewed by Harry. And he said, 'Oh I love Harry, but I don't want to be interviewed.' They said, 'Why not?' And he said, 'Well, the last time he interviewed me, he introduced me as Michael Jackson.'"

"Cub fan, Bud man" was a pitch man's line. We know Harry loved the beer. How 'bout the team, considering he had all that Cardinals red still in his veins?

"He loved the Cardinals. He loved Stan Musial," Roarty says. "But he loved the Cubs, too. Harry could get excited about anything. He was a good salesman because he believed in his product.

"He loved the Cubs and to see him walking around Chicago was incredible. People just couldn't get enough of Harry. He was one of those guys who would visit with you at the table, greet all your guests, make them all feel at home. He was just a terrific guy."

Marty Cohn

Marty Cohn, Harry Caray's attorney and co-executor of his will, had one of the better inside looks at the man.

"I don't think there's anybody out there who would have anything negative to say about him as a person," he says. "Criticize his announcing? That's a matter of personal opinion. But as a person, it's hard to find anything bad about him.

"The worst thing you could say about him is that he was a drinker, and when he was unmarried, he would chase anything that was young and pretty.

"That's all you could say about him. He never stole anything. He wasn't a mooch. He wasn't obnoxious. He drank and he had a good time. If you were in a bar with him and wanted a little quiet, you weren't going to get it. But in a bar you don't expect quiet.

"As a person, he was a super guy. He was charitable. He didn't ask for anything. Nobody knew that he was involved with Maryville (Academy). You never saw a newspaper story or a television story saying here's Harry Caray talking to these kids.

"Most celebrities, if they went someplace and talked to somebody at an orphanage, a hospital or something, would bring their press agents with them. He didn't make any announcements if he sent a check to somebody. He just did what he wanted to do."

Cohn can laugh now about how his client negotiated his first White Sox contract, out (very) loud, with Bill Veeck in

1976. But he wasn't smiling then when the two characters began shouting at each other in a busy restaurant at the Executive House hotel in Chicago. Cohn was trying to speak for Caray at the time, but wasn't permitted.

Marty Cohn *(Photo courtesy of Marty Cohn).*

"I'm a hotshot lawyer trying to build this thing into a new career," he says. "To be just shut out, you wouldn't have thought it was very funny at the moment. Not for me. I lost control. It was a tough evening, I got to tell you.

"I knew stuff was going to happen because Harry couldn't be quiet. I negotiated a contract for him one time and I said, 'OK, now I want such and such as part of his package.' And he was sitting there and he said, 'I don't need that.'

"I said, 'Harry, we had an understanding. You're just going to be quiet and I'm going to negotiate the contract. If I'm going to ask for something and you're going to say you don't need it, we're not going to get very far.'

"And he said, 'Well, just don't get involved in these things. Just ask how much they're going to pay me and how many games am I going to broadcast.'"

A quest for megabucks wasn't a Caray priority.

"He was a different breed," Cohn says. "It wasn't the money. He would have worked for nothing. He told me that a million times and the thought that somebody might negotiate his contract and ask for more than they were willing to pay and lose the deal was frightening.

"That's why all of his contracts of late were based on a handshake. (Tribune Co. executive) Jim Dowdle said at the funeral they would get together to have dinner, talk about how much they were going to pay, shake hands and that was their contract.

"At the luncheon afterward, I said to Dowdle, 'You know, as a result of your action, I'm the lawyer who lost the fee.'

"But that's how Harry was. He didn't want anybody talking about his contract with the Cubs. He wanted to be sure he could play the game. It was 'How much can you pay me?' and Dowdle knew that and was as fair as he could be. Harry knew that and it didn't make any difference to him if he got another $100,000 or if he got another this or another that. He just wanted to call the ball game.

"When Harry got sick and they said, 'You're not going to travel. You'll do the home games and we'll pay X number of dollars,' he said OK. That was it.

"He always told the same thing. He'd say, 'They don't understand. If they told me I can't get paid, but I can work, I'd work anyway. What difference does it make what they pay me?'"

Bea Higgins

Bea Higgins was Harry Caray's personal secretary for 25 years in St. Louis. She worked at Ruthrauff & Ryan, an advertising agency that handled Griesedieck's Brewery, Caray's original sponsor with the Cardinals.

"When we got the Griesedieck account, the boss I worked for, Oscar Zahner, believed that beer and baseball went together," Higgins says. "And he was instrumental in getting Harry here. He came in 1944, doing hockey and a few things. Then the baseball broadcasts started in 1945.

"When Harry started, Gabby Street was with him and none of the articles I've read mention Gabby Street. He really kind of was a father image to Harry, a wonderful man. He was, I think, in his 80s or something when he was broadcasting with him. They just enjoyed each other's company so much.

"I think Gabby died in 1951. Then Gus Mancuso came on. He used to be a catcher with the Cardinals. Then, later,

Stretch Miller was on. And then Jack Buck.

"When Harry first started, he kind of talked a little fast. And the people at the brewery, I remember them calling my boss and saying, 'I don't think he's going to work. He talks a little bit fast.' My boss said, 'No. He's good. He's got something. Just hang in there.' And, of course, he turned out to be right."

Caray also broadcast Cardinals and St. Louis Browns road games via Western Union ticker.

"That was set up in the Paul Brown Building," Higgins recalls. "I'd go over with the engineer and get everything set up, watch him broadcast where the ticker tape is just saying, 'Ball One. Ball Two,' and he's leaning back, saying, 'It might be, it could be, it is.' You know, practically falling on the floor."

Caray's newfound career in the broadcasting booth gave him a bit of affluence for which he had longed.

"One interesting thing right after he broadcast the games for a while, he had never, you know, had these kinds of paychecks before," Higgins says. "And he said, 'There are two things I always wanted to get if I ever had any money.' One was a new suit at this exclusive men's shop in St. Louis and the other was a convertible. And he got both of them.

"I can't remember what the suit looked like, but I remember he called and I met him downstairs on 8th and Olive, where our building was, and rode around the block with him in the convertible. He was so thrilled with these two things that he always wanted and now he was able to buy."

Higgins continued her work for Caray through the years.

"After I got married and started raising my children, I just quit the advertising agency and then I just kept handling all of Harry's mail and stuff out of my home until he left St. Louis.

"He was a fan's person and I know with the mail, he read every letter and signed every letter. And he'd get upset if a fan didn't like him, because he wanted to be liked.

"To me, the mail went either way. They loved him or they hated him. There wasn't any in-between. They loved him, adored him. Or they didn't like him at all.

"When I was answering his mail or doing something for him out of my home, I would always have the broadcast on. But I wasn't really listening to who got a strike or a ball. I was listening to what he was saying. And, by the end of the evening, I'd say, 'Uh-oh, I'd better write that down. I'm going to get a letter.' Or he's going to get a call from the brewery. Or from a player."

Sometimes Caray's anger would well up over a critical letter.

"Somebody would make him mad and he'd want to answer them," Higgins says. "And I'd say, 'You can't say that.' He'd say, 'Well, what do you mean?' I'd say, 'Because you just don't say those things.' And he'd say, 'Well, that's what I want to say.' I'd tell him, 'Answer it yourself.'

"I remember one day I said, 'I'm not going to answer that. Answer it yourself.' And the next day he called and said, 'Are you off your muscle?' And then he'd say, 'Well, answer the damn letter the way you think we should answer it.' A guy would make him mad, because he didn't like it when somebody didn't like him.

"One other thing I want to mention about his mail. We got letters—obviously, people wrote for them—from blind people very often saying, 'We can almost see what you are saying.' And, you know, that's quite a feat.

"It was absolutely amazing. I know when he had his accident (1968), I went to the hospital and I'd say there were 50 big brown bags full of mail. Easy. I've got a picture of me standing there with all this mail in the room.

"I never thought he'd walk again. Or at least for years. And he said, 'I'm going to walk before spring training.' And he did. It was sheer determination. But he had that determination."

After Caray's departure from St. Louis in 1969, Higgins didn't talk to him all that often. But they had a nice meeting recently.

"The last time I saw him, I had been in communication," she says. "He wrote me a nice letter when my husband died and he sent his book when that came out. We really hadn't kept in touch like I wanted to. It just gets away from you. But I did see him in 1993 while I was working at another job in Clayton (Missouri) and he was staying at the Ritz, which was only two blocks away.

"We were talking on the phone and he said,'I'm going to walk up and see you.' He came up and we had a nice visit for a couple of hours and that's the first time I'd seen him since he left St. Louis. He seemed to be very, very happy when I saw him the last time and I was so happy about that.

"They loved him here. People came in droves whether the Cardinals were winning or losing. That's the kind of pull that he had. The main comment about his broadcasting was, 'He makes you feel like you are sitting right in the ballpark.'"

Bill Wills

A longtime friend of the Carays, Tribune Co. public relations executive Bill Wills became the family spokesman during Caray's last days in a Palm Springs hospital.

"The night before the doctors pulled the plug on Harry —I hate that term, but that's what happened—the exec VP of Tribune Co., the man who had hired Harry, Jim Dowdle, had flown in on the company jet," Wills says. "He loved Harry. He wanted to be there, even though I told him there was nothing he could do. He said,'That's OK. I want to be there.' So he flew in.

"He took Dutchie and Harry's boy, Chris—boy, he's a grown man—to dinner at my hotel. Dowdle said I'll take you to dinner to give both of you a break. Pick the best place in town.

"I said the best place in town will be packed and I don't think that's where we want to go, for one. No. 2, it's surrounded by places where press would be and, after being hounded by press all day, that's the last thing we want to do is put Dutchie and me in proximity to the press.

"So I said,'Why don't we go to my hotel, because it's too expensive for any of the press to be staying there and it's a good hotel and I'm sure the dining room is good.' So that's where we went.

"And we sat around talking about Harry stories. We each were contributing Harry stories. And whereupon I said there are so many Harry stories—there's got to be thousands of Harry stories—I think I'm going to write a book.

"Dutchie said, 'It's a great idea, Bill, but you would be writing one book after another book after another. You'd have to quit what you're doing.' And I said, 'Yeah, you're right.'

"Two nights later, following the wake, Dutchie invited a few friends to dinner. I sat next to Jack Buck and of course Jack was regaling us with his Harry stories. And I said, 'See. More stories. I've got to write this book.' And now here you are calling. It's a natural."

Wills witnessed the singing of "Take Me Out to the Ball Game" in church at the Caray wake in Palm Springs.

"Yeah, they allowed us to do it," he says. "In the cathedral here in Chicago, they almost went through the floor when I even mentioned it. They finally condescended to allowing us to have the organist play it his style, which was a little stilted. But I figured if I got it that far, don't push it."

Harry Caray with Bill Wills *(Photo courtesy of Bill Wills).*

Wills was the maestro of the end-act of Caray's life, a huge production befitting a giant of a man.

"I went out four hours after they called me," he says. "I was there for the entire work. And I also handled—produced—the funeral here.

"I handled all the calls (at the hospital). We blew out the switchboard twice. Their patients have included Sinatra, Bob Hope. Red Skelton died there last year. Obviously, celebrity upon celebrity had gone to this very famous medical center. They had never ever had their switchboard blow out. Harry made it blow out.

"They came in pleading with me. You have to make your calls shorter. Is there any way you can hang up? I said, 'What are you talking about?'

"They said, 'Doctors here, they can't reach nurses, they can't check up on their patients. New patients coming in can't find out where they are to report. You are stopping the entire operation of the hospital.'

"I said, 'I'm not stopping anything. This is the popularity of this man.' And I was not taking any fan calls or family calls. I was only taking media calls. They estimated I had over 1,100 media calls in 3 1/2 days.

"I did over 200 interviews myself on television and radio. I didn't sleep more than two hours any night in six nights. I'd get to the hospital, there would be crews waiting. I would leave, there would be crews waiting.

"I knew he was popular because I also had handled the publicity when he had his stroke 11 years ago. Then Mr. Dowdle called me and said 'Guess what? It's déjà vu all over again.'

"Again, I did it for the family more than anything. But also for the love of the man. I truly loved Harry. I was going to try and pull him back to life."

Wills was there when Caray's story ended. He also was there when—at least the Cubs' part of—Harry's saga began.

Then working for Tribune Broadcasting, Wills handled the press conference that introduced Caray as Cubs announcer late in 1981. He had sat on a dynamite story in the days previously.

"It was the best-kept secret ... Well, actually the second best kept secret," he recalls. "The best kept secret was the Tribune Co. buying the Cubs and Wrigley. The second best was Jim Dowdle getting Harry Caray.

"He called me, obviously, and said, 'Get down here.' And he said, 'Now, there's you, there's me and there's one other person besides Harry that knows this. So if it gets out, I'll know I didn't do it and Harry didn't do it, so you had better hope it doesn't get out."

Wills then hopped on the Caray circuit, even risking his neck as a passenger in a car Caray drove.

"When Harry would drive, his hands would gesticulate," he says. "I'd say 'Put your hands on the wheel, Harry.' 'Harrmph, don't worry about it.'"

"I'd been out with him many nights, partying. He buried me every time and I thought I was a party animal. I mean, that's what I do for a living. Harry was unique."

One night Caray and Wills ran into rocker Rod Stewart and a friend.

"We were with some Budweiser advertising executives," he says. "We were having dinner. Harry coerced me. We went to dinner at The Ivy, which is a star hangout kind of place. I've been in the business all my life, so they don't impress me any.

"We were sitting there having drinks and they were talking some business and I was more or less people-watching. And Rod Stewart came in with his new wife or new girlfriend. Very beautiful girl. Absolutely stunning.

"Sort of a hush went over the restaurant. Even though there were other celebrities there, this was sort of the hot celebrity twosome. As it turned out, their table was two tables from ours. And as they walked by the table, the ad guys just stopped talking in mid-sentence, looking at this stunning model. As was I. As was everyone in the restaurant. And Harry was still talking.

"They brought them right in front of our table, sat them two tables away from us. And one of the ad guys said, 'Harry, stop talking. Look at that beautiful woman with Rod Stewart.' Harry sort of like glanced over, took her in with a quick glance and came right back to his story. 'Yes, she's gorgeous. But she has no breasts,' he said.

"Whereupon I spit my wine out and everybody else is falling down. Because Harry's voice is like, you know. The whole restaurant heard it."

Joan Sorensen

Working in the programming department at WGN-TV, Joan Sorensen realized how much Harry Caray increased the flow of paper at the station.

"Harry gets—Harry got, I'm having a hard time talking about him in the past tense . . . at any rate, Harry would get mail by the carloads. Just volumes and volumes and volumes of mail.

"The station had an intern working on it at that time. And I don't to this day know who the baseball player was that she sent one of his post cards to.

Joan Sorenson *(Photo courtesy of Joan Sorenson).*

For example, one that says 'Dear Mr. Stan Musial, Thank you very much for writing to Harry.' She didn't recognize that this was a huge name in baseball.

"And whoever it was called and said, 'Damn it, can't you get somebody at a station like WGN that at least knows who the names are?' So I don't know if Harry called Jim Dowdle or the program manager at that time—it's all very vague in my mind. But he called and said, 'Damn it, you've got to get me somebody who knows baseball!'

"Not knowing what I was getting myself into, I said, 'I'll be happy to help Harry with his mail.' So they come in with this huge ton of mail. I've got one of the busiest jobs at the station a person could possibly have, and I said I can't even begin to do this. But I said I'd take some of it home and do whatever I could.

"My summers ever since then would consist of working at my home—we have a deck and would put lights up and a TV and watch Harry, Steve and the Cubs—and I would work from 6 p.m. until sometimes one in the morning just opening his mail. Opening. Just opening. Not even answering. That's how much mail Harry would get.

"He just got it by the carloads. And when I say carloads, I mean I would load it up in my car and my husband would have to help me carry it in.

"He was a very, very popular person. And I think of all the people in the world that would know that, beside his wife and his family, it was me. People just adored him.

"I'd say 99 percent of the mail came from fans who adored him. Old ladies. Old guys. Little kids. They weren't even Cubs fans necessarily. They just enjoyed listening to him and he converted them to Cubs fans. How many people he must have converted I would not even begin to know."

Sorensen last talked to Caray the day before he collapsed.

"I was going on vacation with my husband to our place down in Florida and I called him to tell him, 'Harry, if you need anything, I'm not going to be around, but I'll be back in two weeks,'" Sorensen says.

"The last thing he said to me was, 'Joan, you come back with that beautiful tan. I want to see all those freckles out.'

"And the second to last thing he said to me was, 'I can't wait for this season to begin.' He said, 'This is the culmination. I always wanted to work with my grandson. I didn't really get to work with my son, but this is close. This is the culmination of a lifelong dream for me.'

"He died on the night we were leaving the following morning for Florida. My husband said, 'We'll stay if you want to.' I said no. I had talked to Dutchie the day before and she told me they were going to disconnect and that would be it.

"I told her I really felt like staying here. And she said, 'Don't you dare. If Harry knew you were going to do that he would be so upset.'

"It was really a tough week, until I saw the highlights of the funeral on WGN. That was such a balm. That was so soothing. They really did celebrate his life and that's the way he would want it. It was great. You laughed through the tears, literally."

Sorensen felt close to Caray even from a distance.

"We had a relationship probably from afar," she says. "I probably met Harry in all my time of dealing with him no more than 15 or 20 times, believe it or not.

"When Harry joined our station, he was at the age where all he wanted to do was go home. He'd go from home to the ballpark then back home again. We had a limo for him. He had a stroke sometime in between so he probably came here even less after that.

"If he came to the station more than once a year, he was doing good. He had earned the right just to lead his life the way he wanted, as much as possible. We hired him to do the baseball games and that's exactly what he did.

"We did most of our dealings by phone, and when we'd see each other, I'd go out to the ballpark and see him occasionally there. Or we'd have occasional parties from the station, retirement parties and such, that he would go to. But I never really met him or spent time with him. When I did meet him, it was usually as fleeting as for other people, because there were always bunches of people wanting to get his attention.

"But I talked to him and Dutchie very frequently in these last years."

Caray was a busy traffic cop in putting names of fans and well-wishers on the air. Sorensen provided insight on how that worked.

"A lot of those names came from people out at the ballpark," she says. "They would bring notes to the administrative offices, a little place they had somewhere on the main floor. I guess there's a little PR department.

"I would get thousands of letters here. Thousands of requests for certain games, people who wanted their anniversaries read, or for someone sick in the hospital. And for the most part, unless it really reached me—and the ones that really reached me would be kids who were sick and needed some encouragement—I would usually type them up on a big long list and give them to the people going over to the ballpark who would then give them to Harry.

"I would word them and he would read them all just exactly the way I worded them. Beautifully. Not all at one time. But one after the other. I never remember a time when he didn't do it. If you asked him, he would always, always do it.

"I would give him photographs to be autographed, 500 at a time. I'm not kidding you. Over the summer it could be thousands. And he would sit there with his bright blue pen and write 'Holy Cow, Harry Caray' over and over and over again.

"I always sent a return, stamped envelope if he was in Palm Springs so he could get it back to me readily and you could count on it. In fact, the day before I last talked to him I sent him a whole ton of them. Because winter or summer, it almost made no difference. People still clamored.

"There was a school teacher in my hometown of Toluca, Illinois, near Peoria. She was an old maid school teacher when I was still in school. And I'm certainly not a little kid. She still teaches. She's 80 years old.

"She wrote a letter to Harry one time. It was all about loyalty. It was when the Cubs were having a very dismal season, losing one game after the other. And he read this one on the air. He said how important it is to be loyal and that loyalty truly means that you are loyal in good and bad times. I'll never forget that.

"That's a case where he read that because I was going through the mail and found this letter from Toluca, and I knew Miss Brandt. She was the highlight of the town. The Peoria paper came and interviewed her.

"It was one of those supreme moments where this little quiet figure that nobody ever paid too much attention to was the absolute heroine in the town. And it was because Harry did that.

"After that, she would take a busload of people up once a summer and I always had Harry make mention of her. And she just preened. Just like a peacock. So when he died, I sent her a holy card, a patch the players wear on their sleeves, the pin.

"They are the unsung heroes of our day. They do things without thought of being repaid or even having an acknowledgment. They do it because they care. Therein lies the difference between a great person and the fleeting stars of our time. You can't give them enough to make them happy."

Chuck McGregor

Chuck McGregor, the bar manager of El Chorro restaurant in Scottsdale, says, "I can tell you a story you are going to like, but I can't tell you any names.

"Harry was in here with Thom Brennaman, and I cannot remember who the other guy was, but we had a waitress working here and she was real sharp and they really liked her. She was waiting on Harry and Thom and a beautiful young girl comes in. They were talking to her a little bit. They were sitting at a table and she was sitting at the bar."

It seems Harry wanted to play matchmaker for his (unnamed) friend.

"Finally, after looking her over—and she was a young, gorgeous gal—Harry called the waitress over and said,'Is that a working girl?' And the waitress didn't quite hear him right. She said, 'Excuse me?' And Harry, trying to be real discreet, said again,'Is that a working girl?'

"The waitress is like,'What?' And Harry said again,'Is that a working girl?' Finally, the waitress realized that Harry was asking if the girl was a prostitute.'I don't think so, Harry. She's my daughter.'

"Harry about fell out of his chair, he was so embarrassed. Thom Brennaman still laughs about that one."

Bill Sullivan

Former Notre Dame basketball player and NBA draft pick Bill Sullivan provides some insight on why Harry Caray was so attached to Maryville Academy in Des Plaines, Illinois.

"When he moved to Chicago, he met Father Smyth," Sullivan says."And when he moved there was when we really started raising money for Maryville. There was a restaurant called Tommy O'Leary's we used to hang around in the '70s. About 10, 15 guys would put $25 apiece in and we took a bus to Maryville to have dinner with the kids. Harry got to know Father Smyth and got interested in (Maryville).

"Harry had a good friend by the name of Ben Stein, who had a lot of money and donated a building up there eventually. There were just a lot of guys who liked Father Smyth, who liked what he was doing. Since then, the thing has grown unbelievably.

"He raises it ($55 million budget), let me tell you. The list of the individuals and companies who donate money now is unbelievable. He's got everything up there now and he never says no to anybody."

Sullivan first linked up with Caray when he made his debut with the White Sox in 1971.

"I had a place in Chicago called Sullys, where I first met Harry. First day he was in town, as a matter of fact," he says. "It was called The Grapevine before that, and every time Harry came to Chicago it was one of his favorite spots.

"So he happened to walk in and he asked the bartender, 'Who changed my favorite place?' Because I changed it so much. He said, 'It's that guy over there.' That's how we met.

"It used to be a piano bar, and I took the piano out. He was with about four or five guys and I picked up his check. The men's room was downstairs at that time and I went to the bathroom and right behind me comes Harry.

"He said, 'Sully, you seem like a nice guy, but I want to tell you something. Don't ever pick up my check or I'll never come back. You can buy me a drink every now and then, but don't pick up my whole check.' So I said, 'Wow, do I love this guy already.' For a sports guy to say that is unbelievable."

Sullivan remembers a Harry encounter with Leo Durocher.

"The first place I had, Jack Pony's Pub in Chicago, I became friends with Durocher," he says. "And, by the way, I loved him. The guy was a gutsy guy, but he hated newspaper guys and broadcast guys—except Harry.

"Harry's in town about six weeks and on his day off, he wants to go to Wrigley Field. We get there early and Durocher is sitting in the bullpen. Harry

Leo Durocher

says, 'Let's go down and say hello to Leo.' So we're walking down the third base line and Leo takes a look at Harry and me and says, 'It was just a matter of time before you two jerks got together.' He didn't use the word jerks, however."

Sullivan was one of the organizers of the 1989 Las Vegas roast of Caray that raised money for Maryville.

"I wanted to do something for Father Smyth," he says. "You know, Harry's a loved guy and also the Cubs were great. So I went to the boss and said 'Here's a new idea, let's try it.' God, it was unbelievable. We had about 5,000 people.

"I did it with our customer base and also a lot of help from WGN. They promoted the hell out of it during games. Everybody just came. That's how much he was loved. I was lucky enough to get a lot of celebrities. Red Schoendienst, Jack Buck, Frank Sinatra, Tommy Lasorda. At the end, we gave —on behalf of Harry—a check for $200,000 to Maryville. So it was very successful. And everybody had a lot of fun."

Dave Dunne

Dave Dunne could always depend on two things come February—the return of the Cubs to the HoHoKam Park he manages in Mesa, Arizona, and Harry Caray getting in his own version of spring training.

"Harry was a great baseball fan and he would come to every game here, whether it was being televised or not," Dunne says. "His last year here, the first year at the new stadium, he would come to every game.

"After the seventh inning or eighth inning, he would be a little tired and want to go. So I would go into his box and take him down the elevator and escort him either to his car or to the HoHoKam Room, where he would sit and relax.

"The last time he was ever here, my daughter, who was 7 at the time, went into the booth with me and the three of us rode down the elevator by ourselves and he was telling her what a beautiful little girl she was, talked baseball to her, and went on about the weather in Palm Springs.

"When he passed away, she said, 'I'll never forget that ride with Harry.' That's a fun story for me.

"She's got flaming red hair. Her name is Shannon. He patted her on the head and said 'Shannon, you are the prettiest redhead I've ever seen.' And he told me, 'Dave you're going to have your hands full.' "

Dunne also recalls Caray needing to shoot a 10-second quickie spot for the Jackie Robinson Nike tribute after a game he broadcast at HoHoKam Park.

"It's after Harry has worked the game and we get him in the elevator and we're going down to get him to the golf cart to take him where the shoot is going to be out in the outfield. He looked at me and said, 'Dave, I'm tired today. I've got to do this commercial. I don't know if I feel like signing any autographs.' I said OK.

"As soon as that elevator opened, there were hundreds of people waiting there. And his whole countenance changed. I mean he went from being tired and kind of dragging to having a big, beaming smile on his face. He walked out into them and he was like the Mayor.

"He walked out into these people, they were shaking his hand, he was pressing the flesh, signing autographs for everybody. He never let these people know he was tired. He never let them know he had to get to this commercial. He never crabbed about anything.

"So finally, he signed for just about everybody. He got in the cart, we went to the shoot. Then the commercial shoot ran a little long, got over, he got back in the cart and said 'Now, I'm going to be a little late for dinner with Dutchie.' She was waiting for him in the HoHoKam Room.

"He said, 'I've got to get to the HoHoKam Room really quick. I can't stop and sign any autographs.' I said, 'OK. Here we go.'

"Same thing happened. We don't get two feet, and the people just mob him right outside where the commercial was being taped. They were all over. He stayed. He signed for everybody. Shook everybody's hand. Told stories. Just did the whole same thing, because he was a fan at heart and he wanted these people to go away feeling good about their day at the ballpark."

Vince Bommarito

Vince Bommarito, owner of Tony's Restaurant in St. Louis, remembers the night Harry Caray came into one of his favorite eateries in his first appearance after his 1987 stroke.

"We heard this clamoring. Everyone in the room stood up and was clapping," Bommarito says. "Harry was crying. Jack (Buck) and I had walked ahead, and we stopped and Jack looked at me and I looked at him and he said, 'Did you ever have anything like this before?' And I said, 'No, never.'

"Later, Harry comes over and Jack said, 'God, Harry, that's really something. Look at this. They are still clapping.' I guess there were 75, 80 people in the room. And Harry said, 'Aaargh, this happens all the time.'

"I've had presidents, I've had all kinds of celebrities and tennis stars and movie stars. I've had people get a little bit of a hand as they came through after an accomplishment of some kind. But never had a standing ovation. So spontaneous.

"When he came with the Cubs for a game in St. Louis, he never missed a night at Tony's. And he invited me up to the booth. I didn't do it for commercialism. But Harry said, 'Come on up Sunday.' And if I wouldn't come up, he'd take it personally."

Bommarito also tells the now-famous story of how even potential muggers had respect for Caray in St. Louis.

"They had an all-night restaurant in the Chase Park Plaza Hotel called The Tack Room," he remembers. "A lot of us would go there and have a bite to eat with our friends when the nights were too busy to eat.

"Well, Harry was a night guy. He'd go there. One night he parked his car on Kingshighway, which is kind of desolate late at night. Kingshighway's fine. But not too far away there were some restaurants that weren't our best.

"Some thugs come by and they see this guy by himself, walking across Kingshighway and they stopped him and were going to rob him. Then they see it was Harry. And they say, 'Harry, what are you doing by yourself this time of night by yourself? Get back in your car.'

"And he said, 'Oh, I'm going to the Chase.' And they said, 'OK. Be careful, Harry.'

"I mean, everybody loved Harry. And that's a true story."

Caray's love of Italian food held forth at Tony's.

"I mean, this guy up until a year ago, he'd come to my place after the game," Bommarito says. "It could be 10:30, 11. Hell, he'd eat pasta with clams. Chicken with the fruit sauce. Vegetables. Tomato and onion salad. Ice cream pie. At 12 o'clock at night, you know?

"When I'd go to Chicago for the restaurant show in May every year, I'd always give him a call and go up and visit in the box. And since he had his restaurant open, I'd always go over that night and have dinner with him.

"And when you had dinner with him, it would take you six hours, almost. Because every single person would come up. He wouldn't just sign their menu. He'd ask their name. He'd talk, you know. I mean he was unique."

Bommarito suspects Caray never lost his love for the Cardinals.

"He had to put up a front," he says. "He'd come in late at night after the Cardinals had beat the Cubs. And people would say, "Oh, we got you tonight, Harry.' And he'd never say anything against the Cubs. But I think in his heart, he was born and raised here . . . "

A pause.

"But he was a true Cubs fan. He loved the Cubs. Yeah, he loved the Cubs."

Jimmy Rittenberg

Jimmy Rittenberg was an impresario for numerous Chicago restaurants. In getting to know Harry Caray, he realized he was an impresario for Chicago baseball, starting with the White Sox.

"When he came to town with the White Sox, he came in as a well-known figure, not a stranger. He got all the restaurant guys together and he said he wanted us to buy tickets in what he wanted to call Restaurant Row. I told him most of us already had tickets right behind first base, where we all hung out.

"He said, "No, Restaurant Row is going to be upstairs by me. So we all wound up buying something like 80 seats in the upper deck, underneath the press box. Harry used to lower that microphone and say, 'Hey, they're here from Restaurant Row. So and so's here, so and so, and so and so ....'

From left: Jim Rittenberg, Don Niestrom, Harry, and Don DePorter *(Photo courtesy of Bill Wills).*

"But the problem was that during April, May and September, when the attendance was down, they'd close the upper deck. So we'd come traipsing up and try to get to our seats and they'd be closed. So they forgot about us.

"We complained to Harry. He went to Bill Veeck and the bottom line was, we got our own usher who ran and got us beer and sandwiches and everything else. So, Harry's clout was substantial.

"I don't remember exactly the first time when we sang 'Take Me Out to the Ball Game.' I wish I could remember that and give you a definitive answer. He used to lower the microphone and we'd sing and all that, but I don't know if the first time it was such a big thing. I wish I could say he had a huddle and said, 'This is what we're going to do.' I think it grew into a tradition, rather than being a planned promotion.

Rittenberg feels that Caray changed the entire atmosphere of the White Sox organization.

"I think every time they had a good year, he made them sound great. And every time they had a slow year, he put asses in the seats. He was the ambassador for the White Sox. He was an ambassador for baseball. But certainly in Chicago, he was a badly needed ambassador for the White Sox.

"Everybody loved the White Sox because of Bill Veeck. Everybody loved the White Sox because they were exciting. But nobody wanted to go the games. It was just a South Side thing. North Side was cool and the South Side wasn't. People just gravitated to the Cubs, and the Cubs always had that sort of hapless puppy-type image. You know, do we want to go see the Great Dane that's fighting the Yankees all the time or do we want to go see the cuddly puppy that always loses its ass. So we had our own underdog in town.

"But when Harry was there, you know, there was some magic there. The ownership loved him. He loved the ownership. The fans loved him. He loved the fans. The players sometimes didn't love him, because he was brutally honest. Especially after (Jimmy) Piersall joined him. Those two guys were pretty outspoken."

Harry Caray for Mayor of Rush Street billboard.

Rittenberg says when Harry left the Sox, it was a great coup for the Cubs.

"I mean, it was the talk of the town. There were no sports talk radio stations then, but on the TV and in the papers, that's all they talked about. Reinsdorf and them, they kind of postured like, 'Well, that's OK. We want our stars to be on the field anyway.' That's when they brought in Donny Drysdale and Hawk Harrelson. Harry loved Bill Veeck, you know. When Veeck sold out, he hated those guys and they didn't like him.

"Look at what Mike Veeck's doing now with the St. Paul Saints. He's phenomenal. A chip off the old block," Rittenberg said. "And Harry fit right in with those guys. What the hell? With Harry, he'd go out in centerfield and take a shower.

"I'm telling you Einhorn and Reinsdorf had huge egos and they believed, maybe they really believed, baseball's a pure thing. The sport should sell itself. If you win, you've got people. If you lose, you don't have people. That's the way they looked at it. Our stars are on the field and da-da-ta-da ... Well, time has proven them wrong.

"The most profitable teams are the ones that have a lot of bars around them. Coors (Field)? A lot of bars. Cleveland (Jacobs Field)? A lot of bars. Wrigley (Field)? A lot of bars. Fenway (Park)? A lot of bars. Those are the ones that are full all the time.

"The Sox go and they build an antiseptic ball park. And their antiseptic ball park is sterile of people and they are having problems. They never looked at the human side of baseball. They looked at the numbers side. As you know and I know, the only side that counts is the human side."

Rittenberg helped Caray promote his "Mayor of Rush Street" image.

"I came up with a whole marketing thing, wrote it out and got ahold of some of Harry's contacts," he says. "One of his buddies, a guy named Leonard Leeds, had an outdoor billboard company. So I had a meeting. I put about four or five people together, a couple who worked for me, and Donny Niestrom and Lenny Leeds, and we put together this little program.

"Lenny said 'I'll give you the billboard across the street from Mariano Park, the big Rush Street billboard, and we'll put Harry Caray for Mayor of Rush Street on there. Donny Niestrom said anything you need from us, from Anheuser-Busch, just tell us.

"We took our cameras out to Sox Park and he put together about a two-minute video. It had Harry singing 'Take Me Out to the Ball Game,' he did a voice-over and it ended up with Harry Caray with the microphone, the flag behind him. What could be better? Harry Caray, baseball, Rush Street and the American flag.

"We took it around to all the bars and those that had VCRs—which weren't too many at that time—and played it. We played it at Faces all the time and up at Jukebox Saturday Night. Donny Niestrom at Anheuser-Busch came up with a trailer and we put it in the park right in the middle of Rush Street—it's called Mariano Park.

"One weekend we took the Budweiser trailer out there, decorated it with posters and banners and called it Harry Caray's campaign trailer. Friday night, he made the rounds of all the nightclubs and bought everybody a Budweiser. And, you know, 'Hey, I'm runnin' for Mayor, I want you all to come out and vote for me tomorrow.'

"And then on Saturday afternoon, we went to all the outdoor joints. Remember this is summer. And Piersall went with him. We were running around with Piersall and him, hit all kinds of joints. Harry walked in and places would just erupt. Harry, you know, he doesn't just walk in and have a beer. He walks in and everybody screams and yells and claps. We'd walk into a restaurant and everybody would be sitting having dinner. You know, $30 a plate. And everybody would start yelling and screaming. You don't get that for ballplayers, but in Chicago you'd get that for Harry.

"So I made up a little ballot that had Al Capone and Bozo the Clown on it—I had to make sure Harry didn't lose. We had campaign buttons, campaign T-shirts, we gave out the ballots.

"On Sunday we set up the voting booth over in the park and everybody came over and dropped off their ballots. Harry won, like 4,000 to 3. Then we had a little ceremony at Faces, announced Harry Caray as Mayor of Rush Street. (Chicago Mayor) Jane Byrne came out with a proclamation, saying that Harry Caray is the official Mayor of Rush Street."

The classic Rush Street really doesn't exist anymore. Rittenberg's remembrance of Caray's hangouts is like a glorious trip to the past, of storied night life days of Chicago.

"The Pump Room," Rittenberg says. "That was a big hangout. The Barkley Club. Faces. Adolph's Restaurant, which is no longer there. A good friend of his there was Fortune Renucci. He went to a place called Hotsy Totsy. He was good friends with Freddy Venrick. Freddy had The Lodge, which was across from Butch McGuire's. He would go into Butch McGuire's. He was friends with Butch."

Rittenberg was confident all along that Harry Caray's Restaurant was going to hit it big—if he could get Harry to agree to the idea. The concept was a long time in the talking stage.

"I've been in the restaurant and bar business for a long time. Before I did Ditka's, I called Harry and said, 'Harry, I want to do a sports bar, but I want it to be a restaurant.' We had sports bars. 'I want to do a place where people will go and sit down and have a steak, a slab of ribs and watch the sports. Because right now there's no place for anybody over 30 to go and watch sports because it's all kids.'

"So I said to Harry, 'We'll have to do one. We'll do a place downtown. I don't want it to be by the ballpark. I want it to be downtown by the hotels.' I said, 'I don't want it to be a player. Players are too young. Players get traded. Players are attractive to kids from 7 years old to 21, 22. I want a coach or a manager. Or better yet, Harry, I want you.'

"He said, 'I'll call you back.' He called me back and told me no. This was in 1984 or '85. I already had the location. It was Ontario (Street) and it was going to be Faces in the back —I was going to move Faces—and a restaurant in the front. Harry turned me down cold.

"He said,'Jim, I'm not going to do it and I'm going to tell you why. I don't want to have a bar or restaurant because of all the other bartenders. I'm their guy. I'm the one they identify with. I'm their customer. I don't want them to think I'm competing with them.'

"Finally, somebody from the Ditka camp came and talked with us and we did the partnership with Ditka. It worked out really well for awhile. But the bottom line was that was going to be Harry Caray's. Now, we open Ditka's and we're doing great. And Ben Stein, who stuttered, says to Harry, 'W-w-w-hy the f-f-f—— don't we do this?' And then Ben asks me to come over and run Harry Caray's. I said, 'I can't do that, it'd be a conflict.' I had 11 joints at that time. Ben said,'W-w-well you got other joints.' And I said,'Yeah, but they're not in the same market as Ditka's is.' If I opened up Harry Caray's for you, what would I do if I got a party for 400 people? Where would I put it? Harry Caray's or Ditka's? If I put it at Harry's the Ditka's investors would be pissed. If I put it at Ditka's the Harry Caray's investors would be mad. I can't win.'"

Harry Caray's Restaurant has shown staying power uncommon in the business.

Rittenberg had second row seats at Wrigley Field and when Harry moved to the Cubs, Rittenberg coveted first row seats.

"Ben Stein was a good friend of Harry's, and a dear friend of mine, my mentor. The second row seats I had (at Wrigley) were great, right behind first base in the sun. First base is cooler at Cubs park because it's always in the sun. Everybody wants first base. And if you're right behind the dugout and you're in the first row, you get to use the dugout for hot dogs, your hamburgers, your beer, what have you. It's like having your own table.

"I had seats in the second row. Now, Jimmy Janek, who also was a friend of Harry's from Restaurant Row, decides to move to Florida. So Janek tells me he's giving up his tickets. So I call the Cubs and say,'If Jimmy gives up his seats, I'd love to grab them.' The Cubs said, 'Yeah, we'll talk about it.' But

Janek was going to make sure by just buying them and reselling them to me.

"Bottom line, when it all gets sorted out, I go to Opening Day and there's Ben Stein sitting in front of me in the four seats I wanted. I said, 'How the f— did you get those seats?' Ben said, 'Who d-d-do you th-th-think you are, you l-l-little s–? Y-you were going to out-c-c-clout me? I'm Harry's b-e-e-e-st friend."

Rittenberg was not astounded by all the charter jets that flew to Las Vegas in 1989 for Harry's roast at Bally's. The 5,000 people came from every where.

"Why would you be astounded? If you knew Harry, here's a guy who spent his life in 24 cities that he called home. American League, National League, every city.

"What did he do in every city?" Rittenberg asked. "He went out and spent money in the bars and restaurants and waved to the fans in every city. The President campaigns for like six months to a year. Harry had been campaigning for 50 years and doing more traveling than any president. He knew guys who started as bus boys and wound up owning joints.

"And with WGN doing this superstation thing, the legend of Harry Caray just grew. And even this thing toward the end, with him mispronouncing names and the controversy of should he retire. All that controversy only made him more famous."

Butch McGuire

Owner of Butch McGuire's Saloon, McGuire is perhaps the most famous barkeep in Chicago history.

"Harry used to come into our saloon and then I'd meet him at Adolph's late at night," says McGuire. "He was always around. He was a late-night person, as I was. Those days we would close at 2 and then we'd go out."

At one time, Butch McGuire's Saloon sold more beer than any single place in the world. He sold only Old Style beer. He brought Meister Brau into Butch McGuire's the year Old Style went on strike. It was the first time the Saloon had sold a beer other than Old Style.

"And Harry sold it to us."

Harry had worked on McGuire to stock other beers that sponsored the White Sox.

"Then Harry went to the Cubs and Budweiser. He'd come in here twice a week and say, 'You've got to sell some Budweiser.' I said, 'Harry, I wouldn't sell Budweiser if you were giving it away.' Then he would announce on the radio, 'Stop by Butch's. He's going to have Budweiser soon.' And he kept doing that.

"I kept telling him I didn't want the damn stuff. Budweiser here in Chicago was a company-owned distributorship. Everything was wrong with it and we just wouldn't have it. One day he brought a bunch of his cronies with him and he went up front and got down on his knees and started singing, 'Please put in the beer. Please put in the Budweiser.

"I said, 'What am I going to do? He's been announcing for a week that we're going to have it.' So I said, 'OK. You can put in a couple of barrels.' So then he really started announcing 'Butch has Budweiser.

"I told him, 'Harry, there's one thing I'm thrilled about.' He asked, 'What's that, Butch?' I said, 'I'm glad you don't sell elephants, because right now I'd have a basement full of elephants instead of a basement full of beer."

"Budweiser didn't sell any beer in Chicago until he started selling it. He brought Budweiser back to the bars in Chicago. They had 'The Bud Man, Cub Fan' promotion and it worked."

McGuire recalls when notorious bad driver Harry spread good cheer on the Chicago Transit Authority's buses.

"We walking down State Street one afternoon after lunch. He ate lunch here a lot. And I don't know why we were walking, but we were walking. People are saying 'Hi, Harry. Hi, Harry, how are you?'

"It was down around Chicago Avenue, a bus pulled over. And the bus driver opened the door and said 'Hi, Harry, how are you?' He said, 'I'm fine. How are you?' And he got on the bus.

"He met everybody on the bus. Shook their hands. Kissed the women. And got off on the back. And I said, 'Harry, we're never going to get anywhere. There's another bus behind him.' So, Harry got on the other bus.

"That's why Harry usually got a free ride."

McGuire, the Irishman, thought he had a compatriot in Caray.

"I honest to God thought for years he was Irish. I didn't know he was Italian until not too long ago. Harry, from all outward appearances, didn't have one Italian trait in his whole body.

"You know, he was a lot of fun. He had a great personality. He was a hard worker. He was gregarious. Outgoing."

Father John Smyth

Father John Smyth is head of Maryville Academy in Des Plaines, Illinois. It has more than 1,000 children under its care at 20 sites or campuses. The former basketball all-American at the University of Notre Dame was a first-round draft pick of the St. Louis Hawks, but turned down the National Basketball Association to enter a seminary. Today he oversees a $55 million annual budget for Maryville.

"When Harry came to the White

Harry and Dutchie Caray with Father John Smyth
(Photo courtesy of Father John Smyth).

Sox, he knew a friend of mine, Ben Stein, who was a very colorful person in the Chicago area. Ben and Harry became very close friends and, consequently, through Ben I met Harry. Harry and I hit it off very quickly. I think a lot had to do with his background, how he grew up on the streets of St. Louis.

"Harry did a tremendous amount of good deeds for Maryville. He didn't like to announce his kindness. In the scriptures, you know, don't let your right hand know what your left hand is doing? He lived that. He really did.

"An example is he wrote an article for *The Daily Herald,* and I'd get a check for about $800, $900. I'd ask, 'Why are they giving us money?' It was Harry. Or we'd get a check for a couple of thousand dollars. And Harry had talked to some hotel. I'd have to track it back. And he never told me. Then I'd find out it was Harry and send him a thank you note. And he'd call and say, 'Don't send me a thank you note. I just want to do it.' He did that for years. He was very generous that way. Anytime he had a fee for talking, he took it, but he always sent it to Maryville."

"I didn't start Maryville, but the diocese was going to close it. They gave me a year, sink or swim. That was 1971. I came here in 1962 and worked with the priest who was in charge. He retired and they said, 'You have one year.'

"I worked my rear end off, and I have been working ever since. And people have been great. Just going out and asking, one piece after the other, we put it together and we are probably now the largest child care agency, possibly, in the United States. First or second, numbers wise."

"I don't go to too many Cubs games. Harry used to announce that I was at the games every day with the Maryville kids and I was never there. Everybody thought I was at every Cubs game. I'd just say, 'Yeah, I went to the game.' I'd go along with it. Whenever there was a Maryville Night or fundraising function, I'd go. I'd probably go to two or three games a year.

"Harry never got personally attached to any of our kids, but he would approach all of them almost the same way. 'You've got to do something. You've got to have a goal in life. You've got to overcome your background.'

Harry Caray and Father John Smyth. *(Photo courtesy of Father John Smyth).*

"Occasionally he talked about his youth to me. He had a tough time with Christmas. And I can understand that, running a place like Maryville. It brought back a lot of memories where there was a void there. See, Harry spent a lot of his early years, his formative years, in surviving. And when you survive, you block out some of the other very human qualities that you should be getting and nurturing in a normal setting. He didn't have that. It took him a while, but he caught up to it finally and got close to his family, his grandchildren, everybody else. Thank God he did. And that's when Christmas meant something to him.

Don Niestrom

Don Niestrom was a longtime friend of Harry Caray who ran the Anheuser-Busch distributorship in Chicago. He currently runs the late Ben Stein's business.

"Several of us were sitting in a bar one day and this guy said to Harry, 'How do you like getting your social security check?' Harry said 'Social security check? What are you talking about?' The guy said, 'It's mandatory you get it at age 70.' And Harry said, 'I'm not 70.' The guy said, 'You f—er, you've been getting your check for 14 years. And I'll tell you how much you're getting. $1,400. It's all they can pay.'"

"I met him when I was with Anheuser-Busch. The White Sox were doing terrible and they brought Harry here from Oakland. We took over the sponsorship of the White Sox. The very first night I met him I got so f—ing drunk with him. We've been buddies ever since.

"We used to sit around and argue. And Bill Veeck, by the way, liked to drink. Of course, Harry did too. Veeck took off his wooden leg one night, he got so pissed, and started slamming it on the table."

Harry Caray and Don Niestrom *(Photo courtesy of Don Niestrom).*

Niestrom says Harry didn't have a contract with the Cubs.

"He had a handshake. He was one of those guys. He always had the theory if you don't want me, I'll walk, because I want the right to go somewhere else. Which, in the last several years, he never would do. But I do know over the last seven, eight years he was contacted by the Mets."

Niestrom also is quick to point a couple of Harry's flaws.

"You know Harry was color blind. He never knew what suit he had on. He also was a terrible driver. I've got to believe the state, as a favor, mailed him a license, because I don't believe any driving instructor would want to take the Harry Caray course. To him, the white line meant that you drove down the middle of it. He could see a ball game to call it, but he couldn't see anything when he drove. But he didn't drive that much. He always threw the keys to someone else."

Niestrom says Harry was always giving.

"There was a policeman who was just shot here in Chicago. He's paralyzed for life. And Harry did some things that no one knew about, but I know for a fact he sent him $5,000 in the mail."

Niestrom recounted Harry's speech upon his induction into the baseball Hall of Fame, in Cooperstown, New York, in 95-degree heat before an overflow crowd. He called the speech, which Harry wrote himself, one of the better speeches he ever heard about sports. Niestrom called it a thank you not just to baseball, but also to the fans who support baseball.

Niestrom, said it went something like this: "'Baseball is made not by the players, managers coaches, it is made up by you the fans.' It was very, very touching."

Niestrom also noted that few people realized Caray's devotion to his wife and family. "Harry loved Dutchie. He also loved her family. He was committed to his family and Dutchie's. Through Harry they became one family."

Freddie Brzozowski

Freddie Brzozowski is a longtime friend of Harry and a part owner of the Chicago White Sox and Chicago Bulls.

"Harry was a guest one time at my place near Palm Springs before he had a place there. He used to get his swimsuit on and about 10 o'clock he'd go sit in the sun. He was a sun worshipper.Then he noticed I had an automatic squeezer for grapefruit. You'd just pour the juice out. So he liked that. He never saw anything like that. I taught him how to work it.

"So he'd go out at 10 o'clock and at about 11 o'clock, he'd get a taste for a vodka and grapefruit. So he'd grab a grapefruit off the tree in my yard, and he'd make himself a vodka and grapefruit juice.Then he'd make himself another.

"One time, my wife went and bought some bananas. Harry was a great banana daiquiri fan. She put them in the fruit basket. So Harry looked at it and ran outside to look for the banana tree. He went bananas, so to speak!"

Abraham Aguirre

Abraham "The Chef" Aguirre is the head chef at Harry Caray's Restaurant and was been acquainted with Harry for nearly 30 years.

"I was at a spring training game in Florida. Several of us went to the park, and then after the game we went out for dinner. We went to a nightclub and around 3 in the morning, Harry said, 'I'm going to take you back to the hotel, then go to the Yankee Doodle in Fort Lauderdale. I've got some friends to meet over there.'

"It was 3 a.m. I was tired. I was dead and I'm 32 years younger than Harry. But he had so much energy. The next morning I didn't want to get up, but the phone was ringing at a 9 o'clock. 'Are you ready?' Harry asked. It was unbelievable. He had so much energy. I wasn't ready, but he said, 'C'mon, get up.' Then we get in the limo and the Budweiser was out. 'Have a Budweiser.'"

Dominic Galati

Dominic Galati, owner of Dominic's on the Hill and several other St. Louis restaurants, knew Harry Caray for more than 25 years.

"Harry used to come into the restaurant and we became friends. You know how Harry is. Harry was a very warm person. He was the guy who never forgot the bartender, never forgot the busboy.

"Every time he came to St. Louis, he would always call and come by. He used to call me The Olive Man. He has an olive tree in the back of his house in Palm Springs. He invited me and my wife to spend New Year's Eve with him about 15-20 years ago. There was a snowstorm in St. Louis so we didn't get there until New Year's night.

"The next morning I saw this olive tree in the back loaded with olives. I said, 'Harry what are you doing with this?' He said, 'We just throw them away.' I said, 'Oh my goodness, I'm going to make something for you.'

"So I picked quite a few olives, cured them in salt water for two or three days, while during the day he'd take me barhopping. Dutchie and I went to the store and bought some celery roots, fresh garlic and oregano. We put them in olive oil and fixed them. Harry, when he tasted these olives, said, 'I'm glad I didn't cut that olive tree down. These are the best olives I've ever had in my life."

Carl Cowles

Carl Cowles met Harry Caray while working as a teenager at St. Louis' Busch's Grove Restaurant, which he now co-owns with his wife, Patty.

"I knew Harry because he lived just a couple of blocks from where our restaurant is. I started working here in '68 and, of course, he was coming in here then. When the Cardinals were in town, he'd come in sometimes twice a day. He'd come in before the game and have lunch and whatever. And then end up here at some point at night after the game, if not immediately after. He used to make the rounds pretty good.

"I happened to be at work the day Harry was fired by the Cardinals in 1969. Harry walked in and nobody at that point had heard he got fired. He asked if he could use our private dining room to have a press conference and I said sure.

"There wasn't a large entourage at that point. He said, 'Have somebody get me a Schlitz.' And I said, 'Harry, you know we don't have any Schlitz.' At that point all we carried was Anheuser-Busch products. He goes, 'Well, I want a Schlitz. Send somebody over to the store to get me a Schlitz.' And I said, 'Harry, you don't want to do that.' He said, 'No, damn it, send somebody to get me Schlitz.' Again, I repeated, 'Harry, you don't want to do that.' He said, 'Damn it, Carl.' And I said, 'OK, you got it. Who am I to argue?' So I sent a guy across the street and he came back with a Schlitz, and Harry during his interview, made sure it was visible.

"Harry regretted that move all the rest of the days, because he was an Anheuser-Busch guy and truly loved Gussie."

"I don't know how we lose some of these games, but we do."

— Harry Caray, 1964

CHAPTER TWO

Baseball People

John McDonough

How popular was Harry Caray?

His appeal was so powerful he could momentarily distract President Clinton's security staff from its solemn duties.

Hillary Rodham Clinton had a gala 50th birthday party staged for her in downtown Chicago after the 1997 season. As a lifelong Cubs fan, the First Lady made sure Caray and Cubs officials and players were invited. The team presented the Clintons a bat and a much prized Beanie Baby.

"We were backstage and we were waiting, waiting, waiting," recalls John McDonough, the Cubs' vice president of marketing and broadcasting, and the Cubs official who had worked most closely with Caray over the years. "Finally, Harry turns to me and says, 'I've got to go to the bathroom. Do you mind taking a walk with me? We can chat. This looks like it's going to drag on.'"

As he and Caray took their walk, McDonough noticed the presence of three armed guards, each of whom was assigned to watch a specific door.

"These security guards, all they were trained to do was be riveted on that one door and don't look at anything else," he says. "We're walking by, and all of a sudden Harry says, 'Hey, fellas, how are you?' All of a sudden, the three security guards

Jay Blunk, Harry Caray, and John McDonough at Harry's Restaurant in Chicago *(Photo courtesy of Jay Blunk collection).*

turned around and said 'Hey, Harry!' It was just for a second or two, and nothing could have happened. They've got the gear on, the flak jackets, the guns, everything. I didn't even know if they'd let us in the bathroom. It was funny to see these big, armed guards rush over to him."

That may have been the highlight of McDonough's many experiences hanging out with Caray on and off the job. Dealing with the broadcaster was one of the highlights of his career since joining the Cubs in 1984.

"I had been a White Sox fan coming over here, so I had all those years of devout adoration of Harry on the South Side," McDonough says. "Being a Harry Caray fan, I maybe had a higher degree of reverence than maybe everyone else here. He had been the competition. This was the ultimate showman, this was baseball's entertainer, this was Sinatra at Madison Square Garden. This was as good as it gets.

"Starting in 1991, when I was assigned to oversee the broadcast responsibilities, Harry and I had a good relationship. I would crave the opportunity of about twice a year to go to his restaurant, have lunch with him, start around 11:30 a.m. and get out of there around 3 p.m. I would just sit there and ask him questions which I felt I could ask him—the relationships he had with Joe Garagiola and Jack Buck and all these people.

"As the years went on, despite all the malapropisms and mispronunciations and calling George Bell, George Bush and calling Sammy Sosa, Sammy Davis, I think he realized it was probably better off just going with it. Self-effacing humor can probably be endearing.

"It was his job for life. He knew it. We knew it. We would never want to sever that tie. He was as big as Wrigley Field. He was as big as the Cubs. Harry was as big as Mark Grace, Rick Sutcliffe, Ryne Sandberg and Andre Dawson. The beauty of it was the players knew it. There was never any friction. The players would never say they were upstaged by an older guy up in the booth."

Any friction involving Caray's standing occurred in 1997. The newly hired Josh Lewin, handling Cubs telecasts on the road because Caray was discouraged from traveling due to his health and age, was not readily accepted by the great announcer. Caray apparently had wanted his grandson, Chip, to join the broadcast team. And, in fact, Chip Caray had applied in late 1996, but could not come to agreement with top WGN management.

The Caray-Lewin situation was potentially stickier than the forced marriage of Caray and Milo Hamilton from 1982-84, when Hamilton did all the complaining while Caray took the high road. As 1997—a disastrous Cubs season on the field—dragged on, Lewin could not get on the air for even one inning of play-by-play at home. By mid-season, McDonough sensed the arrangement could not work much longer.

"I just had a feeling this was not going to be a long-term thing, and Josh knew the fit wasn't right," he says. "Harry just never took to him. Josh did everything possible he could to ingratiate himself to Harry. Finally, about July 1, I asked, 'Where did you think we are with Chip? Do you think he'd be interested in talking to us again?' Harry got on the phone that night to talk to Chip. A few days later, Chip called me back and said, 'Boy, I am interested.' The rest is history.

"It was probably the happiest I had seen Harry while he was here. When he knew he was going to be linked to the lineage, the tradition of the Caray family being together in the broadcast booth. He was so excited to be working with Chip. I think he felt bad about the Josh Lewin situation. It really had nothing to do with Josh. He just wanted his grandson in, for all the right reasons."

WGN-TV officials this time had no objection to Chip Caray taking one or two days per week off to host the Fox Network's baseball "Game of the Week."

When Harry was introduced at the annual Cubs Convention, for what turned out to be the final time, it was memorable.

"It was like the Rolling Stones going on stage. He had this huge, rock-star persona that he took on that he could not get enough of. Don't let anybody kid you that he didn't eat it up."

Caray was indeed compensated with attention at the Cubs Convention, the largest annual team gathering of sports fans. He was named honorary chairman of the confab at its inception in 1986, and held that title through his final appearance in 1998. He received the same fee the entire time, jokingly asking McDonough for a raise, but knowing his real reward would be the fond memories he'd provide the 15,000 convention attendees and the adulation he'd receive in return.

"I get kind of emotional when I talk about this," McDonough says. "I was standing right next to him when he sang 'Take Me Out to the Ball Game' for the last time to start the convention. I've seen it on TV a dozen times."

The Cubs are "toying" with a number of different ideas to permanently memorialize Caray. But in the interim, the "guest conductor" idea for the seventh-inning stretch proved a very fitting way to commemorate its creator, as celebrities far and wide vied to sing off-key and wave the mike like a baton.

McDonough initially looked at playing a tape of Caray's own version. That was tried in spring training. "It just didn't fit. There was something missing," McDonough says. "If we would have played the organ and just gone about our business as if he had never done this, it would have been a slight to his legacy."

Suddenly the light bulbs in collective heads went off to concoct the guest-conductor concept. By late spring 1998, the Cubs had stocked almost their entire season with would-be singers from sports, politics, entertainment and, yes, religion. Chicago Cardinal Francis George took his turn at the unique pulpit late in the season. Soon the Cubs ran out of slots for maestros.

"We turned away some mega-celebrities," McDonough says, declining to name names. The marketing department received calls from the stars, some of whom probably wouldn't have given a baseball team's request for an appearance the time of day a year ago. But in honor of Caray, the scramble to sing was on.

Might this concept catch on throughout baseball?

"The seventh-inning stretch could be baseball's natural intermission," McDonough says. "It's kind of a remembrance of why we're here. It's a pastoral game. It's not lights going off and rock music every 30 seconds. There's nothing wrong with that, but there's a different cadence in this game. I think this has a chance, the longevity of Harry giving this to us, to be the intermission of our game where it's homespun, family and very respectful for the game."

Also reminding all of baseball of Caray's giant shadow was the chin-and-glasses-heavy caricature of Caray emblazoned on Cubs players' uniform sleeves.

"We went to the National League, and they reminded us that a caricature was very unusual, let alone for a broadcaster," McDonough says. "We're not talking about a former Hall of

Famer who was associated with the ball club. That tells you the Herculean impact he had, to put his likeness on a uniform.

"He was bigger than initials. His personality was bigger than H.C."

Sharon Pannozzo

Just about Harry Caray's favorite person around Wrigley Field was Sharon Pannozzo. He couldn't begin his day's—or night's—work without a ritual kiss from the team's media relations director who doubled as his protector and unofficial bodyguard escorting him through the boisterous crowds that swarmed him at the ballpark.

It helped, of course, that Pannozzo was the first woman to advance to director of media relations for a big-league team. You know how charming Caray was around women.

"I also was one of the only girls around, so he didn't have much choice," she laughs. "He was like a combination of your grandfather and your buddy."

Caray was able to practice some of his old lines and double entendres on Pannozzo, all in good fun.

In the open-air press box at the old HoHoKam Park in Mesa, Arizona, Pannozzo sat right next to Caray's broadcast position. There were no partitions.

"It was a hot spring day, in the 90s," she says. "I just kept taking layers of clothing off. He says on the air, 'Every time Sharon Pannozzo walks by, she's wearing less clothing.' I'm thinking, I hope my boss doesn't hear that."

Sure enough, Harry was a big flirt. He'd tell Pannozzo in his faux covetous way, "Boy, I wish I was 30 years younger." But along with "Bud man, Cub fan," that was just part of the act, especially as he got older. So why did women go wild, lining up for kisses and hugs for a man old enough to be their grandfather?

"Dutchie never had anything to worry about," Pannozzo says. "Even though he was always calling you 'Oh, hey, pretty girl, come over here and sit in my lap,' every girl got that. It wasn't as if you got jealous.

"It was hard to explain. Maybe it was because of his reputation of sort of being a ladies man, although you knew because of his advancing age that he really wasn't able to follow up on much of it. He always was very complimentary, always had a nice thing to say about a woman. Even when some 70-year-old woman would come up, they'd almost drool. He would say the right thing to people. He knew how to get a reaction out of them. He had me wrapped around his finger for 15 years.

"He always was very good to me. Whenever anybody wanted something read on the air, they'd always come to me. They knew he'd read my stuff first."

Oddly enough, their relationship got off to a rocky start when Pannozzo first started much lower on the totem pole in her department in 1983.

"We had a run-in over some tickets," she says. "He didn't like the idea there was a 48-hour rule on (complimentary) tickets. He thought he could just call in anytime. I was told it from my boss (Bob Ibach) that it didn't make a difference who you were. I assumed it meant Harry, too. But I guess it really didn't, because Harry got anything he wanted. I figured I'd give him whatever he wanted, when he wanted it. From that point on, we had the best relationship. He'd call me five minutes before the game started and I'd leave him tickets. I didn't do that for anybody else. I still don't."

As Caray got older and his step a bit slower, Pannozzo realized Caray needed help knifing through the masses at Wrigley Field or the Cubs Convention. Everybody wanted a piece of him. If they got their wish, there'd not be much of Harry left.

"He needed a bodyguard, and I decided that was my role," Pannozzo says. "One of the nicest compliments his wife, Dutchie, paid to me after the funeral was that when she sent

Harry to the ballpark, she knew he was in good hands and that I would take care of him until he got back home.

"I had a number of different strategies. On the field, it wasn't so bad. But it was difficult at the convention at the Hilton. Getting him through a crowd of people was next to impossible. He'd never say 'no' to anybody. He wanted to on occasion, because he was tired or needed to get someplace.

"I'd hold his hands, so he couldn't stop and sign anything. To get him to move faster, I'd have him put his hands on my shoulders behind me so I could get a little path for him. At the same time, I'd know where his hands were at all times. It was always important to know where his hands were."

Pannozzo had one of her greatest Caray tasks in handling the media crush in the wake of his death and funeral. Being immersed in her work with Caray again being the center of attention helped allay her grief to a degree.

"It was hard the first day, but then I got so busy," she says. "I had to help Dutchie out. I didn't really lose it until the funeral. I took my place in the pew, and I said, 'Now I'm here to mourn.' When they took the casket out and did the seventh-inning stretch on the bagpipes, Mandy (Cohen, former assistant director of baseball games on WGN-TV) and I really lost it."

But the period of mourning wasn't long, because Caray's life-force was so strong. All of him hasn't really left.

"He led more than one life," Pannozzo says. "He got a second life when he came back from the stroke. He got a lot more than most people got. He had a wonderful life."

Dallas Green

He was almost as bombastic as Harry Caray. Dallas Green pronounced a "New Tradition" as the new Cubs general manager in 1982.

Green also signed off on approving Caray as part of that near total overhaul of the Cubs organization. But it was not a slam-dunk for Caray in gaining Green's—or other Tribune Co. executives—approval.

Yes, it's true—Caray had to modify his act coming over to the Cubs, compared to his wild-man, take-no-prisoners style days in the White Sox broadcast booth. And, doubly true, as long suspected—Green had a talking-to with Caray before he worked his first Cubs game.

Caray had to meet with Jim Dowdle, who spearheaded his move to the Cubs, along with Green, Tribune Co. chairman Stanton Cook, top corporate officer John Madigan and Cubs president Andy McKenna.

"We laid our cards out on the table," recalls Green, now a special assistant to Phillies general manager Ed Wade. "Jim respected my feelings about Harry and my concern about him generating controversy with the Sox. If I had said no to Harry, he would have honored that opinion.

"Both of us walked on thin ice. There was a certain stigma to Harry that the Tribune Co. people weren't used to. I talked

Harry with other members of the Cubs during an off-season promotional tour. Dallas Green is in the back row with sunglasses.

to him. All I said was I don't mind at all the normal play-by-play, say if the player doesn't have his sunglasses on and should have. That's fine. But I didn't want to get into personalities and the personal side of things.

"I think he listened to Jim and me. He recognized that Tribune Co. was different than the Bill Veeck era, but that also this was a golden opportunity for him to enter in on the ground floor and be a part of something special.

"You're not going to change Harry that much. I think he recognized what he had to do. He was a consummate professional and made things happen."

Caray still spoke out. He criticized the corporate parent's move toward lights in Wrigley Field in the mid-1980s, an effort originally spearheaded by Green. But toward the end of his Cubs tenure in 1987, Green began to see the appeal of day baseball, still the predominant feature of Wrigley Field.

"I came to understand what day baseball meant to the Cubs organization and fans," Green says. "I was starting to half-agree with Harry."

Green and his wife, Sylvia, socialized with Caray and his wife, Dutchie, on short vacations in Lake Geneva, Wisconsin. He also finally met Bill Veeck through Caray. "We had a nice dinner, part of a long evening," Green laughs.

So what was the secret to Caray's popularity in the Windy City?

"He was typical Chicago," Green says. "He loved his profession. He loved the people in the city. He was Mr. Showbiz. Chicago loved him."

Jim Frey

Jim Frey couldn't help but be entertained by Harry Caray traveling around the Midwest in the 1950s.

"We played in the low minors in Evansville (Indiana) in the old Three-I League," the former Cubs manager and general

Jim Frey (Photo courtesy of Brace Photos).

manager says. "We'd drive around the Midwest states to games by car, and Harry was on the radio doing the Cardinals. "Even then, he was talking about going out after games and having drinks."

Frey finally get to know Caray when he was named Cubs manager in 1984. He later teamed with him as color analyst on WGN-Radio in 1987, then became Cubs general manager for a four-season stint starting in 1988.

"In 1984, if I walked down the street with Harry Caray, Ryne Sandberg and Rick Sutcliffe, nine out of 10 people would say, 'Hi, Harry,'" Frey says, echoing the experiences of many baseball people.

On August 2, 1984, Pete Rose, then with the Montreal Expos, lined a ball off Cubs reliever Lee Smith's shoulder. The ball ricocheted to shortstop Dave Owen, who tossed to first to double off base runner Mike Stenhouse to end the game. Caray was beside himself with illusions to heavenly interference on behalf of the Cubs.

"The next day, on our pregame show, he said to me on the air, 'Do you think God wants the Cubs to win?'" Frey says. "My reaction was I hope so, because of all the things I had heard about the Cubs syndrome of not being able to win. Then, as the season progressed, he used that (divine intervention) more than once.

Ryne Sandberg, Harry Caray and Andre Dawson *(Photo courtesy of Bill Wills).*

"He was a guy who could agitate and aggravate a manager. He was just like millions of other fans who would question or second-guess. Even if I went out to dinner or drinks with Harry, he would ask questions that other announcers would be a little more tactful about asking.

"I finally realized that he didn't give a s—. That was just his style."

What Harry did care about was preserving his center-stage role when he called a homer. Frey found that out with some Caray body English during his own stint as his color announcing partner. Frey discovered the same thing Ron Santo found out three years later—Caray brooked no interference on "It might be, it could be, it IS!!!"

"Somebody hit a homer," Frey says. "I've been in uniform all my life, and I should have been able to recognize when a ball is hit out and when it isn't. The instant it's hit, I said it's out of here. Harry grabbed my wrist. He went into his home run call. Afterward, he said, 'Don't preempt my home run call.'"

Frey fell in with Caray after-hours, but paced himself.

"If you went out with him more than a couple of days in a row, he would wear you out," he says. "He could wear out a mule.

"It was amazing when his real age was revealed. When I became Cubs general manager in 1988, he was 74 years old, still on the road, still going out at night like that. He just had one of those special makeups."

Frey, now semi-retired and splitting his time between Naples, Fla. and a longtime home in Baltimore, said he can't go anywhere without someone asking him about Caray.

Eddie Einhorn

The most acrimony in Harry Caray's latter years was his departure from the White Sox in 1981. He never patched things up with Sox chairman Jerry Reinsdorf. But at least he had a re-approachment with Reinsdorf partner Eddie Einhorn, and the two even hugged when they greeted each other in ensuing years.

"I was in charge of the radio-TV situation with the Sox then, and a lot of the acrimony was a misunderstanding," Einhorn says. "Harry's agent at the time, Saul Foos, caused most of it. That's the person I dealt with. Saul told him something else compared to what I told him. It was a complicated situation."

Einhorn says he wanted Caray to continue, but he would have had to front the then-new Sox pay-TV operation. Caray knew he would not have the profile he had on over-the-air TV, particularly WGN-TV.

"It was a cause celebre, because people were used to having the Cubs and Sox on free TV," Einhorn says. "Harry did have that in his mind. The truth of the matter was, if that was going to be his attitude, it wouldn't have worked for us. We needed someone selling the medium, selling the product. It wound up being a mutual thing, but it was not about him personally. It was a business thing that we had to go a certain way, we had to be out in front in this area, and he didn't like it. He didn't understand it, and I don't blame him.

"We had no intention of changing that situation at the time. It just happened that way. Our decision to go the way we did was bigger than the announcer situation."

Eventually Einhorn and Caray patched it up, generating more headlines.

"There was more press when Harry and I made up than when we signed Carlton Fisk. That's how big it was at the time," Einhorn says.

Overall, the two seemed to have a decent amount of common ground.

"When I first met Harry," Einhorn says, "he told me, 'I know you. You've been in this business a long time. You always paid scale.'"

Ned Colletti

When Harry Caray came over to the Cubs in 1982, he soon acquired a frequent after-hours running mate in a fella almost young enough to be his grandson.

Ned Colletti, then 28, was just starting out as the Cubs' assistant director of media relations. A lifelong Cubs fan who had become a member of the famed Left-Field Bleacher Bums of 1969 fame, Colletti witnessed a ton of great names in the game. Never, though, had he met somebody quite like Harry.

"From the get-go, I could see this guy had a great zest for life and a great love for baseball," Colletti, now assistant general manager of the San Francisco Giants, says. "Harry was always to me a very, very special guy."

Colletti first met Caray in the latter's earlier incarnation with the Cardinals. A 10-year-old fan, Colletti waited for Caray to leave the field after conducting a postgame interview. He snared Caray's autograph on a scorecard. "His autograph never changed. It was a like a doctor filling out a prescription," he says.

Later, looking at baseball—and Caray—from the inside-out, Colletti says an evening out with Harry was unique. And Colletti didn't sleep all that much accompanying Caray on the road with the Cubs.

"If someone had the opportunity to spend one evening of drinks and dinner with Harry—or drinks, dinner and more drinks with Harry—they'd remember it the rest of their life," Colletti says. "Just one night! And I was fortunate to spend a couple of hundred of them with the man."

Colletti received one piece of sage advice from Caray on how to handle the inflow of spirits over the hours.

"He used to drink a lot of water," he says. "He told me whenever you have a drink, also drink water. He had a great, resilient system for consumption. After five, six years of this, I used to tell him, 'Harry, if we're going out on this road trip, give me a couple of days' notice. So I'll get a little rest, store up some rest."

A typical night out with Harry meant stops at four to five bars or restaurants, depending on the city.

"New York was always one of his favorite places," Colletti says. "He'd go out to a couple of places, then go out to dinner, then go out to two or three after that. He knew everyone. He'd go into any well-known establishment in any National League city, and the bartender would know him, the maitre d' would know him, the cook might know him."

And when closing time came? Often, it came and went, with Harry still entrenched.

"Some places, if he was in there, they'd lock the door, go about their work, check the cash register, balance the books, sweep the floors, clean off the tables," Colletti says. "And when they were done, they probably sat down and had a drink with us. It was an incredible ride.

"He made everybody feel special. That's hard to find these days. There aren't a lot of people who are willing to go out of their way to make people feel good about themselves. It would take you a half an hour to walk a block in some places."

Caray and Colletti talked about "70 percent" baseball. But the wee-hours conversation also covered life, careers and families. "He told me after about three or four years with the Cubs, I should go out to the West Coast to get myself a big baseball front-office job. Little did I know that I would be on the West Coast in a front-office job."

Colletti became a Caray confidant, and not just at 3 a.m. He was one of the few people who was able to see the great broadcaster at his Palm Springs home in the weeks after his stroke in the winter of 1987, after Colletti had been promoted to head the Cubs' media relations department. And he had the uplifting task two years later, in the winter of 1989, of informing Caray he was inducted into the broadcasters' wing of the Baseball Hall of Fame, after years of waiting and protestations from Caray that his family would not accept his enshrinement if it ever came posthumously.

"For two years, there had been stories about whether Harry would be voted in, and he was somewhat touchy on the subject," he says. "He wasn't going to let it ruin his career, but I knew it meant a lot to him if they would elect him. He said, 'I don't want it if I'm gone.'"

When the blessed news about Cooperstown was released, Hall of Fame official Bill Guilfoyle called Colletti at his Wrigley Field office, asking where he could reach Caray, who was not at either of his homes in Chicago or Palm Springs. A few days earlier, Caray had told Colletti he was traveling to Atlantic City for the Italian American Sports Hall of Fame dinner. Of course, Caray asked Colletti to come along. "You're Italian, too, and we can have some fun," he told Colletti, who had to tend to business at the ballpark.

With the Hall of Fame announcement due out any minute and Caray nowhere to be found, Colletti told Guilfoyle he'd call the Atlantic City hotel where Caray was staying. But he found out Caray hadn't checked in yet. All he could do was leave a message. Fifteen minutes later, Caray called back. "Guess who was just named to the Hall of Fame?" Colletti said. Caray's chuckling response: "I hope it was an Italian." Colletti confirmed the good news, and traveled to Cooperstown for Caray's induction speech the following summer.

Caray could have been inducted solely for his enormous impact on the Cubs, with whom his legend simply grew season by season.

Coming off his White Sox years, Caray was hugely popular starting out with the Cubs. But he really took off, along with the team's profile, when the Cubs won the National League East championship in 1984.

"Everything caught on here," Colletti says. "Wrigley Field caught on. There weren't a lot of times (in the 1970s and early '80s) when the Game of the Week (then on NBC-TV) would come to Wrigley Field. WGN was all over the country on cable. The team was exciting. Wrigley Field became the place to be for people who had never been here from out of town. Waveland Avenue and Sheffield Avenue became famous streets, like Flatbush in Brooklyn. But it took until 1984 for that to happen."

In some National League cities where WGN's cable penetration was early and often, Caray became the star attraction of the road show.

"Places like Houston, we'd pull up on the team bus," Colletti says. "We had prominent players like Rick Sutcliffe, Ryne Sandberg, Jody Davis and Keith Moreland and host of others. There'd be 50 to 100 fans by the bus. The players would walk off, and the fans would jam around Harry. Then in 1989, we had Andre Dawson—a Hall of Fame player—along with Sutcliffe, Sandberg and other good players. Still, Harry was the man.

"There are so many popular broadcasters in baseball, football, all the sports. They're synonymous with the game. But I don't think anyone ever went out of their way and did more with the fans, or was more in touch with the fans, and was more a part of the fans, than Harry."

Amazingly, through the entire generation-plus of his popularity on both sides of town in Chicago, Caray kept his home phone number listed. He and Bill Veeck were the top baseball people to remain so accessible at a time when celebrities spent untold thousands of bucks on security aids to maintain their privacy. In an extreme case, Cubs outfielder Moreland objected to sportswriters publishing that he lived in suburban Deerfield —or even a general statement that he resided in Chicago's northern suburbs. "People will come to town, ask where I live, and they'll find their way to my house to bother me," Moreland said in 1986.

In contrast, Caray always believed if a fan wanted to talk to him, he wouldn't duck his call.

"That was a stroke of genius on his part," Colletti says. "Maybe he picked it up from Bill Veeck. No, I didn't suggest to him he get it unlisted. He wanted to maintain his closeness to the fans.

"He was a true character."

Chuck Tanner

The biggest feud in Chicago baseball around the end of the Watergate scandal was Harry Caray-Chuck Tanner. Caray would fire away at Sox manager Tanner on the air, while Tanner would return the salvos in the newspapers the next day.

Funny thing, though. Either the feud was patched up soon after, or maybe some of it was staged. Maybe both. In any case, Tanner now insists Caray "was as good a friend as I had in baseball."

Now special assistant to Milwaukee Brewers general manager Sal Bando, Tanner—still a resident of his hometown of New Castle, Pennsylvania, and living down the street from his star player, Richie Allen—expresses nothing but joy when talking about flapping jaws during his Sox managerial tenure of 1971-75, coinciding with Caray's first five seasons on the South Side.

"We saved the franchise for Chicago," Tanner says. "We'd be together (after games), and he'd ask why the hell did you do things in the game. I told him, 'I'm the manager, Harry.'

"Harry Caray was a fan. I was the manager. I was young and energetic. He was enthusiastic. You're going to get some conversation with that combination. He wasn't really ripping me. He was ripping the game and the team. As a fan, he wanted the team to win so bad, if you didn't have a team capable of winning, he'd say so. He talked like a guy in a bar, a real fan.

"If I ever had a close relationship with an announcer, it was with Harry. We really never had a feud. We cared about each other.

"There were still four daily newspapers in Chicago at the time. They all had to come up with a story. They didn't know what was behind the scenes."

Later on, Caray became a big fan of Tanner's work with the "We Are Family" Pittsburgh Pirates.

"Harry said nobody could have done what I did what that team to get it accomplished," he says.

"Harry would hug me and talk to me whenever we got together. The last time I saw him, I think, was in Pittsburgh in 1994.

"He was one of the greatest ambassadors in baseball."

Ed Lynch

Growing up in both New York and Miami, Cubs general manager Ed Lynch still can't say whether Harry Caray would have made it as a baseball broadcaster on the East Coast.

But Lynch, who also knew Caray as a Cubs pitcher in 1986-87, believes he was tailor-made for the Midwest.

"He was really cut out for mid-America," he says. "He really had his finger on the pulse of Midwest people, their loyalty, openness and honesty. He was more meat-and-potatoes than glitter. I don't really associate Harry with the New York-L.A. kind of lifestyle, or style period. He was really cut out for the middle third of the country."

Lynch had his ups and downs as a spot starter and reliever with the Cubs. But he had no argument with Caray's broadcast style when things didn't go well.

"He was down to earth," he recalls. "He told it like it was. If I stunk, he said I stunk. How can you argue with that? If there was a ground ball that went through the third baseman's legs, others announcers might say it took a tricky hop, or that was a well-hit ball. Harry would say, 'C'mon, catch the ball. You're making $2 million. You should be able to catch a ground ball.' That's what every fan was thinking at home, and that was a big part of his appeal.

"There will never be another Harry Caray. During the 1940s and '50s, he was many fans' only contact with baseball over KMOX in St. Louis. Now, with ESPN and all the cable telecasts of games, there's such a glut of sports programming that no one will be able to have that kind of impact again."

Jay Blunk

Long before he started working with Harry Caray as a Cubs media relations intern in 1986, Jay Blunk enjoyed the best of Caray as a White Sox announcer when Blunk would come up with his father, Dave, and family to old Comiskey Park from their Bloomington, Illinois, home.

"We'd always request tickets by the broadcast booth," Blunk, now director of advertising for the Cubs, recalls. "Harry would lower his fishnet to the crowd, you'd throw things in for him to sign, and give them back during the game, while he was on the air. I've still got those things, scorecards and a red Sox batting helmet.

"I remember when John Allyn tried to fire Harry in 1975. I was in fifth grade, and I was very upset about that. I was very excited—and I still have the paper—that announced Harry was back with Bill Veeck."

That childhood appreciation of Caray developed into a close adult business and personal relationship that had Harry readily agreeing to interview the VIPs that Blunk would bring up to the booth during Cubs games.

"Harry had a great relationship behind the scenes with all the people here," Blunk says of the Cubs front office. "It was because of his relationship with John McDonough (marketing chief) that we developed a good relationship."

Celebrities across the country became Caray fans, and got to meet him through Blunk.

"Harry told me anytime someone (celebrities) wants to meet me, you bring them up (to the booth), even if I haven't heard of them and they have heard of me," Blunk says. "A lot of times, I'd give four or five bullet points to Harry and Steve (Stone), to make sure they didn't embarrass themselves on the pronunciation, and you're in town to do this show, and how's that album doing. It was such an honor for these people, even these mega-, mega-stars, to be seen on the air with Harry."

But the plain common folk, the fans who loved Harry, had their 15 seconds of fame thanks to one plug on the air by the great one.

"He said, 'It will make that guy a star at work the next day,'" Blunk says. "'It's no skin off my nose.' Isn't that a great, refreshing thing where he remembered the fans?"

When Blunk and McDonough had lunch with Caray at his restaurant in November 1997 to ask him if he wanted his own special day at Wrigley Field in 1998, Caray agreed. But there was a stipulation. Instead of any gifts being bestowed on him, Caray wanted a check written to Maryville Academy, the orphanage that became his favorite philanthropic project.

But while the lunch was going on, Caray called a waiter over. He had looked over the menu. "How can a family come here because the hot dogs are so expensive?" Blunk says of Caray's concern. "He understood the steaks and higher end dinners had to be expensive. He wanted some affordable prices, and that was too much for a hot dog.

"Harry was a millionaire, but he wasn't too far removed to remember that. I thought that was impressive."

Another time Dave Blunk was on the field and he was about to take a photo with Caray. The latter insisted that Jay also be in the photo. "'I don't remember my dad,'" Blunk recalls of Harry's statement, and the trio was recorded for posterity. "Don't ever forget, your dad should be your best friend."

Blunk also had to explain modern technology to Caray when the Cubs installed a voice-mail system. "The phone rings, and it's Harry," he says. "'What's this voice-mail system you got? I don't understand it.' He was somewhat frustrated, because he had gone through the switchboard. He pushed this button, that button. 'I just want to talk to somebody. I keep talking to a recorder.'"

But Caray had no problem putting together a video for Blunk's 1993 wedding. "He warned everyone in the room about his two alimony payments and said, 'Jay, be careful,'" Blunk says. "I'll save that forever."

Frank Maloney

Along with business-operations chief Mark McGuire, Cubs ticket director Frank Maloney is the only other front-office executive to have worked with Harry Caray during his entire Wrigley Field tenure. Maloney recalls how Caray so well defined his exuberant self during the winter of 1982, in his introductory trip throughout the Midwest to meet Cubs fans.

"It was his—and my—first Cubs Caravan together," Maloney, former Syracuse University head football coach, says. "I didn't know Harry well then. We'd get on that bus in the morning to go to our first stop in another city, and he'd start drinking mixed drinks. We'd get to the lunch stop, and he'd ask for a Bud. He'd put the can of beer on the dais with the label facing the audience. After lunch, back on the bus, Harry would be throwing down the cocktails again. At the night stop for dinner, same thing with the beer with the label facing out.

"This guy had a wooden leg or something. But I never saw him tipsy or off-color, out of line. He always was on top of his game."

Maloney and his ticket-office staff thank their lucky stars he had Caray, combined with cozy Wrigley Field, on which to fall back when the Cubs plummeted to the nether reaches of the National League in too many seasons.

"There's nobody else in the history of sports, a media person or broadcaster, who brought people in the ballpark like he did," Maloney says. "Wrigley Field and Harry Caray were intertwined as an attraction, and more than the team, except in the years it finished first. He brought 'em in by the busloads."

Jim Riggleman

Cubs manager Jim Riggleman had only three years with Caray. But he'll never forget the sage advice Caray dispensed when the tape wasn't rolling on their pregame radio show.

"We'd sit in the dugout or stand near the batting cage and talk off the record about the ball club or sometimes just about life in general," Riggleman says. "One of the things Harry was always encouraging me to do was getting married. He said you gotta get married, you have to have somebody in your life, you don't want to grow old and be alone. I thought he just cherished Dutchie so much. He would give personal advice. It was a special time.

"He also was enamored with power hitters. He'd talk to me, 'You gotta get this guy, that guy.' He'd be disappointed when the other team would out-homer us at home, as we all would be. It was a real issue with Harry."

No matter what Riggleman was doing in his pregame routine, when Caray came to tape the show, everything else was put on hold.

"Harry's presence superseded everything else here," he says. "The beat writers were always very respectful, allowing Harry to interrupt us and resume when we were finished taping."

Riggleman says that had Caray—knowledgeable about the game as he was—started on a scouting or management track early in his career, he could have had a front-office career.

Dan Radison

Cubs first base coach Dan Radison grew up across the Mississippi River from St. Louis in Columbia, Illinois. He started to get his Harry Caray fix very early.

"At 5 years of age, you're very impressionable," Radison says. "I'd walk down the hill to my great-grandmother's house. She and I would listen to the radio. Harry was at his best on the radio, because he made the game come so alive. I can't explain to you what it was like to listen to Harry Caray on the radio at 5. It was the most exciting part of my day. I couldn't wait for the games to start."

More than 40 years later, with the Cubs in 1997, Radison and his fellow coaches each received a personal note from Caray.

"He said he was sorry he couldn't personally say goodbye to us at the end of a tough year," he says. "It was very considerate of him to do that. It was a handwritten note with the Holy Cow! stationery. It's something I'll always treasure."

Lee Elia

Lee Elia was the first Cubs manager during Harry Caray's North Side tenure, in 1982. Caray, of course, far outlasted Elia—fired late in 1983—but Elia still has clear, fond memories.

"We had a pregame show and he'd have a chuckle, 'A-ha, Lee, I gotta ask you this question, so bear with me,'" Elia, now American League scout for the Philadelphia Phillies, remembers. "He had a special fondness for the game of baseball itself and what it did for people. He'd say, 'When we do the (Cubs) Caravan in January, you gotta meet Harry and Ethel from South Bend, they got a nice place, you gotta say hello to them.' He knew everybody.

"He was very special to me. There were times when he kind of took me like a first-year manager, which I was. He'd say, 'You gotta be careful, sometimes you get a little too vocal. You gotta remember, this is a great, great town, and sometimes you'll be a little misunderstood. But I like your desire, your flair for the game.'"

Lee Elia *(Photo courtesy of Brace Photos).*

One day Elia didn't heed Harry's advice about word rationing during his infamous, obscenity-filled tirade about Cubs fans early in the 1983 season. Uncensored versions of Elia's vituperation have circulated among collectors ever since. Elia eventually lost his job, but his reputation as a good baseball man was unblemished. He's worked in the game ever since.

He also is a survivor of Caray's after-hours grand tours.

"There was many a time when we'd sit down after the game and have a drink," he says. "I marveled at guys who could hold their cocktails at night like he could. He was in the Top Ten.

"He was the one extension of the Cubs in 1982 that really got everything going. I was glad they got a couple of division championships while he was there and played well for him."

Nancy Faust

If Harry Caray first began singing "Take Me Out to the Ball Game" off-key in 1976, at least Nancy Faust kept up a rhythm

Harry Caray and Nancy Faust *(Photo courtesy of Nancy Faust).*

accompanying him. Faust, in her 29th year as White Sox organist, provided the instrumentals and pacing for Harry's warbling for six years until his move to the North Side.

But the Caray-Faust show didn't just begin and end with the seventh inning sing-alongs. Caray liked to do his own version of boogeying in the booth, pulling it off with Faust's expert musical cues.

"I had the advantage of having visual contact with Harry," Faust says of her organ loft in the left-field upper deck of old Comiskey Park. "If the timing was right in the middle of the game and things were going right for the Sox, I'd catch his eye and go into something like 'Rock Around the Clock' or 'Jailhouse Rock.' He'd start dancing. He'd have his own style of what you'd call the disco bugaloo or something. That would catch the eye of the fans, and they'd turn their backs to the action, because there was more action in the booth.

"When Bill Veeck realized the popularity Harry had from dancing, I suppose he thought he could augment it with a vocal rendition of 'Take Me Out to the Ball Game.' That was quite an unforgettable experience. He did focus attention on what had been going on all along without much ado. We always played the song on the organ in the seventh inning before. Give Harry credit for reviving 'Take Me Out to the Ball Game.'"

Faust also played another role for Caray several times—chauffeur.

"Harry seldom drove, and I heard he entered on an exit ramp the one time he did. So after a game every once in awhile, he'd ask if I could give him a lift back to this bar, that restaurant, or his hotel, which I was glad to do. And he shared a lot of feelings about the game and management with me. He was candid."

Caray was good for the White Sox—and good for Faust's profile as an organist.

"He was a one-man marketing department for baseball and beer. He built up the opposition just to get you out there. He'd say 'Come out Sunday. Nolan Ryan's pitching.' He wasn't intimidated. He didn't let an owner say, 'Don't build up the opposition.' He would always say whatever it took.

"He was always referring to Miss America, Miss This and Miss That in Chicago just to make the ballpark seem like the place to be. He'd build up any aspect he could. And he never sang 'Take Me Out to the Ball Game' without saying, 'Let me hear you, Nancy.' And that's how I gained the recognition I did. I was very grateful for that."

Gary Pressey

Wrigley Field organist Gary Pressey, who provided the music bed for Harry Caray's seventh-inning singing for the past 12 years, was in tune with him long before he worked the keyboard at the ballpark.

"As a fan, I listened to the games on KMOX—'the Cardinals are coming, tra-la, tra-la,'" he says. "I listened to the top of the ninth when the Mets clinched the division in 1969 and the double-play Joe Torre hit into, with Harry announcing."

It was relatively easy to coordinate organ with seventh-inning maestro.

"He told me, 'Just hold those keys down, I'll pick up that tune,'" Pressey says. "It was the key of B. As long as he heard those two notes, he picked it up pretty well."

Always, a-one, and a-two, and a ...

Wayne and Kathleen Messmer

The "other" noted singer at Wrigley Field was Wayne Messmer, who specialized in great baritone renditions of the National Anthem in addition to serving as public-address announcer for a decade. Often Wayne was joined by wife Kathleen for duets of the "Star Spangled Banner."

"We saw Harry for the last time at the Cubs Convention in 1998," Wayne Messmer says. "He stops the conversation, walks across the room, and says (in Harry voice) 'Hey ... there's the best voice ever!' I'd say, 'Ah, my voice coach,' and I'd give him a hug.

"He said, 'We ought to switch songs at a game. You sing the seventh-inning stretch and I'll sing the anthem.' Both of us started laughing. Harry thought better of it: 'My job is to try to bring people in the park. If I sang before the game, everybody would clear the joint.' Little did I know I'd get a chance to sing in the seventh inning, in his memory. I get a feeling every time I sing the Anthem, he's up there getting a little chuckle, that maybe he's singing along.

"He was the guy you'd always look forward to seeing. In the P.A. announcer's booth, you'd always leave the door open until Harry arrived, just because of the chance he'd walk by and say something funny."

Kathleen Messmer, called "pretty lady" by Caray along with every other woman he met, remembers a long rain delay in a game in which the promotional giveaway was children's ponchos. "Harry put on a kid's poncho, including the head part, and hung outside the window and started singing and carrying on," she says. "Here's this kid's poncho surrounding his head, and all that was peaking out was his little face. It looked like he was going to rob a bank.

"I'll miss most him trying to pronounce the name, 'Galarraga.' It's really hard to come here to Wrigley Field and not have him here."

Mary-Frances Veeck

Wife and sometimes creative partner to Baseball Barnum Bill Veeck, Mary-Frances Veeck got a special insight into her husband's ever-fertile promotional mind set—including the time when Veeck decided to secretly mike Harry Caray singing "Take Me Out to the Ball Game" at Comiskey Park.

"Bill had wanted to do it for a long time," she says. "Harry told him he couldn't sing, but Bill said that's exactly the idea. Bill had an exquisite sense of timing."

Bill Veeck ensured Caray's White Sox career would continue after previous owner John Allyn tried to fire the announcer during a live interview on Chicago station WBBM-TV. But that didn't mean the two always saw eye to eye.

"Bill used to laugh," Mary-Frances Veeck says. "He said to Harry, 'You don't say how cool it is at the ballpark.' But Bill was a big believer in freedom of the press.

"For me, I hated as a fan (announcers) getting on players. You blow the play, you don't get a hit, you feel bad enough. One of the basic precepts of any players is you put it behind you, you forget it. But the announcers will talk about it four innings later."

When Caray decided to jump to the Cubs from the White Sox, Veeck was consulted by the new employers. "He'd said they'd be crazy not to take Harry," Mary-Frances Veeck recalls.

Starting in 1981, Veeck took up summertime residence in Wrigley Field's centerfield bleachers, just above the ivy he had planted in 1937. Caray's arrival meant Veeck could sing along with Caray as a fan, with his brainstorm of the mid-1970s developing a life of its own during every seventh-inning stretch.

Tony La Russa

"We have a photo of Bill singing in the bleachers with the whole family," Mary-Frances Veeck says. "Bill was a pretty good singer."

To Mrs. Baseball Barnum, "Take Me Out to the Ball Game" should stay while every other ballpark song ought to be tossed out.

"I'd like to see some civic-minded person offer a great amount of money to songwriters to come up with new songs and throw these other ones out," she says. 'Charge' is a football song. You don't charge in baseball. The 'Mexican Hat Dance?' Yuck. Carmen? That can go, too. We should really get some wonderful music in the ballparks."

Tony La Russa

Tony La Russa still finds it's hard to talk about Harry Caray. Even after nearly two decades as a big-league manager, the on-air zingers that Harry Caray tossed his way about his strategy and lineups when he first worked the dugout for the White Sox in 1979-80 still sting.

"I was a young manager, and Harry needed to be shown that I could do something to help a club," the present-day Cardinals manager says. "There were a lot more important things in his life besides the manager of the White Sox. I don't think I was a big part of his life.

"I think he was like a lot of the fans: 'Who is this guy? He's got no credentials. Let's make him earn something.'"

Did Caray second-guess him unfairly?

"I don't have any opinion on that," La Russa says. "I don't think there was enough importance there for somebody to pay that much attention to him."

Did La Russa at least have a working rapport with Caray then?

"I was manager of the club, and we communicated, certainly."

Could La Russa at least see what Caray and Jimmy Piersall were providing the listeners, in the context of entertainment?

"Yes."

Did the pair at least have civil conversation in the ensuing years, after La Russa moved on to Oakland and Caray to the Cubs?

"I was in California and he was in Chicago. Your paths don't cross."

Doesn't La Russa believe Caray was more positive than negative in helping the White Sox franchise at the gate?

"I'm sure people who have followed the club for a lot of years have opinions on that. You're asking me stuff that I don't know. I'm a baseball guy who pays attention (to things) on the field."

As a more mature person and manager, do you now pay attention to what announcers say?

"I pay attention to as much of the game as I possibly can. I have opinions about announcers, just like I do writers, just like I do players. But understand my place is on the field. That's where I pay the most attention."

Bill Bartholomay

As chairman of the Atlanta Braves, Bill Bartholomay had a box seat that anyone would have paid a princely sum to sit in. However, he preferred his seat at early morning meetings with two of sports' all-time characters—Harry Caray and Ted Turner.

"I introduced him to Ted," he says of Turner's first season as Braves owner in 1976. "Budweiser was a significant sponsor of the baseball team. We had a lot in common. We all liked beer. Ted was a Bud man, and his sailing crews were Bud men. He and Ted became very good friends, and I became kind of like the referee between them. I had to referee good times—who had the most staying power, who had the best jokes. I just sat and listened after putting them together."

Was this a Liars Club meeting?

"No," Bartholomay says. "A very high percentage (was true). One thing about the exciting lives Harry and Ted had was they didn't have to exaggerate. All they had to do is relate what they did. They were two great personalities who got along famously."

The meetings took place in Chicago, New York, Atlanta, wherever Turner's and Bartholomay's travels intersected with Caray's. Bartholomay himself didn't have to go far at all to see Harry in the Windy City. He lived in the same apartment building.

Bartholomay credited the Turner-Caray friendship with helping in the hiring of Skip Caray as the mainstay of the Braves' announcing crew. Years later, the connection benefited Chip Caray, Skip's son, who broke into baseball announcing on regional Atlanta cable telecasts. "Ted did the final sign-offs on our broadcasting teams, and that relationship was very, very important," Bartholomay says.

"Harry was beyond baseball. He was the ultimate people guy. He just loved people and they loved him. He'd be in a restaurant, and most people don't want to be bothered in restaurants. But Harry would be upset if you didn't come to talk with him. He had the reverse psychology."

Jerry Colangelo

Growing up a Cubs fan in Chicago Heights, Illinois, Jerry Colangelo only could hear Caray through the static at night on KMOX-Radio in St. Louis. By the time Caray came to Chicago to work White Sox games, Colangelo already was general manager of the fledgling Phoenix Suns of the NBA.

But he made sure he tuned into Caray via cable TV.

"He was synonymous with baseball," Colangelo, now doubling as head of the new Arizona Diamondbacks, says. "Harry related to the common man. It didn't matter what he said or how he chopped it up. You weren't sure what he'd say next. Whatever, it was acceptable. I can't ever listen to 'Take Me Out to the Ball Game' the same way anymore. Harry brought that song to a new level."

Mark McGuire

Mark McGuire, executive vice president of business operations for the Cubs, is the top team executive to have worked Caray's entire North Side tenure. McGuire was hired at the same time as Caray.

"Clearly, Cubs fans made the transition to Harry (from the White Sox) more quickly and stronger than anyone would have thought," he says.

McGuire says Caray "modified his act," toning it down a bit, in moving to the Cubs. But that didn't make Caray a house man.

"Sure, he was critical," McGuire says. "Here was our No. 1 spokesman, and he was coming out against night baseball at Wrigley Field at a time we were trying to get the lights approved. Harry was so big, so popular you couldn't put the clamps on him."

Arthur Richman

It figures that Art Richman would go full-circle. Growing up hating the Yankees in New York, he became an unabashed St. Louis Browns fan—even stowing away on the Brownies' Pullman car on road trips with the help of the players. Many decades later, he's now—figure this out—senior adviser to the Yankees' public relations department. The Yankees always were known for acquiring cagey veterans from their opponents.

It was on one of those trips to St. Louis that the teenage Richman first met junior announcer Harry Caray at the Melbourne Hotel, where the ballplayers stayed.

"Being around the ballplayers, I started drinking at an early age," Richman says. "I was at a place called the Happy Hollow in St. Louis. Harry, as you know, liked to have a drink every once in awhile.

"As the years went by, I ended up working for the *Daily Mirror*, on East 45th St. in New York. There were about 10 great steak houses in that area. One place I knew the bartenders very well. Harry started coming in. He knew I was there and a lot of baseball guys were there, because where the ballplayers went, the gals would follow. Harry was a popular guy with everyone."

Bob Howsam

Bob Howsam was the Cardinals general manager from 1964 to '67. He later helped put the finishing touches on the famed Big Red Machine in Cincinnati.

Howsam witnessed some interesting card duels between Harry Caray and August Busch, Jr., that came out in Caray's favor.

"Harry used to fly—Mr. Busch and I did, too—down to Florida for spring training," he says. "He loved to play cards and Mr. Busch loved to play cards. And they would play cards. And Harry would get the biggest kick out of beating Mr. Busch, because Mr. Busch didn't like to lose. And Harry would stick it right to him.

"One time he won quite a bit of money. A thousand dollars or something. And boy did he let him have it. He didn't let him forget it."

Bing Devine

Bing Devine preceded Howsam as Cardinals general manager. He later returned to the job for Caray's farewell two seasons. But he had gotten a great insight on him when Caray was Harry Carabina, with fame still a couple of decades into the future.

"I knew him when he was in school," Devine says. "He went to Webster Groves High School here in St. Louis. I had a cousin who went to Webster Groves. Harry and my cousin were a couple of years older than I was and through my cousin I met him.

"As a matter of fact, at one time he was kind of a wanna-be basketball player. This was before the days of the NBA. It was AAU ball, good basketball. He was on a club with my cousin and several

***Bing Devine** (Photo courtesy of St. Louis Cardinals).*

other athletes from Webster Groves High School. Through my cousin, I ended up on the team, too. Harry and I kind of sat on the bench together."

Years later, Devine was instrumental in the broadcasting career of a young Ohioan named Jack Buck. The Cardinals had two Triple A teams at that time—one in Columbus, Ohio, where Buck was working, and the other in Rochester, N.Y., where the general manager was Devine.

"The guy who ran the club in Columbus called me and asked, 'Do you need a broadcaster?' I said, 'Well maybe. We've got one, but we're not satisfied with him.' He said, 'I've got one here who's not going to have a job. We don't have any advertisers or stations interested. So if you're interested, I'll send him up and you can interview him.' And it was Jack Buck.

"So we hired him in Rochester. And then a year later, Anheuser-Busch bought the Cardinals. They were looking for another voice to go with Harry, because Harry had been broadcasting for another beer. So they wanted somebody to give a transition to the broadcast. Harry stayed on and suddenly changed his sponsor. We sent in Jack Buck for an interview. He ended up getting the job and the rest is history."

Mike Veeck

Mike Veeck, son of former Cleveland Indians, St. Louis Browns and Chicago White Sox owner, Bill Veeck. Veeck currently owns several minor league baseball franchises. He worked with Harry when both were with the White Sox organization in the 1970s. Veeck also calls himself the "worst play by play guy Harry ever worked with". He gave himself that label after his performance near the end of the 1978 season when Harry gave every White Sox front office employee the chance to do a half inning with him in the booth.

Veeck described Harry's reaction to "Disco Demolition Night", a now infamous promotion in which White Sox fans were given the opportunity to bring their disco albums onto the field between games of a doubleheader to be blown up by a Chicago disc jockey. The event resulted in chaos with significant damage to the field and caused the White Sox to have to forfeit the second game of the evening. "Harry was absolutely amazed. There were so many people there; he had no control. Both he and Dad went down to home plate at different points to try to get the crowd to return to their seats.

"But Harry was a performer. He knew that to get 65,000 into Comiskey Park and another 35,000 outside for a twinight doubleheader on a Thursday night with Detroit was a pretty good hustle. I think though that he was embarrassed because Jimmy (Piersall) attacked me and the promotion during the broadcast. Piersall was relentless, and I think that Harry, being the pro that he was, began to soften it and cover.

"That is one of the reasons why I have always been appreciative of Harry because very few people came to my defense. Harry and, interestingly enough, Jack Brickhouse, were two who did. You remember those little things. Harry did everything that he could and I was appreciative.

"When it was all over Harry said, 'I can't believe that many people hate the Village People.'"

Veeck also recounted how Harry came to sing "Take Me Out to the Ballgame" during the seventh-inning stretch. Legend has it that a hidden microphone was used. However, Veeck says that was not the case.

"My Dad, who had a voice that made Harry sound like Perry Como, would look over at Harry during the seventh inning and notice that Harry, like himself, was always singing.

"So Dad called the station one day and said, 'Do you have a copy of Harry singing?' They went back and edited it out of a previous ballgame and sent him a copy.

"Then Dad said 'Harry why don't you sing?' Harry refused. And Dad said, 'Well, I got a copy of it, so they are not going to know if you sing anyhow.'

"The sound system at Old Comiskey all came from center field. So we ran everything through the eight horns that came off the green wall out in center. So that is where the sound would come from.

"So Dad kept asking Harry, begging him for a full week. He finally told him, 'We will play the tape; they won't know. They'll look up, see you just standing there swaying, think you are singing it.

"So Harry finally agreed to sing it, and he was absolutely thunderstruck at the reaction of the crowd. They went wild. And, of course, Dad's theory was the crowd would love it because Harry is every man. The fans related so well with him. He called the game much more skillfully than people realized, but that is the mark of a real talent. And he made it look easy, so we all thought we could do it just as well."

However, Veeck's favorite story involved a practical joke he and several others played on Caray in the late 1970s. "Harry was living at the Ambassador East. Because Harry was color blind, Dutchie used to match all of Harry's outfits when she came to town.

"We got the bright idea to bribe the concierge to get into Harry's room while he was out. So for a double sawbuck we got access, shall we say, to Harry's room and created havoc with his wardrobe. And, of course, he would get this funny look on his face because people would just look at him. They did not know whether to say hello to him or slap some cream cheese on him and put a bagel under him."

Andy McKenna

Andy McKenna, former Chairman of the Chicago White Sox and Chicago Cubs recalled one of Harry's visit to Notre Dame for a football game.

"Harry was on the Notre Dame campus in the late 1980s for a football game. He was walking around campus and someone observed 'There's Harry Caray.' and people got in line behind him like they get in line behind the band. People, who didn't know him, but had heard him; and people who knew him by reputation or by sight or by his voice, just started following him.

"Well, Harry loved it. Here Harry was walking through the Notre Dame campus to see the Sacred Heart Basilica and there behind him is a group of people who are there for a football game and wind up walking behind Harry Caray. Harry was the attraction."

Summing up his thoughts about Harry and his special relationship with the fans, McKenna added, "Harry loved who you were. That part of people. He had respect for what you were doing in life."

"Lonborg at the belt ... The pitch ... There's a long drive, way back ... It might be out of here ... it could be ... It is-s-s! A home run. Javier hits one off the screen in left field. And the Cardinals now lead 7-1."

— Harry Caray, Game 7, 1967 World Series (Photo courtesy of Steve Green).

CHAPTER THREE

Players, Past and Present

Mark Grace

Much of Mark Grace's favorable public image with the Cubs was intertwined with Harry Caray's play-by-play descriptions of his .320 hitting style and slick glove work at first base.

And the Grace family returned the favor. On the answering machine of Mark's parents, Sharon and Gene Grace, at their Arkansas home for years was Caray's call of a Grace game-winning homer against Randy Myers of the Mets in the middle of that glorious 1989 National League East title season.

But Caray didn't hop on the Grace bandwagon when he began spraying base hits all over Wrigley Field in 1988. Two years earlier, Caray spotted an up-and-coming talent in Grace at Class-A Peoria, then owned by ol' buddy Pete Vonachen.

Grace and his future (and now ex-) wife, Michelle, were invited to dinner with the Carays and the Vonachens at Agatucci's Pizza in Peoria.

"Here's a snot-nosed A-ball kid talking baseball to Harry Caray," Grace says. "It was a big honor for me to be there. I was a little nervous being in his presence. But he made me feel so comfortable and at ease talking to him. He's one of the most famous people in the world, but he was going out of his way to include me. Harry called me to go out for dinner. It wasn't like Pete invited me.

Mark Grace *(Photo courtesy of Brace Photos).*

"The thing I noticed about Harry was the passion he had for baseball. The whole conversation for three hours of dinner and drinks— maybe 30 minutes of dinner and 2 1/2 hours of drinks—was baseball. He talked about who was the greatest player he ever saw, and Pete talked about his greatest player. Harry's favorite player was Stan Musial. He thought Stan was the best overall player he had ever seen. And then he said (another Harry mimicry), 'Mark, I think you're going to be a lot like Stan Musial.' Obviously, it hasn't worked out that way.

"I was happy to be taken out for dinner. I was making $700 a month and thought that was all the money in the world at the time. If I got a free meal, I jumped at the chance."

Grace later accepted Caray's hospitality at a private table in his restaurant and hopped rides in his limo. "Dinner with him was usually a three- to four-hour shindig," he says. "When he was still drinking, there was no way I could keep up with him and Pete. They had a special gift as far as that is concerned."

Over the years, Grace realized how much great publicity Caray gave him.

"When we lost Harry, for me personally, I lost a big fan," says Grace, one of three Cubs players (along with Sammy Sosa and Scott Servais) permitted to leave spring training for his funeral Mass. "He really thought the world of me, for some reason. I don't know what it is I did. Maybe it was the fact it was the Cubs broadcaster, but also because he was a friend of mine. We spent a lot of time together. He appreciated the fact that even though I was a big-league player and had time constraints, I always had time for him. I always had time for dinner with him or had time to spend with him at the ballpark.

"Not all Cubs players appreciated Harry. A lot of the guys who maybe weren't playing too well or were on their way out didn't appreciate Harry's candidness. Every game is rebroadcast or is taped. Somebody you know would have seen it. If he says something derogatory about you, your phone is going to ring.

"My situation is if I was playing stinky baseball, and Harry says Mark Grace is playing stinky baseball, well, my goodness, how can I get mad at it? All he's doing is telling the truth and doing his job. If I'm playing bad, I don't expect Harry or any announcer to say, 'Mark Grace is just unlucky.' If I'm not playing well, I expected him to tell the whole WGN audience I'm not playing well."

So why didn't other players adopt Grace's attitude toward broadcast criticism?

"Those people have to look themselves in the mirror. That's all I can say," he says. "When you do something poor enough to be booed, then Harry felt the same way. Harry was the ultimate Cubs fan. If you can look in the mirror and ask yourself whether I deserve this criticism, the answer should usually be 'yes.' I have no problem with it. Harry saw a lot of baseball in his time. He knew the game. Nobody knew the game as much as he did.

"Harry was a lot like Vin Scully or Jack Buck, guys who have seen a lot of baseball. Harry didn't like the new-fangled player, all the showboating and all the shenanigans. He didn't like all the gold and the sunglasses and the zebra shoes and all that flash. Harry liked ballplayers, he liked throwback, down-to-earth baseball players, like Vin Scully does, like Jack Buck does, like Ernie Harwell does, guys who have been around a long time.

"That's why Harry appreciated me, because I'm just a ballplayer. I'm a baseball player who goes out there and plays every day, whether I'm injured or whether I'm healthy. I'm not flashy, I'm not going to set the world on fire and make you gawk at 500-foot home runs and I'm not going to steal bases. But I'll do all the things it takes to win games."

Many of those complaining players come and go. But as Caray himself pointed out, the game goes on and outlasts everybody. He was as close to an exception, though, as was possible, as judged by the fan reaction to him compared to the stars at hand.

For an example of the public feeling toward Caray, Grace cites one pregame photo session involving himself and Hall of Famers-to-be Ryne Sandberg and Andre Dawson a few years back in the Houston Astrodome.

"There were about 100 fans over our dugout there," Grace recalls. "They were waiting for us to finish the photo shoot. 'Mark, Ryno, Andre, sign, sign, please,' they were calling out. So we're signing five, 10 minutes. All of a sudden, Harry peeked his head out from behind the home-plate area. Someone hollered, 'There's Harry Caray.'

"Every single person just rushed over to Harry Caray. Ryne Sandberg, Andre Dawson and Mark Grace did not have one more person in front of them for autographs. Two Hall of Famers and me, every person left. We kind of looked at each other and said, 'That's where we are on the totem pole. He's way above us.' It was a reality check right there. It was really something to see how popular he was.

"The greatest thing you could say about Harry is whether you liked him or disliked him, you listened to him. It was like Muhammad Ali. Whether you loved or hated Ali, you watched Ali. That is an icon, that's a legend."

Like most Cubs fans, Grace is heartbroken that Caray was never fated to see a Wrigley Field World Series.

"It's upsetting that he didn't get to see it," he says. "It's like Kerry Wood's 20-strikeout performance. I said after the game that I wished Harry had been there to call it. He'd have been so excited. Whenever the Cubs do win a World Series, it's a shame that Harry won't be there to call it.

"But do you know what? I'm really a believer that Harry's watching and he's probably calling the games up where he is now."

In the end, though, no tears should be shed for a full life. Or, in the case of Caray, a number of lifetimes rolled into one.

"If you told me today that I would live to be an old man, work until the day I die, doing what I'm doing, I'll take it. Harry lived a good life."

Sammy Sosa

Famed for his frenetic body English in the dugout after his homers, Sammy Sosa had no problem adding a salute to Harry Caray for the 1998 season.

After Cubs right fielder Sosa finished blowing kisses to his mother in the Dominican Republic—and then all the mothers out there in the worldwide TV audience—he flashed a "V" sign to the camera to salute Caray.

"They loved Harry in the Dominican," Sosa says. "They understood what he said; a lot of people are bilingual. He gave everything for the game, for the fan. He always had a smile on his face. I'll miss him."

Sosa made some glaring fundamental errors in his early Cubs seasons and has always been strikeout-prone. But Caray never roasted Sosa on the air like

Sammy Sosa *(Photo courtesy of Brace Photos).*

other favorite targets of the past. Sosa believes Caray liked his hustle and willingness to play every game.

"It's the way I played and went out there and took care of my business," he says. "I consider myself a good person and he liked the way I played. That was the key."

Sosa and wife Sonia, regular patrons of Harry Caray's restaurant, had dinner with Caray several times at the eatery. "I'll never forget him," Sosa says.

Kerry Wood

Long before he could have conceived of throwing a fastball 100 miles per hour and striking out 20 batters in a game, Cubs pitching phenom Kerry Wood was a fan of Harry Caray's complete broadcast presentation. It wasn't just the nuances of the game that drew Wood to WGN-TV's cablecasts coming into his Irving, Texas home.

"One of the reasons I watched is that you never knew what he'd say," Wood says. "He'd talk about everything but the game."

While at Triple-A Iowa in 1997, Wood and his teammates chuckled at Caray's attempts to pronounce their strongest player's name. "With Brooks Kieschnick, we'd see how Harry would botch up his name," Wood says.

Almost everyone around Wrigley Field, from players to cynical press box types, has regrets that Caray had not lived long enough to announce Wood's record-tying whiff spree against the Astros. Wood includes himself in that group.

"I wish he'd have had a chance to announce my games," he says.

Greg Maddux

Every so often during the winter, the Atlanta Braves' Greg Maddux takes out an old game videotape from his Cubs days. Of course, the announcer is Harry Caray, who was lucky enough to describe the first of Maddux's four Cy Young Award seasons in 1992.

"It was an honor to have him call a game you're pitching," Maddux says. "My last game as a Cub was special. I've watched that, you hear Harry, and it's great."

Maddux is big, but he freely admits Caray was bigger than just about any big leaguer on duty during his time.

"Seeing him at the Cubs Convention, Harry was above everyone," he recalls. "You had Ryne Sandberg, Rick Sutcliffe and Andre Dawson, all great players. But the only one everyone cared about was Harry. There was something special about him. He set a lot of picks for us (on the road where he was mobbed for autographs). He was special.

"When you come to think of it, Harry sang (via WGN-TV) in front of more people than anybody, more than Michael Jackson."

Scott Servais

Cubs catcher Scott Servais got to know Harry Caray a lot better when he came over in a trade from the Houston Astros in 1995. But Servais already was a Caray fan. After all, he hails from the LaCrosse, Wisconsin, area—and you know how well Caray plays in smaller-city America.

"Every afternoon, the Cubs were on TV," Servais says of his early high school days of 15 years ago. "You'd watch other players and learn from them. Along with that came Harry. That was an added treat.

"Harry could relate to both the blue-collar and white-collar people. Coming from the smaller towns in the Midwest, people could relate easily to his style, and how he went about explaining things bluntly and right to the point. I thought it was hilarious and a lot of fun. Harry just enjoyed the game and people enjoyed listening to him.

"He used to come down to the batting cage at least once a series, talk to the guys, joke around a little bit. One of the fondest memories I have is my oldest daughter, Jackie, who was only 6 or 8 months old, and getting a picture of Harry kissing her on Family Day."

Servais, one of three Cubs players who attended Caray's funeral Mass, called it an "honor" to represent the team. "It's something I'll never forget," he says.

Lance Johnson

A longtime wish was granted when Lance Johnson was traded to the Cubs from the New York Mets in August 1997. He was a Cubs fan, and now he was playing for his favorite team.

So how does a fellow who grew up in Cincinnati, get signed and developed by the Cardinals, and achieve stardom with the White Sox and Mets end up rooting for the Cubs?

Simple. Harry Caray won him over some 15 years ago.

"I was at Triton College (in west suburban Chicago) in 1982 and '83, and listening to Harry day in and day out kind of grew on me," Johnson says. "I found myself watching all the Cubs games. I became a Cubs fan from Harry, not from the players, at first. Then, I got into the players more. Ironically, I'm over here and I'm a Cub. I've spent half my life in Chicago now.

"I was really excited and thrilled about meeting Harry. He was always nice to me and said good things about me. I'd go up to him and tell him even though I was on the other side —the South Side—I appreciated the good things he said about me."

Ryne Sandberg

Cubs Hall of Famer-to-be Ryne Sandberg and Caray both broke in on the North Side together on the same day—Opening Day 1982 in Cincinnati. The pair soon would connect as the top two figures in Cubdom for the next 15 years.

Ryne Sandberg *(Photo courtesy of Brace Photos).*

"Harry came to the ballpark each and every day with the same attitude and same enthusiasm and same love for the game," Sandberg says."He was just a guy I enjoyed being around. I spent half my life with him, at the ballpark, at the airports and on the buses. Just his overall impact on the game, love for the game and love for the fans was tremendous."

Stan Musial

This was as clear as anything Harry Caray ever said. Stan "The Man" Musial was his favorite all-time player, no ifs, ands or buts.

"Well, we were together 25 years," Musial says. "He saw my entire career and saw my good years. We had a lot of great years together.

Harry Caray and Stan Musial.

"I guess it was probably after my career was over when Harry thought I was a great player and talked about. He sang my praises very highly through the years."

Caray was the main conduit for Musial's prime years to a multi-state audience.

"Harry made a lot of great Cardinal fans back in those days, because after the war there weren't many cars around and people didn't travel," Musial says. "Harry made all these fans in Arkansas, down in Tennessee, all the southern states, Kansas and other places. We were the team for the west. We had all those fans.

"But Harry made them great fans through listening to him and Cardinal baseball."

Musial admired Caray's ability to come back from his 1987 stroke.

"He made a remarkable recovery, because when I saw him his mouth was turned, his arm was down and he couldn't do much," he says. "I figured this thing is serious. Six or eight weeks later, he was back doing the games again. He was tough."

Musial didn't go out on the town with Caray. But he was a worthy opponent across the card table.

"I would be with Harry and Gussie Busch and Jack Buck," Musial says. "We played cards quite a bit after my career was over. He was a pretty good card player. We'd play Honors, a game that Busch kind of invented. Face cards count so many, you could go high or you could go low. You could go around King-Ace-Deuce, play that series or you could go down the other way. It was an interesting game because you didn't know if a guy could go high or low."

Lou Brock

Lou Brock's emergence as a Cardinal star almost immediately after the disastrous (for the Cubs) trade from Chicago on June 15, 1964 provided plenty of grist for Caray's excitement in the broadcast booth.

But Caray wouldn't know Brock as the all-time base stealer. He also worked with Brock in 1981 in the White Sox TV booth, when the latter briefly toiled as a color analyst.

"My best memory was 1964," Brock says.

Lou Brock.

"In '64, the thrill and excitement in his voice in the last game (pennant clincher) was something.

"I got to know Harry very well as a person. I always knew him as a broadcaster, because I grew up in the Cardinals' broadcast area. I found he was friendly to players. He was always there. He'd go to bat for you. As a broadcaster, he went to bat for me, too.

"In the booth, I found out Harry never made a comment about something he didn't have backup information about. He always told me to be equipped."

Mike Shannon

***Mike Shannon** (Photo courtesy of St. Louis Cardinals).*

Mike Shannon knew exactly what to expect from Harry Caray when he joined his hometown Cardinals as an outfielder 36 years ago. After all, Shannon grew up enthralled, like everyone else in the St. Louis area, with Caray's play-by-play.

"Harry made the games exciting, whether you were out in Podunk Junction or Festus, or wherever," says Shannon, who since 1971 has occupied the Cardinals broadcast-booth seat once held by his senior partner, Jack Buck, alongside Caray. "Harry kept you on the edge of your seat. He may not have been watching the same game you were watching. But it didn't matter. When you were down there and listening to the radio, Harry had you excited about the action."

Shannon was a reliable player until an illness shortened his career. Caray did not spare him because he was a hometown boy. And if the truth be known, Shannon expected Caray to be tough on him.

"Harry was Harry. You knew exactly where you stood with him," he says. "I accepted him as a fan. I accepted him as a player.

"One day, Harry came to me and interviewed me. He said, 'Mike, I've been getting a lot of letters and a lot of calls that say I've been too rough on you.' I told him, 'When I'm struggling, I look pretty bad. I'm a streaky player. When I'm going bad, I'm going bad. When I'm going good, I'm going good.' From that day forward, he became a Mike Shannon fan. I didn't disagree with him."

In his prime, Shannon was nicknamed "Moon Man." He was a nocturnal creature, enjoying night life and all its attractions when not putting in a full shift with the Cardinals. Chicago's day games were particularly to his liking. Shannon would play at Wrigley Field in the afternoon, go back to the hotel and sleep, wake up at midnight and hit the down. A post-dawn nap would precede his return to the ballpark, usually to torment the Cubs with the long ball.

"We ran in different circles, no doubt about that," Shannon says of his post-midnight circuit. "But if you were out and about, sooner or later you'd run into Harry."

Both enjoyed Chicago even more because of the 1 a.m. closing time of St. Louis bars. Their counterparts in Chicago locked up at 4 a.m. But even the early closings didn't deter Caray. "They'd stay open for him if they knew he was coming," Shannon says.

Later, as broadcasters, Shannon patronized Caray's Chicago restaurant, while Caray graced Shannon's St. Louis eatery. Fair trade for the two lords of the night.

"Harry was one of the all-timers," Shannon says of Caray's night-shift wanderings. "I really thought that was a part of his mystique. He liked to be out with the fans. He was out as a baseball fan. He figured his job continued after a game."

Shannon says Caray is still revered in St. Louis.

"Chicago is No. 1, but I think St. Louis is a close second," he says. "Of course, Harry was international. Everyone knew him."

Joe Torre

Joe Torre became friends with Harry Caray—despite being traded for one of Harry's favorite players.

Torre, now New York Yankees manager, was dealt from the Braves to the Cardinals for Orlando Cepeda in spring training 1969. All Cepeda had done was win the National League Most Valuable Player award in 1967 for the world-champion Redbirds—and have Caray constantly sing his praises.

"He was a big Orlando Cepeda fan," Torre remembers. "I used to meet Harry after a game, at a restaurant. He would proceed to tell me what Orlando did that night. 'He hit another home run. He hit another

***Joe Torre** (Photo courtesy of St. Louis Cardinals).*

home run,' he said. I was uncomfortable with it, but that was Harry.

"It wasn't a matter of winning him over. He didn't dislike me. But it was just his way of conversation, what 'Cha-Cha' was doing. Plus, the Braves won the division."

Torre had a bit of wit about Caray's firing at the end of his first season with St. Louis in 1969.

"I said, 'You guys had him for 25 years. It only took me one year to get rid of him,'" he recalls.

Over the ensuing years, Torre and his wife socialized with Caray and his wife, Dutchie, in both Palm Springs and Chicago.

"I enjoyed being with Harry," Torre says. "He was a passionate guy and loved what he did."

Ferguson Jenkins

*As an ace pitcher with the Cubs, Boston Red Sox and Texas Rangers, Hall of Famer Ferguson Jenkins was the opposition for Caray when he broadcast the Cardinals and White Sox.

But in 1982, Caray and Jenkins joined up on the same side in the latter's second tour of duty with the Cubs. Caray called Jenkins' 3,000th career strikeout in San Diego in '82 and his final, 284th big-league victory the following season. Later, in 1995 and '96, Jenkins worked with Caray again when he served as Cubs pitching coach.

The affable Jenkins stayed away from Caray's controversies. He stayed back—as a spectator around the batting cage.

"One afternoon, Harry said we had the slowest guy around in Keith Moreland," Jenkins recalls. "Keith's wife phoned him to tell him what Harry said. The next day, around the batting cage, Keith wanted to choke Harry. They got into a heated argument. Fortunately, Harry did the right thing, apologizing and saying he didn't choose his words correctly. Keith kind of accepted that. But for a second, I thought we were going to have player-sports announcer fisticuffs."

Fergie Jenkins.

Billy Williams

Jenkins' longtime Cubs teammate and fellow Cooperstown enshrinee Billy Williams had some sage advice to give Cubs pitcher Dickie Noles back in 1982: Don't take on Harry Caray.

Williams, then in his first go-around as Cubs hitting coach, sat in the dugout one day with the emotional Noles when the latter spotted Caray coming out on the field. Noles' anger welled. Seems that Caray had said some not-so-complimentary stuff about the right-hander on the air.

"Harry was the kind of guy who didn't hold back," Williams says. "He said something about Dickie not getting people out. Dickie wanted to approach Harry, discuss something, maybe start an argument. I told Dickie don't do that, because Harry's a little bit too big for that.

"You couldn't change a guy like Harry, because he'd been in the game so long. I remember real good singing (Harry's voice), 'The Cardinals are coming, tra-la, tra-la' back in 1969."

Williams was never a big nightclubber. But in 1991, he and Ron Santo went out one night to celebrate Harry's birth-

Billy Williams.

day. "We didn't get back in until later that morning," he says, shaking his head.

Williams has one lasting image of the unabashed Caray.

"I always remember him wearing those shorts on hot days and those burry legs."

Larry Bowa

Shortstop Larry Bowa came over with Ryne Sandberg from Philadelphia in a famous trade in the off-season of 1981-82, and thus got his eyes opened—day and night—by the new broadcaster for Dallas Green's "New Tradition."

"He was the show," Bowa, now a coach with the Anaheim Angels, says. "We were trying to get some credibility here.

Harry was all that people talked about, coming over from the White Sox. That summer I met him, I could understand why everyone fell in love with this guy.

"No question, without a doubt, he was more popular than the players.

"It was unbelievable how he was treated when we went into different cities. A couple of times I was at dinner with him, it was unbelievable. Harry was Chicago. We thought he was as much a success to the Cubs in 1984 as the team itself, because people would literally come to see him. Once they saw the product, they continued to come out.

"At least to us, he was never on an ego trip. He just told it like it was. A couple of times, he ripped a couple of players. The thing that I admired was the next day, he'd be down on the field. He said, 'Don't take it personally, I just report the game.' He knew the game inside and out, so you could accept it more as a ballplayer. He would say, 'This is a good place for Bowa to be pinch-hit for,' and I agreed with him, because I wasn't swinging very well. But he'd also praise you, and he pointed out my leadership qualities, how important it was if I wasn't in the playoffs.

"He was a great man, and I'm glad I was able to share part of my time in Chicago with him."

Al Hrabosky

No way could Al Hrabosky keep his "Mad Hungarian" act going off the field as well as on. But just to make sure, cagey baseball man Birdie Tebbetts used Harry Caray as a stalking horse to determine if Hrabosky was just a regular guy off the mound to relay in his scouting reports.

"The first time I ever met Harry Caray was at Wrigley Field. I had come up with the Cardinals in 1970, so I just missed him in St. Louis," ex-reliever Hrabosky, now a Cardinals announcer, says. "He came down to the bullpen corner with

Al Hrabosky *(Photo courtesy of St. Louis Cardinals).*

Tebbetts. They sat down in the bullpen for a little bit. Harry got my attention and was just talking to me a little bit. I found out later it was for the benefit of Tebbetts. Birdie just wanted to find out if I could talk, to see if I was human in some capacity."

Eventually, the Mad Hungarian act met up with master showman Caray when Hrabosky went to the Kansas City Royals while Caray broadcast the White Sox.

"Harry was a little intrigued with me, because I, too, had a falling-out with August Busch, Jr.," Hrabosky says. "Harry saw something that he kind of liked in that sense. I stood up to Mr. Busch for something I believed in, and I think Harry always kind of took that under his wing. Without that, he might have criticized me or jumped on me. I think he never did.

"Once I got into the broadcast booth and got to know him a little more, he couldn't have been nicer to me. Stan Musial and I both flew up for Harry's wake, the night before the funeral. I said then that Harry probably symbolized baseball, and the youth of America could probably identify baseball through Harry better than any player today."

Ed Farmer

Native Chicagoan Ed Farmer did not grow up listening to Harry Caray. Bob Elson was the top White Sox announcer in Farmer's formative years.

But Farmer, who now teams with John Rooney on Sox radio broadcasts, enjoyed his best year as a Chicago relief pitcher with Caray in the booth in 1980 at Comiskey Park. And briefly, Farmer shared a vinyl label with Caray. The pair made a how-to-pitch record together.

"Harry would ask five or six guys questions, but I don't know how many it sold. Certainly it didn't sell a lot," Farmer recalls.

On his first day in a Sox uniform, Caray introduced himself to Farmer. The latter laughs at the memory. "Like I didn't know that," he says.

Another time, Farmer pitched for the Cleveland Indians while Caray broadcast from Comiskey Park's centerfield bleachers on a blazing hot day. Bill Veeck had installed the famous shower out there.

"Every half inning, he'd come down there, pull the chain, take a shower, try to cool off, and go back to his microphone," Farmer says.

"It's legendary that he'd broadcast from Comiskey Park and say, 'Six of my best friends just walked in and they're all named Bud.' That was the amount of beer he was going to consume during the game."

Ed Herrmann

As the incumbent White Sox catcher when Harry Caray joined the team as broadcaster in 1971, Ed Herrmann had good rapport—unlike some of his teammates—with Caray. In fact, he joined him as a fill-in color announcer while disabled with an ankle injury for three weeks in 1974.

"Both of us liked to have a beer, so we had some things to talk about," says Herrmann, now baseball coach at Poway (California) High School.

Herrmann had suffered through the Sox's worst-ever season—56-106-in 1970. So he was happy to see someone, anyone, bring fans and fun back to Comiskey Park.

"I don't know if they were White Sox fans, but they were baseball fans," Herrmann says of the huge, Caray-inspired jump from 495,000 attendance in 1970 to more than 830,000 the following year. "Harry thrived on being the main attraction. He was the main attraction for a few years.

"He was great for the fans, going out to the centerfield bleachers to do the broadcast and taking his shirt off, which I think was a mistake (because of his chubby physique). That was as close to a superstar as the fans were going to get, and it was good for them."

Herrmann applauded Caray's on-air honesty, while admitting that many of his baseball contemporaries couldn't handle a broadcaster like him.

"Athletes, especially today, don't like hearing the truth," he says. "We're catered to. So it makes it hard for someone to come up to you and say, 'You can't pitch or you can't hit.' He didn't pull any punches."

Caray's play-by-play, of course, bothered third baseman Bill Melton, Herrmann's road roommate. But Caray was not a constant subject of conversation among the early and mid-1970s Sox as it was later on.

One player in particular was affected negatively by Caray.

"Harry called Tom Egan the worst catcher he had ever seen, and one of the worst hitters," Herrmann says of his 1971 and '72 teammate. "I think it hurt him mentally and might have hastened the end of his career. His wife told him what Harry said. He'd say to me, 'He got me again last night,' with some expletives you couldn't print. We were a very close knit group. Twelve or 14 of us would be out someplace together on the road, and our wives were the same way."

Caray's style can't be criticized in the end, Herrmann says. The only difference between him and the fans was that he had a 50,000-watt radio station for his opinions.

"Harry told it into the microphone what all the fans were thinking in their seats," he says.

Wilbur Wood

Herrmann's frequent batterymate, knuckleballer Wilbur Wood, got far more praise than damnation from Harry Caray. And for good reason—Woody won 20 or more games in Caray's first four seasons with the White Sox from 1971 to '74.

"I got along great with Harry," Wood, now a salesman in the Boston area, says. "If you were going well, he was with you 100 percent. If you were going bad, he told it like it was. He probably elaborated a little too much (on ballplayers' failures).

Wilbur Wood
(Photo courtesy of Brace Photos).

"I can't knock the man. He did an awful lot to bring people to the ballpark. He helped revive Sox franchise."

Larry Monroe

More than two decades ago, Larry Monroe had an eventful break-in to the majors.

The White Sox's No. 1 draft pick in 1974, Monroe already had rubbed shoulders with Caray as a minor-leaguer by dating his stepdaughter, Gloria, nicknamed "Tuney." Then, he was summoned to the parent club from Knoxville for a Sunday, August 12, 1976 doubleheader—and a pregame TV interview with Caray.

Monroe, now the Sox's vice president of free-agent scouting, had to do the interview in the latest Bill Veeck-inspired garb—shorts. Baseball's Barnum had introduced the game's first and only uniform shorts for the '76 Sox. Caray could get away with garish, mismatching shorts on his job, but the ballplayers were fair game for humor.

"I met him behind home plate," Monroe recalls. "The camera clicked on, and he said, 'Hi, this is Harry Caray at the ballpark. We're going to do an interview with the newest call-up for the White Sox, right-handed pitcher Larry Monroe. We'll be back in one minute. But before we break, Larry, I want to ask you one question: Do you feel as stupid in those shorts as you look?'

"I was a 20-year-old kid in my first day in the big leagues, scared to death anyway, and it added some levity to the conversation. He just had that chuckling laugh. I probably turned all red-faced, dumbfounded."

Monroe, who along with his date went out to dinner several times with Harry and Dutchie Caray, also remembers "little mutterings" among the players about Harry's on-air comments. "But we weren't too good as a team at the time anyway," he says.

"Ba-a-a-l-l, inside. Ball three."
— Harry Caray

"Three balls and one strike on Ralph Garr. Write that down."
— Jimmy Piersall

"History is about to be made. There's Ziggy Czarobski, the great star from Notre Dame ..."
— Harry Caray from a White Sox broadcast, July 26, 1977 (Photo courtesy of Brace Photos).

CHAPTER FOUR

Broadcast Partners and Coworkers

Jack Buck

Jack Buck, of course, is the broadcast partner most closely associated with Harry Caray, joining him in the Cardinals booth in 1954, then succeeding him as St. Louis' No. 1 baseball voice in 1970.

But he figures he might have been a second choice. Chick Hearn, now the Harry Caray of pro basketball play-by-play with the Los Angeles Lakers, apparently was Caray's first choice at the time. Hearn was working in Peoria then. "I am almost 100 percent certain that's who Harry wanted in 1954," Buck says.

Nevertheless, Buck got the job, and the rest is history — all the way to enshrinement alongside Caray in the broadcasters' wing of the Baseball Hall of Fame and the knowledge Buck's own son, Joe, has worked his way into the top-dog role on Cardinals games as his father cuts back his schedule.

"I was in Rochester and the ball club was sponsored by Anheuser-Busch in 1953," Jack Buck says. "I did their commercials for Budweiser and the team was owned by the Cardinals. It was the Triple-A farm club for the Cardinals. I had been in Columbus (Ohio), which also was a Triple-A club for the Cardinals. So I was in their farm system as well.

Jack Buck.

"A fellow by the name of Bill Walsingham, a brewery executive who became a Cardinals executive, sent me a tape of Harry Caray when I was broadcasting in Rochester. It was a play-by-play with the bases loaded, two out, a pop fly hit behind short. Marion going out, Terry Moore coming in. Marion and Moore collide, the ball falls. One run scores. Two runs score. Three runs score. Holy cow! How could that have happened? And you can hear Harry screaming on it, right?

"And (Walsingham) sent me a little note. 'This is the way we want you to broadcast.' And I said, 'Well, hell, I'm finished.

My career is over.' Because I could do that for one game. Or maybe a week or even a month. But not for a year. And certainly not for 50 years."

Yet Buck adapted to Caray's style. Soon Buck learned why Caray connected so well with the fans at old Busch Stadium.

"Our booth was right behind the crowd, the same level as the back row," Buck recalls, "People used to stick their heads there to say hello to Harry. And, of course, the microphones would pick them up. 'Hi, Harry, I'm from Mississippi.' 'I'm from Louisiana.' 'I'm from Oklahoma. Good to see you, Harry.'

"He really was a hero to everyone on the Cardinal network. He just appealed to them. His honesty was something they hadn't heard before. You talk about 'tell it like it is,' as (Howard) Cosell professed to do. Harry was the first one in the business to ever do that, the first to ever defy authority. And that's why Gussie Busch liked him so much.

"They played gin together. They were the same kind of people."

Two's company, but three often is a crowd. And three is exactly what Caray got when Joe Garagiola joined the broadcast team.

"All during that year (1954), he was campaigning to have Garagiola" Buck says. "And Garagiola did come that next year. We had Milo Hamilton with us that first year. He got fired when Garagiola came along."

Buck also soon discovered why Caray eventually made the limousine business wealthy wherever he went.

"Ben Stein, one of Harry's best friends, was a stutterer," Buck says. "And Harry was driving the car in Palm Springs and Ben said to Harry, 'H-h-h-arry, I d-don't know about P-p-p-alm Sp-p-p-rings, but in Ch-ch-icago, it's illegal to drive a car on the sidewalk.' I always drove. I wouldn't ride with him. He used to start fires with those glasses he wore."

Yet by taking the wheel, Buck didn't avoid eventful experiences with Caray—including a close brush with the law one night in Houston.

Jack Buck with Harry Caray.

"I was driving," he says. "I went through a flashing red light and a cop stopped us. I was getting along OK with the cop and all of a sudden Harry got out of the car and said, 'What's going on here? Break this up.'

"Well, we'd been drinking. The cop told him to get back on the sidewalk. He said, 'I don't have to get back on the sidewalk. This is a free country.' By that time, there were six police cars there. Somebody pointed a finger in his face and said something to him and he finally calmed down. But he was always very feisty."

If Caray and Buck had any disagreements while a Cardinals broadcast team, they had long forgotten them by the time both were senior announcers—and icons—in the 1980s. Buck filled in as a guest announcer on the Cubs telecast while Caray recovered from his stroke in 1987. He suffered the ignominy of calling a game-clinching Andre Dawson grand slam off Todd Worrell in Busch Memorial Stadium during the guest stint.

"We ended up on pretty good terms," Buck says.

Jimmy Piersall

Caray already had earned acclamation as the "Mayor of Rush Street" by the time Jimmy Piersall joined him as color analyst on White Sox broadcasts in 1977. But the pairing of the bombastic Caray and the often-controversial Piersall, who bragged he had papers to prove he was crazy (after his *Fear Strikes Out* book and movie) transformed baseball broadcasting into guerrilla theater of the air for five seasons on Chicago's South Side.

With the two master critics in the booth together, players whose ears were singed by Caray alone had to develop an even thicker skin. One summer night in 1977 against the Detroit Tigers, Sox outfielder Ralph Garr worked the count to 3-and-1 against pitcher Dave Roberts. Both Caray and Piersall wanted to freeze the moment; they claimed the act of patience was a career first for Garr. During the same game, Piersall made fun of Tigers second baseman Tito Fuentes as the two broadcasters called him a hot dog.

And when the two had to fill time during a long at-bat, anything might come out of their mouths. As the Rangers' Mike Hargrove worked the count full against Steve Stone one summer night at Arlington Stadium, Caray speculated why the wind had changed so abruptly. "There are no lakes or mountains nearby," he said. Piersall then offered his own theory: "Must be the planes taking off from the airport."

In this famous pairing of characters, Piersall had to fight for mike time. Caray was in his absolute prime in cramming dozens of names of ballpark visitors and cronies into a single half-inning of play-by-play. Such minor notables as Ziggy Czarobski and Tommy O'Leary had their names dropped innumerable times by Caray. Piersall had to be creative to get a word in edgewise.

"I took the names from the usher and hid them," Piersall, now in his 13th season as the Cubs' minor-league outfield instructor, says. "I couldn't do any talking when the names were on. Harry found that out, and he chewed me out."

But that bit of subterfuge was about the worst of the discord between Caray and Piersall. They worked like a charm together, and kept interest in the Sox going while a cash-strapped Bill Veeck allowed the team to decline after 1977.

Caray helped mold Piersall's announcing talents.

"I learned by watching him, watching him prepare," Piersall says. "It took me a year to learn how to get in and out (on the air). Harry told me don't go in unless you have something to say. I learned how to get in and talk with him. I'd touch him on the arm when I wanted to talk.

"At first he wasn't very patient with me. But we got used to each other. Dutchie (Harry's wife) said I was good for him and gave him a new image."

The Caray-Piersall pairing broke up after the 1981 season when Caray jumped to the Cubs. Piersall continued on for a season as an in-studio analyst for SportsVision, the ancestor of the present-day Fox Sports Chicago. But his days were numbered with Jerry Reinsdorf and Eddie Einhorn now running the Sox—and de-emphasizing the role of announcers in the ball club's appeal.

Piersall soon began hosting his own nightly talk show on WIND-Radio in Chicago, and almost was re-united with Caray in the Cubs broadcast booth.

"They called Jan (his wife) and me in for a meeting," Piersall said of WGN brass. They kept us there two, three hours. They asked if I could get along with Chuck Swirsky (top WGN-Radio sports voice of the day). I told them what you see is what you get. I couldn't change. But I still think they wanted to hire me to work with Harry again."

Piersall never did get the job, but was hired as a Cubs outfield coach. He could depend on seeing Caray every spring training, occasionally at Wrigley Field, and in a Lake Geneva vacation outing or two. But in any form, Piersall, who had an active social life of his own in his day, did not dare run with Harry after hours.

"I didn't drink. I didn't like the smell of smoke," he said. "I liked women.

"I don't know how Harry had all that endurance to go out most of the night. I know one fact. He was a good sleeper and did get his proper rest. He was a perfectionist on the air, and he wouldn't have done anything to interfere with his broadcast. Competition was fierce, and a lot of people wanted that job."

Piersall knows one thing about his association with Caray: His post-playing days wouldn't be nearly as productive without him.

"I was broke at the time I started with Harry," he said. "So it really made a tremendous change for me because Harry was so well-known, that he helped me become very popular. I started doing a lot of promotional things in Chicago, commercials. It was important to me that I got popular. People really didn't know me (in Chicago).

"So now, after 20 years of doing my own TV show, my own radio shows a couple of times, I find out I owe an awful lot to Harry. I've got two houses paid for, four cars all paid for, some certificates of deposit, some IRAs. What else can I say except that, 'I love you, Harry!'"

Steve Stone

Second to Jack Buck in seniority as a Caray broadcast partner was Steve Stone, who worked with Harry from 1983—three years after Stone won the Cy Young Award with the Orioles—to 1997.

Steve Stone and Harry Caray *(Photo courtesy of Steve Green)* .

He provided some insight as to how he got along with Caray as a White Sox player and how that relationship paved the way for the Caray-Stone broadcast pairing.

"Well, apparently, I handled it pretty well (with the White Sox)," Stone says. "Harry was the motivating factor in me getting this job. Harry realized I wasn't going to make any excuses, and like everyone else when you pitch poorly, you just say you did that. And when you pitched well, you try to accept whatever credit was due you.

"I was the leading pitcher in 1977 and '78. Although I had my bad moments—because we had one of the worst defenses in history on those teams—our hitting made up for it. My relationship with Harry was always a good one. He gave them three names when they were looking for a partner here at WGN. I was one of the three, and the rest, shall we say, is history."

Like others who witnessed Caray's handling of player relations, Stone marveled at the man's willingness to talk face-to-face with those who had problems with his commentary.

"Harry had no problems being controversial with anyone," he says. "Probably the greatest story about Harry was with (Sox manager) Chuck Tanner. Harry was sniping at Chuck, and Chuck would then use the newspapers to snipe at Harry. Harry went down on the field and said, 'Look, we're wasting a golden opportunity to get some great ratings. Instead of me talking about you on television and you talking about me in

Harry Caray, Ernie Banks and Cubs announcer Steve Stone discuss 1996 Spring Training *(Photo courtesy of Bill Wills).*

the press, let's just go head-to-head before the game every day. You can air your grievances, I'll air mine, and it will make for great television and radio.' That's the kind of guy Harry was. Always had an eye for the ratings and never dodged controversy."

Arne Harris

Along with Carlton the Doorman from the old "Newhart" show, Arne Harris is one of the most frequently recurring off-camera characters in TV. He has directed Cubs telecasts and won local Emmy awards since 1964. Harry Caray and predecessor Jack Brickhouse have made Harris a star without his face ever being seen live.

Accustomed to working with a consummate pro like Brickhouse, Harris had known Caray over the years. But he didn't get an absolute, proper introduction to the Harry style until the latter's introductory press conference as Cubs announcer late in 1981.

"The first thing he said to me was, 'I've got a question for you,'" Harris recalls. "I thought it would be something really profound. And he said, 'You think that song I sing at Comiskey Park will go at Wrigley Field?' Here's someone who gets one of the biggest jobs in the world and the only thing he's worried about is that cockamamie song. In my infinite wisdom, I said, 'I don't know. Let's see what happens.' It worked out pretty good."

Harris and Caray didn't plan out the telecast, pregame or inning-by-inning. "Everything was right off the cuff, on the air," Harris says. "Obviously, I tried to lead him into some stuff, and he loved it. If he liked something, he'd tell me about it.

"I fed him stuff that I thought was essential to help the telecast. I'd be on the field, particularly on the road, and I'd pick up some stuff from the players. Harry wasn't necessarily with them all the time. The combination of Harry, Stoney (Steve

Stone) and I talking to people was what made the show. But most of the stuff Harry did was his own."

Harris did not jump on the intercom from the remote truck to correct most of the famed Caray malapropisms and mis-identifications.

"We just let it correct itself," he says. "They're watching television, and they could see who it is. People knew who he was talking about.

"I'm convinced that once in awhile, when things got dull, he did it (mis-identify names) just to see what the hell would happen."

Harris' trademark shots of hats and attractive women continued from the Brickhouse days, with the added flavor of Caray's unique commentary. "I probably did a little more rooftop shooting, because he loved the rooftops," Harris says. "I never shot limo shots for anyone but Harry, because he always had a limo."

Harris, Steve Stone and Caray were frequent postgame dinner companions. Here, Harris noted an eccentricity that rivaled Wade Boggs' fanatical devotion to a daily chicken diet.

"Harry's the only guy I know who ate Italian food 365 days a year," Harris says. "He always had to have his couple of martinis. The game would end at 10:30 p.m. or so, and we'd get to the restaurant at 11 or 11:30. He wouldn't be ready to eat until 1 or 2 in the morning. I was pooped out. Stoney and I were tired and ready to go to bed. If Harry would have been ready to eat the meal right away, it would have been all right."

At least the entourage didn't have to pay in their bleary-eyed state.

"He was great at picking up the tab," Harris says. "I've never seen a guy like Harry. He would not take a freebie most of the time. Some guys are tight, but he was the best I've ever seen."

Harris, who haunted racetracks far and wide, providing grist for on-air humor, never lured Caray out to help him handicap the horses. Caray attended a special night in Harris' honor at Sportsman's Park in Chicago, but that was it. "Harry told me once that when he was young and very poor, he got hurt making a bet, and it drove him off gambling," he says.

Mandy Cohen

Here's Mandy Cohen, not long out of college, up in the WGN-TV booth, giving Harry Caray and Steve Stone cues as the floor manager in the broadcast booth. Scary? No, because Harry took to Mandy from Day One.

"When I went on my first road trip, I was very nervous. It was my first time with the team," says Cohen, who now directs baseball for Fox Sports in Detroit. "We arrived in Atlanta, and I asked what do we do next? I was told we would get on the buses and go to the hotel.

"Suddenly Harry turns around and says (in Harry voice), 'No, no, Mandy, you come with me.' I was saying, 'That's fine, I'll take the bus. Oh, no, this is the worst!'

The lamb with the wolf? No, Mandy was now a fully vested member of the Harry Caray after-dark traveling troupe. She was ushered into a limo with Caray, Steve Stone and Arne Harris.

"The entire team was screaming," Cohen laughs. "I think it was Mark Grace yelling, 'I've been with the club a long time. He's never offered me a limo ride!'"

Like all the other assistant directors who worked with Caray, Cohen ran to the Wrigley Field press lunchroom to get him drinks. One cold day, he chose tea.

"It was time to come on camera for the game open, and Stoney plugged in his ear piece and turned around," Cohen says. "Harry also turned around. Stoney and I both saw it at the same moment. Somehow, he got this ear piece tangled up with the tea bag string. So if he picked up the ear piece and put it in his ear, the tea bag would be dangling down like an earring.

"I come flying down the stairs. We're about a minute to air. Steve reaches over. Harry says, 'I got it, I got it!' The three of us were all over it."

All grappled with the tea bag and ear piece as the clock ticked down.

"I hear Arne saying, 'Thirty seconds,'" Cohen says. "Everything was in slow motion. Harry says, 'I got it!' Bam! The teacup tips over, tea's all over Stoney's scorebook, all over Harry's scorebook. Arne's going, 'Three, two ...' The three of us are laughing so hard. They're laughing so hard they couldn't talk. Harry finally got it together enough to say, (in Harry's voice) 'Holy mackerel, we had a little accident up here.' He went on to explain how he spilled tea everywhere. He slipped right from that to the game open. All the pregame notes he had written out were smeared from the tea. We spent the whole game laughing about it."

Cohen rates Caray one of the all-time greatest broadcast ad-libbers.

"That's why people watched," she says. "No matter what was happening on the field, he always made it interesting. It was a fun show. That's what he always thought it was—a show."

Kathy Kerr

Kathy Kerr succeeded Mandy Cohen giving Harry Caray his cues in the booth full-time in 1996. She got to see the sentimental side of Caray in 1997.

"The first time I saw Harry show affection for Dutchie was the day he walked into the booth glowing from head-to-toe," Kerr says. "He said, 'Kathy, Kathy, get down here, I've got to show you something, this is so exciting. I just got here. I opened up my scorecard, and look what I found inside.' It was a very sweet anniversary card from Dutchie. He had kind of forgotten at the moment that it was their anniversary."

Dutchie Caray was able to surprise her husband with the card by packing his bag in the morning and slipping the greeting in with the scorecard.

"You could tell how much he was in love with that woman. He kept pulling everyone over and showing them the card. 'I've got to show you what my sweetheart did,' he said. And did he ever talk about it on the air! That was probably the most exciting thing that happened to him on a personal basis. I've never seen him so overjoyed and so emotional."

Pat Hughes

Present-day Cubs radio voice Pat Hughes, in his third season in Chicago in 1998, rates Sunday, May 5, 1996, as the day Harry Caray officially "welcomed" him to the job. Sammy Sosa broke a window across the street on Waveland Avenue with a game-winning homer. More importantly, Caray relayed the blessings of others to Hughes when he stopped into his booth.

"After exchanging pleasantries for a few moments, he told me the real reason he came over was to tell me that people really love the work I was doing. 'When you're new in town, you don't really know how people are accepting you and receiving you,' he told me. 'I just want you to know you're doing great, keep it up, and that you and Ron (Santo) are a great team already.' It really was one of the nicest things that he could have done. It was so sincere, to go out of his way like that, to make me feel welcome. It's something I'll never forget. I'll always love Harry Caray because of that.

"After that game, after the game-winning homer, I'm in the booth doing the postgame show. I'm right in the middle of a sentence when I hear that familiar voice bellow out (a Harry imitation), 'How about those Cubbies!' And he just left, kind of strolled on out."

Hughes, who grew up on the West Coast, still got exposed to Caray on trips to his mother's hometown in Colum-

Pat Hughes *(Photo courtesy of WGN).*

bia, Missouri. "There's Harry Caray, doing Cardinals games in the 1960s," he says. "He was such a great talent in those days. His voice almost forced you to listen.

"If you were to put together a list of five people who popularized baseball, more than any other individuals, Harry Caray would have to be in that group along with Babe Ruth, Jackie Robinson, maybe Mickey Mantle, Joe DiMaggio, Willie Mays, and you can throw Vin Scully in there.

"There was only one Harry Caray. There were so many things I learned from Harry when he was a radio man in St.

Louis. He was right on top of the call. He was dramatic, he was fun, he was enthusiastic. There's so much about Harry in his later years, he was so unique that you couldn't copy it. You just appreciated him and loved him, but you couldn't really adopt that kind of style for yourself.

"It only worked for Harry. I don't think it would work for anyone else."

Ron Santo

Since he grew up in Seattle, out of range of St. Louis' KMOX-Radio, and later was busy during the season as a player, Ron Santo never heard Harry Caray—not until one day in 1969.

The Cubs team he captained as an All-Star third baseman was beaten in St. Louis. Reflecting on the game in the clubhouse afterward, the players' attention suddenly turned toward a radio.

"The Cardinals were maybe seven games behind us," Santo says. "We're sitting around having a beer. You can hear Harry, but you're not really listening. And then all of a sudden, at the end of his show, he goes, 'The Cardinals are coming, tra-la, tra-la.' We all stopped. It was unbelievable."

Flash forward to 1990, after Santo was hired as color analyst for WGN-Radio's Cubs broadcasts as part of a three-man booth with Thom Brennaman and Bob Brenly. At the time, Caray still handled the fourth, fifth and sixth innings on radio, switching over from WGN-TV when the latter broadcast games.

"I was so nervous getting the job. I was more nervous getting in the booth with Harry," he says. "But before we even started, he put his arm around me and said, 'You were a great ballplayer. I know you're new at this. I'll give you all the leeway. I want you to be yourself. I'll help you out. Relax, we'll have fun.' He relaxed me so much. It was like my first hit in the big leagues. Everything was lifted off my shoulders."

Ron Santo *(Photo courtesy of WGN).*

Santo soon learned, though, that no one, positively no one, upstages a Harry Caray home run call. A Ryne Sandberg spring-training blast provided the grist for Santo's first lesson in broadcast-booth etiquette with Caray.

"When he hit it, I hollered 'Yes!!' (over Caray's call)," Santo says. "The game's over, he turns to me, and he says, 'That's my call.' He was very serious, but not to the point of embarrassment.

"That's fine. Six years later, Pat Hughes comes into the booth. Harry's up above me in the booth. Someone hits one out and Pat gives his call. But as soon as he hits it, Harry yells, 'Yesss! Yesss!'" Santo was about to give some pay back, with humor. "As soon as the inning was over, I turned around and said to Harry, "That's his call.' He laughed. He was as emotional as I was.

"The biggest compliment I could give him was he could do both play-by-play and color. He knew everything about the game."

Like most of Harry's friends and colleagues, Santo says he couldn't keep up with Caray after hours. And, like everyone, he was amazed at Caray's stamina and recuperative powers.

"Don't forget about his stroke," he says. "Nobody else comes back from that. Nobody. I said one thing about Harry when he died. He lived a full life. Then I said, stop. He lived three full lives. He was almost like a cat. He'd come back from adversity, he willed himself."

Rich King

Rich King reports sports for WGN-TV. But almost 20 years ago, when he was a play-by-play partner of Harry Caray during White Sox broadcasts on Chicago's WBBM-Radio, King could have been a science correspondent—reporting sleep deprivation. Test subject: Mr. Holy Cow! himself.

King, Caray and fellow announcer Joe McConnell did a 6 o'clock game at Comiskey Park one evening, knowing they'd have to catch a 7 a.m. flight the next morning to Baltimore.

"I got to the airport at about 6 a.m., and Harry was there," King recalls. "He was wearing the same clothes he had on the night before. I asked him what happened. He said, 'I was out on Rush Street all night long. I didn't even bother going home.' He didn't sleep at all.

"I figured he'd get some sleep on the plane. But he and (Sox coach) Bobby Winkles always played gin rummy on the plane. They played gin and he was drinking Bloody Marys on the plane. Then I'm at the ballpark at 5 p.m. to do some pregame stuff. Here comes Harry, and I asked him if he got any sleep. He said he hadn't, that he had gone to lunch at one of his drinking spots.

"Now he does the game. It's a long game that ends around 11 p.m. Joe McConnell and I were dog-tired from getting up real early to catch the plane. We're at the hotel at 12:30 a.m., dragging our bags. We see Harry running out to get a cab. I asked him where he was going. 'We're going to Little Italy to get some sausage.' Here's a guy who had never slept, and I'm 20 years younger than I am now, and I'm dying."

Baltimore also was the sight of another Caray conspicuous consumption story, but one that you wouldn't expect from him.

"We had a technician who was a vegetarian, Harry McIntyre," King says. "Harry (Caray) got hungry on the air, in the middle of the game. There was nothing for him in the booth until he turns to Harry McIntyre, who gives him a big bag of yogurt-covered raisins. He says, 'I can't eat these, they'll kick me off Rush Street!' He puts them away for half an inning, then takes them out. 'I'll try one of these things,' Caray proclaimed.

"He tries them, and says they're tasty as heck. So he keeps eating them for two innings on the air. In the process, he's dropping them everywhere—on his chair, his table. He got up. He had on this powder-blue suit. As he left the booth, he had crushed raisins hanging off his butt, off the back of his suit, off the back of his shirt. It was one of the funniest things I've ever seen."

Lou Boudreau

Hall of Famer Lou Boudreau finished out his WGN-Radio announcing career as Caray's partner in the 1980s. He suggests Caray should be remembered with a special honor.

"I suggest the Cubs, as well as Major League Baseball itself, should dedicate all seventh-inning stretches to Harry," Boudreau says. "They should do it in honor of Harry, for what he's done for baseball. He brought the fans together.

"Harry just loved the game. Remember, the number of miles he traveled as a broadcaster was tremendous. Baseball should remember that.

"He always told me that one thing he despised and hated was not to see an athlete perform at his best. He knew when they were hustling. Harry had studied the game not only as a broadcaster, but also having played himself. He knew whether they were putting out. And he had an encyclopedic recall."

Lou Boudreau, Harry Caray and Vince Lloyd at Spring Training, 1982 *(Photo courtesy of Bill Wills).*

Vince Lloyd

Vince Lloyd hobnobbed with Harry Caray all the way back to 1950, when he joined Jack Brickhouse for Cubs games on WGN-TV. He later would team with Caray for five seasons on WGN-Radio after Caray joined the Cubs.

But the encounter Lloyd remembers the most took place on the Cardinals' last trip into Wrigley Field in September 1969. Lloyd and WGN-Radio partner Lou Boudreau suddenly had an unexpected visitor to their booth in the middle of the game.

"I remember when Harry barged into our booth," says Lloyd, now retired in his hometown of Sioux Falls, S.D. "He said, on the air, 'You guys won't believe this. I've been fired.' We asked him why he's being fired. He said he didn't know why. 'They can't get away with that. I've been here too many years,' he said. I told him August Busch, with all his money, could do whatever he wanted and could afford it.

"Can you imagine anyone else in the business getting on another station and announcing he'd be fired? So typical of Harry to announce it on the air, on another station."

Oddly enough, the startling news made Lloyd think of a tip that he had dismissed at the beginning of 1969.

"I had heard at the beginning of the season that he would be fired," Lloyd says. "Someone who lived in downstate Illinois, a fan, told me. I thought that was preposterous. It was in the back of my mind."

Lloyd and Boudreau had been an on-air team for 17 seasons when Caray joined them in 1982. He did not try to push either one out.

"In the booth, he couldn't have been better to work with," Lloyd says. "That first spring training, we had a game in Tucson. I drove him down. We hadn't done a broadcast yet. I asked him how he wanted to work it. He said we'll split it down the middle, flip a coin to see who goes on the air first. That's how we did it."

When WGN summoned Lloyd out of retirement in 1994 for some fill-in work, Caray asked Lloyd to consider a full-time comeback.

"I walked into the press box," Lloyd says. "He came running over and said, 'I caught your broadcast last weekend. Outstanding. Why don't you tell them you're coming back?' I told him I appreciated it coming from him. But I was finding out why I retired. It was the fourth straight weekend I was on the road. I know why I quit.

"I really enjoyed him tremendously. Out on the road, dinner and drinks. He was tremendously entertaining, and very straightforward and honest."

Wayne Larrivee

Wayne Larrivee probably thought he was a pretty good adlibber after working pro sports broadcasts, including the Chicago Bulls and Chicago Bears, for the better part of two decades.

But when he was matched up with Harry Caray on Cubs telecasts starting in 1994, Larrivee couldn't have been prepared for the line with which Harry Caray set him up one afternoon.

During the three-headed game broadcast introduction involving Caray, Larrivee and Steve Stone, Caray first asked Stone a question. Then he turned to Larrivee.

"As he was making his turn, he was thinking about, 'What am I going to ask this guy?'" Larrivee says. "It was in the middle of one of the Bulls' playoff runs. Dennis Rodman's in the news. But I'm expecting a baseball question. And Harry says, 'Well, did you go to Crobar with Rodman last night?'

"It came out of left field. But that's the way it worked. It was one of those situations where I knew what he was thinking. He was thinking, 'Hey, if it was me, if I was the Bulls broadcaster, that's exactly where I would have been after last night's game, at Crobar with Rodman.'

"That was the beauty of the opening of the ball games. It was never rehearsed. Most of those opens on TV are rehearsed.

They go through the graphics and everything else. Everything with Harry, though, was fresh. You had no idea what he was going to say or ask. Through the summer, it became a great exercise in ad-libbing.

"You always tried to think of a clever line, because chances were good he was going to hit you with a clever line going in. What a great privilege to work with him."

Larrivee also admired Caray's work ethic.

"He'd go down on the field to interview the manager," he says. "He'd come back up to the booth. He didn't go back up to the pressroom to kibitz much with the writers and scouts. He'd go into the booth and do his lineup card. He had two or three things written down that he wanted to talk about. He was all business.

"The other thing was he was tremendously loyal. In spring training, he only had two or three games to do on TV. But every day, he'd go to the ballpark, watch the game, and sing that song in the seventh inning. He knew the fans would enjoy it and were expecting it. He felt it was his duty. The Cubs didn't require him to do that."

"Now the stretch, the pitch ... There's a long drive, way back, might be out of here ... It is! It is! He did it again! The game is tied. The game is tied. Holy Cow!"

—Harry Caray after the second of Ryne Sandberg's two homers off Bruce Sutter, June 23, 1984 (Photo courtesy of Steve Green).

CHAPTER FIVE

Other Media Members

Vin Scully

For oh-so-many decades, Vin Scully ranked second to Harry Caray in seniority among all baseball announcers. Now he's No. 1. Caray began in 1945, while Scully broke in as Red Barber's junior partner on Brooklyn Dodgers games in 1950.

Scully and Caray's styles were like night and day. But both were all-time greats in their own way. There's no right and wrong way to broadcast baseball. Yet both Hall of Famers have earned the enduring loyalty of millions of fans. And both kept going through the grind because they simply loved the game.

"What impressed me the most about Harry was the fan reaction to his work," Scully says. "I first met Harry in the pressroom in St. Louis my first year, where I was in awe of everybody. The impact Harry made on the community was remarkable. The people in St. Louis, they just loved him."

Scully didn't cross paths much with Caray for 12 seasons after the latter was fired from the Cardinals in 1969. The reunion, so to speak, in 1982 was like a whirlwind.

"When he came to the Cubs, it was like a marriage truly made in heaven," he says. "The people in Chicago, the outpouring of love day after day, the network where people all over the country were able to see him. Even in Dodger Stadium in the seventh inning, the crowd would holler, 'Hey, Harry, sing!'

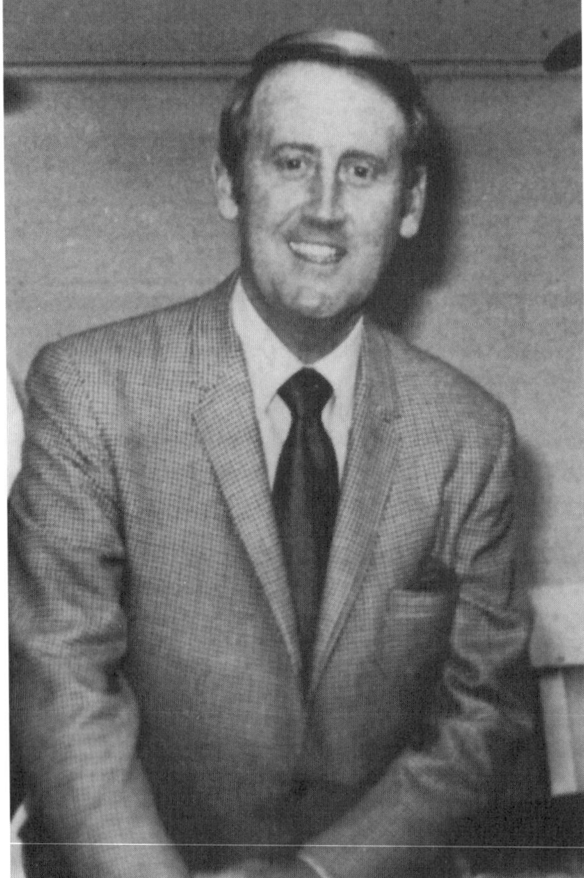

Vin Scully.

"The other great thing was he would be a fan on the air. He rooted openly. That kind of shocked me, because I was brought up by Red Barber in New York. Our whole idea was you don't root at all, because there were three teams in the city There are people coming from all over and we don't want to be selling product only to Dodgers fans. We want to sell them to everyone. To see someone like Harry go completely the other way was remarkable.

"And if he was annoyed with the team, he would say it. I remember one time in St. Louis, the Cardinals were just furious at him because he said, 'Once you get past (Ken) Boyer and (Stan) Musial, it's like having the weekend off.' The other seven players were livid. But that's Harry."

Scully has worked only on the East and West Coasts, while Caray logged just one season on the West Coast, in Oakland in 1970. Was Caray's style cut out just for mid-America?

"Without putting a label of provincial on the Midwest—and I don't mean that—I think over the years if the announcer is in any community long enough, something happens," Scully says. "There is some chemistry. The people get the announcer they want, and he knows what they want. He follows their direction. For Harry and Chicago and St. Louis, it was absolutely perfect.

"But knowing him, had he gone to New York, he might have had the love and affection there, too, for all I know."

Scully theorizes that Caray may have just been a natural-born, after-hours bon vivant, at least starting out.

"I'm sure he paced himself," he says. "Maybe in his early days, like all of us, he had the ability, or God-given strength, to abuse your body up to a point. But there's no way to last that long with continuous abuse."

Ross Porter

Ross Porter, Scully's longtime Dodgers' broadcast-booth partner, can remember being riveted to Caray's far-flung Cardinals play-by-play growing up in Oklahoma.

"I wasn't a Cardinals fan, but I was a baseball fan, and I thought he brought a great deal of excitement to the game," Porter says. "Then I got to know him later, even when I was working in Oklahoma City. When I got to the majors, I'd always tried to sit down and talk to him when we were either in Chicago or Los Angeles. He always remembered my Oklahoma background and he'd always say, 'Are your folks listening today in Oklahoma?' And he'd always say hello, time after time."

Porter lives in the off-season in Rancho Mirage, California, across the street from Eisenhower Hospital, where the stricken Caray was taken for his last days. "I went over the Sunday afternoon after he collapsed to try to see him, but of course the nurses wouldn't let me do that because he was very critical," he says.

Porter says Caray "wanted to be the people's voice, and he never forgot that."

Bob Uecker

When you're hitting .198, you start beginning to think of your next career. And when Bob Uecker, little-used backup catcher of the 1964 St. Louis Cardinals, had show-business thoughts, he started out as a mimic—of Harry Caray.

One of the classic moments of the Cardinals' 1964 pennant-clinching clubhouse celebration at old Busch Stadium was Harry, conducting live radio interviews, summoning, "Uke! Uke!" Obligingly, he played straight man.

"Here we are in the Cardinals' clubhouse," Uecker roared in his best Harry voice, to the guffaws of the real thing, "with Jack Buck."

That was a peek into by-play between Uecker and Caray that lasted more than three decades, well into Uecker's own career as "Mr. Baseball"-funnyman on the "Tonight Show," co-star of "Mr. Belevedere," wacky broadcaster in the "Major League" movie, and real-life radio voice of his hometown Milwaukee Brewers.

"For awhile I really had him down pretty good," Uecker says. "I did him every day. We got a kick out of it. I did it in front of Harry. I did it on the team bus. When people imitate you, you've got to be somebody. They don't imitate people who aren't anybody."

Since Uecker didn't play much with the Cardinals in 1964 or '65, he escaped the verbal lightning bolts that Caray often cast at his own players for their on-field foibles. But Uecker understood that Harry's zingers weren't zapped out of anger.

"He loved baseball to the point where he thought fans sometimes might be cheated by lackadaisical play," he says. "He was not ashamed to talk about it.

"I remember things he said about (Cardinals third baseman) Kenny Boyer. He loved Kenny Boyer. Harry never said anything because he disliked somebody. He said it because he thought they could do a better job. It wasn't malicious."

Caray was never afraid to face players who disagreed with his on-air criticism.

"If he ever said anything about you, and he heard you were looking for him, he was right there for you," Uecker says. "He'd come walking into the clubhouse. He'd stick his face right in your face. He was not embarrassed to put his face in your face and say, 'You got a problem with something I said?'

"He did that with Tracy Stallard (in 1965). Tracy was supposed to do Harry's pregame show. He didn't show up. Harry marched right in the clubhouse. I was there; I saw it. Harry walked up to Stallard and got right in his face. He said, 'If you ever do that to me again, I'll bury you. If you don't want to be on my show, tell me. But don't ever try that again.'"

Later, Uecker saw Caray in the latter's travels throughout the American League with the White Sox and in spring training, when the Brewers and Cubs played each other.

"I don't think I saw him in anything that matched," Uecker says. "That's why I enjoyed him so much, to see him in a pair of shorts out there. I always looked forward to seeing him in the spring. I called him 'Coach.' I called him that for a long, long time.

"I think Harry made a lot of people better people, by either coming out to the ballpark or listening to a broadcast. I was glad to be a friend of his. I learned a lot from him.

"He'll be remembered for a long, long time. Baseball has lost a lot of great people, front-office people, broadcasters. It will go on forever. But baseball will always have a place for people like Harry Caray."

Jerry Coleman

Longtime San Diego Padres announcer Jerry Coleman is famous in his own right for on-air malapropisms. But no way could he screw up on the air like Caray—and be beloved as much.

"What people heard at the end of his career was nothing like what he was as a young man," he says. "The best way to describe Harry Caray was as a great broadcaster and a guy who really worked at his craft.

"Nobody could be a Harry Caray. He was a one of a kind. He could say things that if I said them, they'd run me out of the booth, maybe out of town. But he could get away with it. How many people could say what he said and get away with it?"

Tom Cheek

Toronto Blue Jays announcer Tom Cheek has broadcast every game his team has played since its inception in 1977. But his endurance streak can't compare with Caray, who showed up every day for work from the start of his career until his stroke in 1987.

Every day was a banner day for Caray—especially one bleary Sunday morning in old Comiskey Park.

"I remember that Stroh's Beer was Harry's sponsor at one point with the White Sox," Cheek says. "He'd always have a cooler in the broadcast booth. I'll always recall it was Sunday morning and it was Banner Day. We were getting ready to do the game, they opened the gates out in centerfield, and all these kids came parading in. I wasn't paying too much attention until I heard this little commotion and stir.

"The first banner that came by in the parade said, 'Harry, stop drinking before it's too late.' And Harry was saluting them with a bottle of Stroh's, kind of waving it from the broadcast booth."

Charley Steiner

ESPN on-air personality Charley Steiner's best memory of Harry Caray came when he helped put together a feature for the inaugural season of "Baseball Tonight" for his network in 1990.

"It was a piece on the dying art of great radio baseball broadcasters," Steiner says. "I had the pleasure of traveling around the country to see all the greats. We came to Wrigley Field on the night the Dodgers were playing the Cubs. I had a chance to talk to Vin Scully, who I grew up listening to when he did the Brooklyn Dodgers.

"And I also talked to Harry Caray, who could be a cantankerous sort. But he was really charming and wonderful to me and for me. We were both talking about something we both had this visceral pleasure in—broadcasting baseball through the mind.

"The moment I remember the most about this piece is we had a camera in the booth next to Vin Scully. And next to Vin's booth was Harry's booth, calling the very same game. Our camera guy, Jeff Israel, was focusing on Scully at that moment. He was miked for us. Someone hit a homer. He's telling a story and (in Scully voice) 'And there it goes ... and ... it ... is ... gone.'

"At that moment, our camera guy decided to pull back, and you could then see Harry making the exact same call in his way. He's leaping out of his chair and (Harry's voice) 'It might be ... it could be ... it is! Hey!' There were two right ways to say the same thing. That was the beauty of that moment, to hear these two masters describe the exact same situation in their own unique style."

Caray saw the piece and praised it to Steiner. "I was blessed because there was somebody old enough to call me 'kid,'" he says.

Rick Rizzs

Seattle Mariners announcer Rick Rizzs grew up in Blue Island, a south Chicago suburb, listening to Caray handle the White Sox, then the Cubs.

"The biggest impression I had of him was how much fun he had on the air," Rizzs says. "I was working at a downtown Chicago insurance company one day. Harry was doing his broadcast from the bleachers and he had a six-pack of Falstaff with him. Suddenly he cried out, 'Holy Cow! Someone stole one. Just ask me for one!' "

John Sterling

Famed for his "Yankees Win! THHHEE Yankees Win!" calls, New York radio play-by-play voice John Sterling offers up one Caray story that "tells you how much Harry loved doing what he was doing."

When he was part of the Atlanta broadcast team with Skip Caray, Sterling recalls sitting in the dining room near the broadcast booths with the father-and-son Carays, Steve Stone and Ernie Johnson after a Cubs-Braves game in old Fulton County Stadium. Pete Van Weiren had to stay behind to do the final scoreboard show on Braves radio.

"Here's Harry Caray," he says, "at that time of night, after his own game, yelling at Pete as he came out of the (booth) door into the lounge, (in a Harry mimicry), 'Pete, what was the final Oakland score?' " Sterling laughs heartily. "He really cared if Oakland beat Seattle, or Minnesota, or lost to them.

"Another time, I was doing a game in Wrigley Field when the press box hung from the upper deck. I had a break between innings and I went to the men's room along the catwalk. I stopped to watch Harry and the fans sing in the bottom of the seventh. I looked down and saw young, old, male, female, black, white, all singing, and I almost cried. I thought it was sensational, just sensational.

"Harry Caray was a spellbinder, a dream-weaver. There won't be another Harry Caray."

Ken Singleton

Caray remembered the days when Ken Singleton was a slugging switch-hitter for the Montreal Expos and Baltimore Orioles. Caray's memory, though, didn't stop there. He never forgot Singleton's grandmother, Panella Hathaway, in Maywood, Illinois. Hathaway turned 99 in 1998.

"The first time I asked him to say hello to her on the air, he did it," Singleton says of his debut as a Montreal Expos announcer. He's working for the Yankees and Fox Sports now.

"And I never had to give him a note all the next times I came to town. He always said hello to her on the air. He always remembered. And he'd always say that her grandson was doing a great job.

"When he reached his 50th year in baseball broadcasting, she wrote him a letter thanking him for all the hellos. It wasn't that she heard all the hellos on the air. But she went to church every Sunday and someone would always remind her that Harry said hello to her during the week. She's one of the few persons around who's old enough to have seen the Cubs win a World Series."

Singleton recalls his first interview as a broadcaster was Caray in 1985. "He said players come and go, but people come to see the game."

Jerome Holtzman

They were the two "deans" of their respective professions—Harry Caray, dean of baseball announcers, Jerome Holtzman,

Jerome Holtzman *(Photo courtesy of the* Chicago Tribune*).*

dean of baseball writers. Befitting their status, they squared off in post-midnight gin rummy games throughout the 1970s when both covered the White Sox.

Holtzman began on the baseball beat in 1957 for the *Chicago Sun-Times*, 12 years after Caray started his Cardinals broadcasts. He's still writing columns for the *Chicago Tribune.* But another talent he had was battling Caray down to the wire over cards on the road.

"Harry was pretty good, and one of the things he always said after a few hours' playing was, 'The Big Possum walks late,'" Holtzman says. "I hated when he said that, but he ended up using that on his broadcasts quite a lot. He'd also say: 'What are martinis mixed with?' He'd lay his cards out on the table and say, 'Gin.'"

Holtzman also notes how Caray had some prescience about a move that changed the landscape of Chicago baseball. Move the time machine back to about 1980 when they were on the road with the White Sox.

"He said, 'Why doesn't WGN or the Tribune Co. buy the Cubs? It would be a natural,'" Holtzman recalls. "I told him I hadn't even thought about that."

Sure enough, Tribune Co. did buy the Cubs in mid-1981. Then it hired a guy named Harry Caray.

Irv Kupcinet

Chicago's all-time gossip columnist frequently ran into Caray on Rush Street. But "Kup" had an edge in seniority in service on his job to Caray. He began his column, still in the *Chicago Sun-Times*, in 1943, two years before Caray started with the Cardinals.

"He instilled a spirit of baseball that very few players have, because he was such an ideal man for telling the story of baseball and telling it in a very grand fashion," Kup says. "At Sox Park as well as Cubs Park, he was an idol. More important than players at that time, because he drew so many fans. He drew more fans than the players during his two segments here."

Bill Gleason

Longtime sports columnist Bill Gleason, also the creative force behind the syndicated "Sportswriters on TV" talk show, was a kindred spirit of Caray's. You might find Gleason at his post in the press box with a cold one at the ready.

But Gleason, who had a long run at the *Chicago Sun-Times* and the old *Chicago American* before switching to the *Daily Southtown* and *The South Bend Tribune*, insists Caray was not just fun and games.

"I was most impressed by a characteristic of Harry Caray that most people don't mention—his willingness to work very hard," Gleason says. "Harry had so much fun and boasted about the fun he was having, his night life. It often was not clear to people that this man was a very hard-working person.

"When I used to cover spring training in Sarasota on an annual basis, I tried to be first out there in the morning and get my work done. Sometimes I would be second, because Harry would be first. And this was after a very long night, as most of Harry's nights were long. Sometimes I was with him.

"Harry knew what he was doing, a consummate professional. He did not call pitches. He did not call sliders, he did not call curve balls. He just said the man winds up and pitches, and the batter hit it. I'm so tired of these guys analyzing pitchers' stuff. Harry never did it.

"Everyone knows Harry was fun. But I want everyone to understand he was great in his profession because he worked hard. If Harry had a cold, what difference did it make? It wouldn't affect his voice. His voice wouldn't get any worse."

But what's the scoop, Gleee-son, as they call him on the TV show? How much did Caray imbibe after hours?

"That was exaggerated," he says. "He was a good drinker, but he could hold his drink. He was a gentleman drinker. After hours, though, I never saw him have a beer. It was Scotch and water or a mixed drink. All the times I was around him, I never saw him intoxicated. That might be at 3:30 or 4 in the morning."

The wee-hours Caray was not a story-teller like Bill Veeck.

"He was just like he was behind the microphone," Gleason says. "he was criticizing the players, he was criticizing the manager, he was criticizing the management. 'How we gonna win with this club, Bill?' Harry didn't tell stories about baseball's past, at least not to me. Veeck lived in the present, but he also told stories to entertain people. Harry entertained people by his rigid belief in how the game of baseball should be played.

"He was more than a purist. He had extremely high standards."

A vocal White Sox fan by his birthright, Gleason credits Caray for helping save the South Siders for Chicago by his arrival in 1971.

"Absolutely. He was the biggest drawing card," he says. "People would buy tickets just to sit in the upper deck by the broadcasting booth. It was so much fun to be around him and

Bill Gleason *(Photo courtesy of Bill Gleason).*

listen to his off-the-microphone caustic comments about his personnel."

Bob Broeg

Not all media types got along with Harry Caray. And one of St. Louis' most famous scribes, *Post-Dispatch* sports columnist Bob Broeg, got off on the wrong foot with Caray early on. There's a sense of regret.

"We didn't have a very good experience with each other, it's unfortunate to say," Broeg says.

"I was in the Marines in '44. I came out happily assigned by *Leatherneck* magazine to cover the Cardinals-Browns World Series. He was just doing a daily sports show for KXOK before he had gone into play-by-play baseball. He did such a nice organized job with setting up his night's editorial. I told him I thought he'd have a great career and he obviously did.

"He started covering (baseball) the next year and I came out in '46 covering it. He was awfully tough to deal with. His nightly editorials he'd say, 'Despite what you read in the newspapers ...' Well, after a while you get pretty sick of that.

"I know Bob Burnes of the *Globe-Democrat* finally did the most insulting thing. We just cut him out of the news, which didn't help. But he was tough. He was very competitive."

That even extended to after-hours meetings with Caray.

"I found that his exaggerations of the game were one thing, but he was difficult to go have a drink with in those days," Broeg says. "You'd say black was black and he'd say it was white. All of a sudden his eyes squinting behind those thick glasses, he'd say something derogatory.

"One time Gus Mancuso, who succeeded Gabby Street as his associate, had to pull me off of him. Another time, Dixie Walker, coaching for the Cardinals had to pull me off of him. I don't mean that he wouldn't have fought, but I just said, 'Harry,

Bob Broeg.

the hell with it. You go your way and I'll go my way.' And that's what we did."

Their quarrels couldn't dampen Caray's popularity.

"Obviously he had a great stranglehold on the public," Broeg says. "And the Chicago market was better for him. And I think by that time, he was wiser. He went there, in effect, with his hat in his hand, dealing with the press and got along admirably, which he hadn't done here. Harry was very competitive and almost cunning. He was critical of almost everybody except his boss.

"He was like a fan. I give him his credit and his due compared with those of us in the press box. When I was angry I could kick the furniture and then sit back down and write with detachment. But his venom and his frustration came out directly into the microphone, which was one of the reason the players didn't like him.

"He'd take umbrage at little things. He got on (Ken) Boyer repeatedly because one day Harry wanted to do a gimmick from the Los Angeles Coliseum where he would do a late game from a box seat next to the dugout and he wanted the players on deck to talk with him and he wanted Boyer to talk with him. And Boyer said, 'Not now, Harry.' And he took offense at that.

"He was a little unreasonable in that respect. And I guess their wives at times would tell them some of the things he said about them and that didn't help either."

Even with their differences, Broeg praised Caray's announcing talents.

"He could make any game better than it was," he says. "Which, of course, is a hell of a point. It was more effective, I always thought, in the country areas than it was in the city areas, where we used to have two or three stations competing at one time.

"His third year on the job, 1947, (Cardinals owner) Sam Breadon granted exclusive rights to a network that set up on the grounds. I think Breadon himself was one of the men involved in picking Caray and Street over Johnny O'Hara and Dizzy Dean. And, of course, that gave him an opportunity to be heard by people who hadn't heard big-league games regularly.

"He's a little bit like Ring Lardner ... I think it was at the '25 World Series where Ring Lardner said, 'They played a doubleheader today—the one that was played and the one Graham McNamee broadcast.'

Broeg figured Caray survived a lot of pot shots by enemies until his last season in St. Louis in 1969.

They hardly spoke after that, but Broeg eventually communicated in writing to Caray, offering advice at a crucial time in the latter's life.

"He was amazed when he suffered the stroke. I happened to know that hospital. I banged a letter out to him—I'd had a stroke previously—and I think he was taken aback because I not only commiserated, but gave him some tips as one who had had a stroke, that I could be that considerate of him. But I'd learned, too."

Fred Mitchell

Chicago Tribune sports columnist Fred Mitchell got to both cover and hang around with Harry Caray when he worked the Cubs beat for his paper from 1983 to '88.

"I was impressed mainly with his energy and his ability to have a good time and enjoy every moment of his life," Mitchell says. "The travel was arduous for even younger men, as I was at the time. But I marveled at

***Fred Mitchell** (Photo courtesy of* Chicago Tribune*).*

his ability to go out to dinner, have drinks, and have fun late at night.

"I remember a trip from Montreal to New York, a charter flight that arrived in New York around 2:30 a.m. Most of the players were dead tired on the bus from the airport to Manhattan. They were sleeping. Before we got to the Grand Hyatt hotel, Harry asked the bus driver to stop and pull over to the nearest corner so he could get out and meet some friends in the wee hours. I remember watching him walk away and wondering how in the world he could muster the energy to keep going.

"But that was typical of Harry. He lived and thrived on friends, and he made friends wherever we went. That's a lasting memory that will stick with me."

Mitchell offers up a theory— "an amateur psychiatrist" —about why Caray developed such stamina for nocturnal wanderings and staying on the job for life.

"The fact was that he was an orphan and had these enduring memories of being left out and not being part of a family, a traditional family," he says. "Baseball became his family—the players, coaches, management, writers and broadcasters. All represented a family to him. He was willing to do anything he could for a family member. That's what kept him going as long as he did. He never wanted to formally retire as a broadcaster. He was doing something he loved doing and he was around people he loved more than anything."

Red Mottlow

Red Mottlow is Jerome Holtzman's counterpart as dean of Chicago's radio sports reporters. He says some of his own broadcast style was influenced by Caray.

Mottlow's first broadcasting job was in 1950 at WGIL-Radio in Galesburg, Illinois. The station carried Bert Wilson's Cubs broadcasts by day and Caray's Cardinals games at night.

"Harry's style was just great," Mottlow recalls. "I was trying to develop a style of my own. The things I listened to Harry for were his enthusiasm, his feeling for the game, and how he described the game. You don't copy anyone's style in this business. You try to be your own person. But Harry's enthusiasm, his love for the game that he couldn't check through the microphone, impressed me the most."

Thirty-seven years later, when Mottlow worked at the old WFYR-FM in Chicago, he suffered a stroke around the same time Caray was afflicted with his stroke. Oddly enough, both were scheduled to come back to work the same day.

"Our news director called up WGN and told them I was coming back from illness that day," Mottlow says. "Would Harry please mention that on the air. And Harry did. That was a wonderful thing on his part. He welcomed me back. "Those were two experiences that just enriched my feeling about him."

Les Grobstein

Harry Caray was many things to many people. But counter-espionage agent? The most ubiquitous fellow in sports journalism in Chicago, Les Grobstein of WSCR-Radio (The Score), witnessed Harry's act of pro-White Sox patriotism back in 1977 as he caught a "spy" for the Yankees.

"In those days, walkie-talkies for scouts in the stands were illegal," Grobstein says. "The White Sox were accused more than any other teams of using illegal recon stuff, eyes in the skies in the scoreboard, that kind of stuff.

"Well, Harry Caray was the only guy who spotted Gene 'Stick' Michael, then already working for the Yankees, working in the upper deck in a sellout crowd. Nobody from the Sox organization saw him. Harry spots him, turns the microphone over to Lorne Brown, and gets up.

"I watched him leave the radio booth, walk into the stands, and go over to Stick Michael and start smiling, kind of like a cat with feathers on his face from the canary. He put his arm around him and pointed to the walkie-talkie. He let Bill Veeck know about it and the Yankees got into a little bit of trouble. The so-called color-blind Harry Caray found this. When Stick Michael got the Cubs managerial job in late 1986, he remembered Harry busting him."

Six years later, on April 29, 1983, Grobstein gained fame as the radio reporter who recorded Cubs manager Lee Elia's classic expletive-filled postgame blast at fans. Minutes after Elia's tirade, he played the uncensored tape for Caray, Vince Lloyd and Lou Boudreau, all of whom had just gone off the air on their Cubs broadcast.

"Vince has that cigar wiggling around in his mouth and his eyes are rolling," Grobstein says. "Harry's just standing there straight-faced, frozen. Lou's got his eyebrows rolling. The first words out of anyone was from Vince: 'Gee-zus, Lou, he's gonna get his ass fired.' Lou says, 'This is true, Good Kid.' And then Harry just looks at me and says, 'That's really him? It's not an impersonation?' I say, 'I think you know his voice.' He says, 'I have a feeling the Lee Elia pregame show might be in danger of getting canceled.' We were rolling on the ground."

Still another time, Caray tussled with umpire Harry Wendlestedt at Wrigley Field. "One of the nicest guys of all the umpires," says Grobstein. "One day, around 1993, they should have started a game (on a rainy day). It stopped raining, wasn't even drizzling, not even a trickle, but the umpires were afraid it would start up again and refused to allow them to take off the tarp. Harry (Caray) is on the air, going bananas on the air, saying 'Harry, get that tarp off, let's play ball.' They send it back to the station, and Harry (Caray) comes right into the press box lunchroom.

"Wendlestedt calls up there, looking for Harry, because he heard what he said downstairs. Wendlestedt says, 'Harry, since when are you going to become an umpire and tell us what to do?' Harry shoots back on the phone: 'C'mon, what are you doing, start the damn game.' Wendlestedt told Harry that his crew knew how to run a game. And Harry says back, 'You got to start the ball game to run it. Obviously, you have nowhere to go tonight.'

"Wendlestedt raved on, which was very much unlike him. Harry then says, 'Just remember who always promotes the hell out of your umpiring school.' Finally, Harry slams down the phone. He went on the air later just before the game started and just trashed Wendlestedt. But bygones were bygones. The next time Wendlestedt's crew came into town, here's Harry back on the air promoting his umpiring school once again.

"I know he disliked Jerry Reinsdorf to the very end. Maybe Reinsdorf had no desire to patch things up with Harry. But let's say he did, I bet Harry would have done it. Maybe if Harry had gone to Jerry, maybe Jerry would have done it. It's unfortunate the two didn't get along. I think Harry got along OK with (Eddie) Einhorn. I think he felt his problems were with Jerry. But everyone I've seen Harry get into it with, when that person wanted to patch it up, he was willing to do it.

"I'm also convinced that if Milo (Hamilton) wanted to bury the hatchet with him, Harry would have done it, no questions asked. But Milo dislikes him. There were times in the past with the White Sox where Chuck Tanner and Johnny Sain were vastly criticized for overusing pitchers like Wilbur Wood. He would criticize Tanner, and then Tanner would go off in the paper and rip Harry. What would Harry do? Come on the show and let's talk about it.

"Bill Melton would get P.O.'d. He asked Melton to come on. No thank you, he wanted no part of it. Then there was Ralph Garr, one of the nicest guys you'd ever meet. He says, 'You got guys like Piersall and Harry always talking stuff on us and ripping the players.' The next day, who does Harry have on the show? Ralph Garr. He respected the fact that even after he ripped Harry, that Harry had him on the show.

"He never ducked anybody. If somebody ripped him, he'd say come on the show, you've got an open forum."

Tom Shaer

A sports anchor-reporter for Chicago's WMAQ-TV, Tom Shaer had an inside look at the silly and serious sides of Harry Caray.

He'll start with Harry the Flirt, still practicing lines on women as a septuagenarian.

"I was out to dinner with a group of us in spring training," Shaer says. "There was an attractive woman, also in the media, in our group. She knew Harry. He said, 'Y'know, tomorrow is my birthday.' She said, 'Not a chance.' She knew him. He said, 'She knew I was kidding.'"

Funny anecdotes aside, Shaer gives Caray the lion's share of credit for publicizing him as he tried to establish himself in the Chicago media after moving from the Boston area.

"I came to Chicago in April 1983," Shaer says. "Nobody knew me. The biggest name in broadcasting was Harry. I told him, 'You broke my heart with the 1967 Cardinals (beating Shaer's Red Sox in the World Series). All I heard every day was his voice on the broadcasts. 'Gibson, H-e-e-e strikes 'em out.'

"I'm doing a nightly show on WGN-Radio with Jack Brickhouse. Harry starts mentioning me on the Cubs broadcasts. More people were coming up to me saying, 'I heard Harry talk about you' than were mentioning they heard me on my show. He was helping establish me, using his tremendous platform to make a conscious effort to promote me. I thanked him. He said, 'What are you thanking me for? I'm not doing anything.' So, Harry gives me these plugs and helps me get established.

"Harry had extreme power, but I never saw him abuse the power. I was at WGN in 1983. You never mentioned the call letters of another station during your broadcast. I quit WGN suddenly to work at WBBM. He told me he didn't want me to leave, but also that you've got to go for the best offer. He gets on the air during a Cubs game about me leaving WGN, and says he wishes me well at WBBM. I can't believe this guy is plugging me and my new station. No other broadcaster could get away with that."

Shaer also tried to enter into several business relationships with Caray.

"In 1984, the Cubs were wildly popular," he says. "I had this idea to do Harry Caray phone answering tapes. Harry would have made $100,000 on the deal. I would have made $50,000. I went to Channel 5 a couple of years later. I told him I don't have enough time for this project. All right, Harry said he didn't care. He didn't need the money. If Harry didn't need the money, why would he do it? He was doing that to help me.

"Also, Harry's restaurant has been extremely successful. They were going to build another Harry's downtown, Harry's Seventh-Inning Stretch. I wanted to invest in it. He said, 'Don't let my involvement play a role at all.' He wanted to keep our friendship out of it. Harry's concern was to make sure I made a sound business move."

Shaer says Caray became Chicago airwaves' four-ton gorilla.

"Harry had more power than any broadcaster in this town —ever," he says. "He was able to dictate his terms. But it wasn't always that way. He was almost fired by John Allyn of the White Sox after the 1975 season. When he chose to leave the Sox after the 1981 season, he was at a crossroads. He achieved his greatest success with the Cubs and WGN. He didn't start that until he was 68 years old! That's unbelievable.

"On Harry's worst day, he appealed to more people than any other broadcaster. That's the bottom line. You can rest assured that if Harry did not remain popular, he would not have remained on the air.

"The timing was just right. There was open warfare between the two Chicago baseball teams. The White Sox did long-lasting damage to their image by not offering Harry a deal he could accept. Even though the Cubs had lousy teams for his first two years, Harry was doing 150-plus games on TV, plus all on radio. You could barely find the White Sox on over-the-air TV. Harry was the people's broadcaster who was not retained by this new Sox ownership. He goes over to the Cubs and he's on all the games. He was in the right place at the right time.

"This is the great secret of Harry Caray. He was not the same broadcaster with the Cubs as with the Sox. He cherished his reputation as an objective critic. To be sure, to his last day on the air he was more objective than most play-by-play men. But he was much more of a booster."

Paul Sullivan

Chicago Tribune Cubs beat writer Paul Sullivan conducted the last extensive print-media interview of Harry Caray at the Cubs Convention in 1998.

But the tape of that hour-long conversation at the Chicago Hilton & Towers Hotel almost was lost to history, but for Sullivan's switching of the tape to another bag in his Scottsdale, Arizona, condo as he covered the start of spring training—and reaction to Caray's death—a month later. There was this little matter of a burglary of the condo while Sullivan slept, in which his laptop computer and another bag in which the Caray tape had been kept were swiped.

Sullivan already had filed a story for *Sport* magazine from part of the interview, focusing on Caray welcoming his grandson, Chip, to the broadcast booth for the 1998 season. Now, a rattled Sullivan, already shaken with the news of Caray's collapse, was somehow able to compose himself to transcribe the complete interview for the *Tribune*.

Caray had invited Sullivan to his hotel suite during the convention to talk.

"We sat down, talked, and we went on and on for an hour," Sullivan says. "He was great. We started out talking about Chip. He was so ecstatic about doing a year of baseball with Chip. He was so proud. That's all he wanted to talk about. Then he got into his past, his White Sox days."

Sullivan did not feel a sense of urgency in interviewing Caray at that time.

"I thought he was totally immortal," he says. "He seemed to be in such good health and in great spirits. The idea of working with Chip made him feel younger, and he was looking forward to the season with all the free agents the Cubs got.

"I don't ever remember a day when he came out to Wrigley Field when he wasn't in a good mood. That's what I liked about him. I remember thinking that after I interviewed him. I had an hour's worth of interview, but it was going to be a short story.

"And then I went to spring training and got the call at 4 in the morning from my editors that Harry had collapsed. It was like your grandfather or someone close you know. I thought he would recover. His auto accident, heart attack, stroke. How many times has the guy defied death? You didn't even think about his age.

"It was very strange, listening to it. I did feel that Harry said all of this, and that I owed it to readers to hear this."

David Kaplan (Photo courtesy of WGN).

David Kaplan

WGN-Radio sportscaster David Kaplan conducted the last broadcast interview with Caray, via phone, early in February 1998.

"He was looking forward to going to spring training," Kaplan says of the session on the "Sports Central" show. "He was excited about Chip coming to Chicago and working with him in the booth.

He was pretty excited about some of the Cubs' acquisitions. He was just glad the season was back. We saved the tape, as we do with all our shows.

"We also had him on the air at the 1998 Cubs Convention on a Friday night. We got a chance to talk to him for 20 minutes to a half hour. As usual, he had the crowd in stitches.

"During that interview, I was asking more questions than my partner, Tom Waddle (former Bears receiver). Harry says, 'Hold it a minute. Tom, I enjoyed watching you play. How come every time I come on with you, you don't ask as many questions?' Tom says he wasn't a baseball guy and that he was in awe of Harry. And then Harry says, 'I was in awe of you, because you were a great player.' The crowd erupted and went crazy. It was really a neat moment to see Harry paying tribute to a guy who was 30 years old, was a great player, but obviously not as big of a name in this town as Harry was.

"Whenever we interviewed him, he didn't give the stock answers like a lot of people do. He'd say, 'We don't have enough pitching.' He was great.

"With Chip coming here, I thought that re-charged his battery. I don't think he would have left. He would have stayed as long as his health permitted."

Dave Eanet

Dave Eanet had plenty of chances to rub shoulders with Harry Caray as sports director of WGN-Radio.

But his best memory of Caray hops into the way-back machine to 1981, when Eanet, a young sportscaster at rival WBBM-Radio, the CBS all-news station in Chicago, filled time during the mid-summer baseball strike with live broadcasts from ChicagoFest on Navy Pier.

Caray was the life of the lakefront party even then, during his enforced sabbatical from White Sox broadcasts.

"Harry would sing 'Take Me Out to the Ball Game' each night and people would come from all over Navy Pier to

Dave Eanet (Photo courtesy of WGN).

watch," Eanet says. "There were two levels of catwalks above where we were broadcasting from, and people would pack both levels. They'd gravitate toward us whenever he'd sing, around 8 p.m.

"He'd also take questions from the audience. I remember all these beautiful young women would ask Harry if they could kiss him. Of course, Harry was very reluctant to allow that. After much prodding (Eanet rolls his eyes), he'd agree to it. What amazed me was a lot of the time these women were with husbands or boyfriends. They were the ones pushing the girls up to give Harry a big kiss."

One year before, Eanet was breaking in on the air in Chicago, co-hosting a talk show on WBBM with Caray.

"He could have just hammered me, just been difficult on me," Eanet says. "But he was great to me. After we were done, he'd invite me to dinner. He'd always pump me up on the air. He called my boss and put in a good word for me. It was as great an ego boost as I ever got."

Marc Silverman

WGN-Radio sportscaster Marc Silverman's first experience with Caray wasn't at his station.

"I got to meet him at 12 or 13 when I was at a restaurant on Rush Street with my parents and grandparents," Silverman says. "I always saved the autograph and photo I took with him that day. He wrote the autograph, 'To Marc and Melissa (his sister) ... I love you, Harry Caray.' That sums him up. It wasn't 'best wishes' or whatever they write. He genuinely loved the fans. He was the same way when I worked with him. He treated me with respect."

Bob Verdi

Bob Verdi authored *Holy Cow: The Autobiography of Harry Caray* in 1989. He had a nice vantage point of Caray—often across drinks and dinner—in his years as a *Chicago Tribune* sportswriter and sports columnist.

"I remember one I always tell about the time I was covering the White Sox as a beat reporter for the *Tribune* and Harry was doing the games," Verdi says. "We had a day game and he said 'Let's go to dinner tonight.'

"I think we went to Adolph's, some place on Rush Street. I think I meet him at 7 o'clock. We start bulls—ing. Drinks. 8 o'clock. 9 o'clock. 10 o'clock. More drinks. Now, I think it's midnight and I haven't had a cracker. I haven't had a saltine. And we're talking. I'm just listening. I'm having a ball, except I'm starved. So, finally, it's got to be 1 o'clock and I have to get the hell out of there. I still haven't eaten and I've got one eye open.

"I said, 'OK, Harry. It's about time. I want to go home.' And he goes, 'You're right. Waiter. Menus.'"

Verdi says the book idea half-originated with Caray.

"He sort of came to me," Verdi says. "I think he had some-

***Bob Verdi** (Photo courtesy of the* Chicago Tribune*).*

thing in the works. I did some of it with him during spring training in Arizona and I remember distinctly a couple of nights we went out and we'd start drinking. He'd start telling me these great stories. His childhood.

"And, of course, I didn't bring enough to take notes with. So I'm writing this s— on cocktail napkins, little notebooks, scribbling it and thinking, God this is great stuff. And I'd go back home and the next morning the phone would ring and it'd be, 'Bob, you know that stuff we were talking about last night? I don't think that belongs in the book, you know? I don't think anybody cares.' I said, 'Harry, that's great stuff, I thought, and not incriminating.'

Harry's response: "Naaah, I don't think so, buddy. I'll see you at the ballpark."

Like many other Caray associates, Verdi marveled at the announcer's work ethic.

"He worked at his craft," he says. "Anybody who thinks he just fell out of bed in the morning, showed up at the ballpark 20 minutes before the first pitch and didn't know what was going on is missing the essence of Harry.

"He did breathe the game. He was this Hall of Fame announcer who basically could get by just laughing and reading names of people at the ballpark. He could have cruised. And yet, every day you would see him in the booth and he's pasting those freaking box scores in his notebook. You know? I mean, he knew what was going on around baseball."

Chet Coppock

If anyone could show bombast like Harry Caray, it's Chet Coppock, who has had as many incarnations on the air as anyone in Chicago's broadcast history.

"When he arrived in Chicago back in 1970, the White Sox were absolutely at their lowest ebb," Coppock says. "In fact, the 1970 ball club went 56-106 and I believe drew 495,000 paid. You couldn't give away their radio rights. I mean you could not give them away for love nor money.

"So here arrives this icon from St. Louis, who had done a year in Oakland. Harry Caray. And he is broadcasting, if you can believe this, on a suburban radio outlet. I mean people can barely hear the guy.

"But, a month into his run with the Chicago White Sox, you already were seeing bumper stickers being passed around Comiskey Park, 'All of Chicago Loves Harry Caray.'

"I have a lot of respect for the great ones. Jack Brickhouse. Ernie Harwell. Mel Allen. Vin Scully. But I have never seen anybody galvanize a market as quickly as this guy galvanized Chicago. If ever a marriage was made in heaven, it was Harry and Chicago."

Coppock saw several sides of Caray.

"I think what impressed me most about him—above and beyond the fact that he was Peter Pan, above and beyond the fact he was in many respects a guy who because of his orphan upbringing in St. Louis always thought the other shoe was going to fall and thus he figured I better cram 28 hours into every day—was the fact that when you had the opportunity to visit with him in a casual but private atmosphere, you found another man. His voice would change. His octave level would change. He was always remarkably honest.

"I recall a good story when Jerry Reinsdorf and Eddie Einhorn bought the ball club back in January of '81. My gosh, about a month later, Harry was negotiating a contract with Eddie Einhorn. The *Sun-Times* ran this column 'Caray: Einhorn a lying bleep.' You know, a lying b———. And the whole town was jumping up and down. Is Harry going to be retained? Do the White Sox want him?

"And when he came back to town—and this is the essence of Harry—he couldn't understand why people were so concerned. To Harry, it was all sort of a joke. In fact, I think he thought that when he called Eddie a lying bleep it didn't mean anything to him."

One day, Coppock, then hosting a nightly radio sportstalk show, thought he had the scoop du jour.

"I remember once he came on a Friday, about two hours before the Cubs opened their convention," Coppock says. "He said 'Chet, I think you should be the first one to know because you have always been such a good friend. I think this will be the last year in the booth. Fifty years is enough for anybody.'

"We run it and, bang, it's picked up by AP, every sports news service in the country. Rudy Martzke the following Monday would make it his 'Hustle of the Week' Award in his *USA Today* column.

"And the beauty of it is, two hours after Harry said this on our air, he opens up the Cubs Convention, he's besieged by the pen and mike club and the first thing he does is say, 'Well, I haven't talked to anybody about retiring. What are you talking about?'

"That was the essence of Harry. Harry loved tweaking us. Harry loved being a Peck's Bad Boy and I think this goes back to an environment of his childhood, which wasn't very comfortable. I've read innumerable stories about Harry crying during the holidays over very acute feelings of loneliness."

Coppock believed Caray was one of a kind in being able to speak his mind without consequences.

"Harry had one quality very few of us ever achieve," he says. "Harry developed the ability to tell management and tell the people he worked for to go straight to hell, and get way with it, because he was so damned talented. And sponsors were so in love with this guy. His relationship with Budweiser. He literally kept Falstaff Beer on the map with the White Sox back in the early 1970s. True Value was in love with him.

"Chicago has been blessed to have three guys who are truly remarkable baseball announcers. Actually four, in my opinion. One being, obviously, Jack Brickhouse. Along with Vince Lloyd, who was just a sterling silver, concise, fan friendly announcer. And Bob Elson, who was perhaps the ultimate wordsmith, the ultimate broadcast craftsman.

"Then arrives Harry Caray. Harry was disco before disco. Harry was bell bottoms before bell bottoms. Harry was remarkable in that he was very contemporary in his late 70s and early 80s."

Coppock recalls when a nearly 60 Caray tried to act 30 years his junior.

"I remember one time being in spring training down in Sarasota in 1972," he says. "And the late Jack Drees, who himself was a legendary broadcaster, and I were having dinner. Then we began going down Highway 41, stopping at a couple of joints. Finally, it's about 1:30 or 2 in the morning and Jack said, 'Do you want to have one more belt?' I said, sure.

"We stopped off at this little honkey tonk, walk in and there are about 10 hardbodies dancing on the dance floor. I look over and do my basic young gawk and then sit there talking to Jack and having my drink.

"Dance one becomes dance two, then dance three. I said to Jack, 'I've got to see what the hell's going on here.' I walk over and here's Harry standing in this pack of girls dancing. And he yells out, 'Come on, kid. There's plenty for everybody.'"

Michael Jordan may be synonymous with Chicago, but Harry Caray is synonymous with baseball.

"I remember being in Scotland for the British Open in 1989," Coppock says. "We took a day to go into Edinburgh to see the castle and just pick up some odds and ends. I walked into a McDonalds in Scotland. I begin talking and the clerk says, 'So Yank, where you from?' I say, 'Chicago.' And he goes, 'Isn't that the home of that Mr. Harry Caray?'

"That's when you realize you're big."

Mike North

Not staying out quite as late as Harry Caray, but still trying to make after-hours grand tours, is Mike North, the top talker at all-sports WSCR-Radio in Chicago. After a rough start, North and Caray found out they had more in common than not.

"When I first came on the air, Harry didn't like me," North says. "He didn't. And he let it be known that he was not a big fan. Then he found out some things about me, started listening more and I grew on him.

"He found out that I was a high school dropout, like him. That we both had similar type of backgrounds. Only he was an orphan, I had both my parents. And we became buddies. We went out to dinner. We hung out. He knew that I went down to Rush Street a lot. Like he used to and stuff like that. Even though it's like generations apart, I've led somewhat of the same life he led, you know.

"And we're very opinionated. He called me one time and said, 'You protest too much,' and I said, 'Who do you think I learned that from?'

I had the TV show at Hollywood Casino in Aurora on SportsChannel (now Fox Sports Chicago) for 31 weeks. And he was the only guy we brought back twice. That's how popular he was. We had Ditka on, Wilt Chamberlain, Walter Payton. We had Frank Thomas, Jerry Reinsdorf, guys like that. And this guy was the most popular guy. There was nothing phony about Harry. He'd tell you it like it was, you know."

But the meeting of the minds didn't always mean Caray would agree with North.

"We never got into any trouble together, but one night he did my show and he called me Reinsdorf's bobo," North says. "He did not like Jerry Reinsdorf at all. And I like Reinsdorf. On the air, he called me Reinsdorf's bobo. It was hilarious. I said 'You're the Tribune Co.'s bobo, if that's the way we're going to go about this.' We never backed down from each other.

"He loved my wife, Bebe. Loved her. She's a pretty girl and every time he'd see us, he'd say, 'It's beauty and the beast.' He was a good ball-buster, he really was."

A rabid White Sox fan, North applauded Caray's arrival on the South Side in 1971.

"When he came from Oakland, we were thrilled about it," he says. "But we didn't know what to make of him. But I'm a Sox fan, big time. And it was bad when he left. We were not happy at all when he left and when Reinsdorf got rid of him. And that's one of the things that still hurts them today.

"Everybody knew it was a bad move for the Sox. Everybody. He goes to the Tribune Co. and Harry was a smart man. He knew he was going to get more exposure over there. It was a terrible move. Like with the Cubs, he was the Sox MVP for a long, long time."

Paul Hagen

Longtime baseball writer Paul Hagen, now of the *Philadelphia Daily News*, was witness to a story that suggests Harry Caray would have been comfortable as a crafty rewriteman, disguising himself as a different character in the ol' "Front Page" days.

In 1978, Hagen was covering the Texas Rangers for now defunct *Dallas Times-Herald.* He traveled with the Rangers for their first trip into Chicago that season—and the return of Richie Zisk, a folk hero popularized even further by Caray on the South Side in 1977. Zisk had defected to the Rangers for a lucrative free-agent contract Bill Veeck could not afford.

"Harry was outraged by it. He thought it showed a terrible lack of loyalty," Hagen says. "All throughout the game, he was on Richie pretty bad. What he didn't realize at the time was Jon Matlack was pitching for the Rangers. He kept coming into the clubhouse when the Rangers were at bat to change shirts. He heard the whole thing. After the game, Matlack went off on Harry, and it made all the papers in Chicago."

Matlack must have thought that was the end of that. Resting in his hotel room the next morning, he had put a "hold" on his phone calls until 12 noon.

But at 10 a.m., the phone rang.

"Harry had called the front desk of the hotel and asked to speak to Jon Matlack," Hagen says. "He was told Matlack had a hold on all his calls. Harry then said, 'You don't understand, m'am, I'm Brad Corbett. I own the Texas Rangers, you got to put me through right now.

"Harry does get through. He tells Matlack, 'Jon, Jon, this is terrible, you said all these terrible things about me, they're in all the papers. We're going to Texas next week, and they shoot presidents down there, Jon!' They talked it out and settled it. That to me was a classic Harry story, because he wore his heart on his sleeve and said what was on his mind. And when the s— hit the fan, he would call the player and talk about it, and didn't hide behind anyone."

Joe Goddard

Joe Goddard, then and now a *Chicago Sun-Times* baseball beat writer, couldn't figure out why Harry Caray put him under a microscope one day in the early 1980s when they sat down the left-field line in Seattle's Kingdome to tape Caray's pregame radio show.

"Before we said anything else, he said, 'Aren't you one of (Sox manager Tony) La Russa's boys?'" Goddard says. "I was amazed. I told him I'm not a columnist, I just write what the manager says, as a beat writer."

But Goddard and Caray got along overall, even after Caray called him "Bob Goddard" one day. "I think that was a St. Louis columnist," he says. "I told Harry my name is Joe, and he said, 'You know what I mean.'"

One day in Cubs spring training, Goddard, Caray and other media folks were having dinner in the dusty desert town of Yuma, Arizona. Goddard then embarked on a harrowing after-midnight experience with Caray.

The pair went from bar to dance hall to bar again. "I was starting to run out of money and wanted to get back to the hotel," Goddard says. "But Harry wanted to go into this one more place.

"It didn't look good, like a biker bar. There were motorcycles in front, horses tethered in back. We walk in, go up to the bar and Harry orders. There were these rough-looking guys playing pool. I don't think we should be there. But at the end of the bar, another rough-looking guy comes up to Harry and says, 'Don't worry, Harry, I know who you are,' and went back to his seat. He didn't ask for an autograph or talk to him like a regular fan. Finally, Harry says he doesn't think we should be in here and we left."

Dan Cahill

Harry Caray's broadcast malapropisms and mis-identifications were recorded most frequently in the early 1990s in a weekly feature called the Harry-O-Meter in the *Chicago Sun-Times.*

Steve Rosenbloom, now a *Chicago Tribune* columnist, once was the *Chicago Sun-Times*' sports assignment editor. He asked staffers Dan Cahill and Mark Gaffney to do a weekly sports media column, with an emphasis on critiques and humor.

"I went home that night and felt it would be great to run Harry's gaffes every week," says Cahill, now Sunday sports editor of the *Sun-Times*. "It was right after the Shawon-O-Meter was popular in the left-field bleachers of Wrigley Field. So I called it the Harry-O-Meter. It was without a doubt the most popular part of the column. One year we had a preseason Harry-O-Meter. Ninety percent of the people who read the column would always mention it.

"A lot of times we'd hear mistakes ourselves, but soon other writers, editors and readers would send it in. We had no shortage of material."

Cahill's all-time favorite is Sammy "Sofa," for Sosa. Caray went on the air one day identifying his broadcast partner as Steve "Santo," for Stone.

"Usually, when you caught him messing up names, it was at the start of the game when he was rattling off lineups," Cahill says. "Arne Harris was in his ear, and something might have been happening on the field. You could see where he messed up names.

"He was kind of like Willie Mays in his last few years. Willie was hitting .200, but people still wanted to come out to see him."

Caray initially was miffed at the Harry-O-Meter. But in the long run, he and Cahill were able to carry on cordial conversations when the latter needed Harry's comments for other angles in his column.

"He sent us a letter on his Holy Cow! stationery," Cahill says. "He cut out a Cubs article in the *Sun-Times* that had a mistake in it and circled the mistake, saying that even writers make mistakes, but that we don't highlight that.

"After talking to him the day after Red Barber died—I was hesitant, worrying that he would end up being pretty short with me—he was great. He was always quite gracious to me."

So why did fans forgive Harry's goof-ups? Why did his popularity simply increase over the years?

"The whole appeal was Harry, the ballpark, the bars, and Harry played into that ambiance," Cahill says. "He was this robust guy who lived life, drank, went out and partied. All of that went together. The fans showed up and ate it up. In the seventh, everyone's got a six-pack in them, and they're singing this goofy song."

Bruce Levine

A longtime reporter for Chicago's WMVP-Radio, Bruce Levine has seen all types in sports. He's witnessed very few who compare with Harry Caray.

"ZZ Top was visiting Wrigley Field one day," Levine recalls. "They were sitting on the bench. Harry came by to do his pregame show with the manager at that time, Jim Lefebvre. Here's two guys with Blues Brothers hats, blue jeans and long beards and mustaches and sunglasses. Harry sees them and says (in Harry's voice), 'Hey, who are you guys? I'm Harry Caray.

Are you guys rabbis?' They said,'No, we're ZZ Top.' Harry asks, 'What kind of a religion is that?'"

Noted for his love of Italian food at odd hours, Caray momentarily switched to Cincinnati's specialty—chili—one night in 1987 when he bumped into Levine and fellow sportscaster Ben Sherman after a Cubs-Reds game.

"It was midnight and we were coming out of one of those Skyline Chili places," Levine says. "And Harry's walking down the street with Ned Colletti and Jim Frey. 'Hey, where you guys coming from?' Caray called out. When Levine told him about the chili parlor, Caray asked to sample the local delicacy.

"We go in there, he has two bowls of chili with onions, cheese, the works," Levine says. "Then he tells us, 'Let's go have some nightcaps.' We went out, he had at least four or five drinks on top of that. He took us to an after-hours place there. It was a hole in the wall. You wouldn't even know it was a bar. Knock three times and give the password."

Spike O'Dell

Almost everyone who encounters—or is exposed to—Harry Caray for the first time comes away with a story they love retelling. No exception is Spike O'Dell, midday personality at WGN-Radio in Chicago.

"Before I moved to Chicago and WGN," O'Dell recalls, "I was the big loudmouth known as 'Spike at the Mike' at the big 100,000-watt blowtorch in the Quad Cities, doing a morning show. And I also was an honorary president of the Quad Cities Cubs Fan Club.

"So we took a busload of Cubs Fans up for Quad-Cities Day and they wanted me to throw out the first pitch. I was obviously excited.

"As we all know, Harry Caray has his way with words. Or mispronouncing words. Or never saying them right.

Spike O'Dell *(Photo courtesy of WGN).*

"I told everybody back home to set their VCRs. I was going to throw out the first pitch and be on TV and it was a big deal for me.

"When I got home, my wife said 'I've got a surprise for you. You're not going to believe what Harry called you.' We re-wound the tape and there's a picture of me throwing out the first pitch and Harry says, 'Mike O'Neal. Mike O'Neal throws out the first pitch from the Quad Cities.' So, to this day, my best friends still call me Mike O'Neal instead of Spike O'Dell."

Rory Spears

Harry Caray the hockey announcer?

He told the boys at Wrigley Field it actually happened.

Free-lance sportscaster Rory Spears was rehashing a double-overtime Blackhawks-Redwings game he had attended the previous night.

Caray noticed Spears and two colleagues talking hockey as he picked up some media information in the press room.

"What are you all talking about?" he inquired.

Spears and Co. told him about the exciting playoff game. "Hockey's a great sport, too," Spears said to Harry.

"Of course it is, but it's a booo-tiful day for baseball," Caray responded.

Spears then asked Caray if he ever called a hockey game.

"Did I ever call hockey games?" Harry shot back. "Of course I did. I called the old St. Louis Flyers, playing in the Checkerdome. They had a couple of good teams, but then the NHL came to town with the Blues." Harry then launched into memories about frantic rushes up and down the ice, a Flyers late goal, a wild crowd.

"He was really getting into it," Spears said. "Then WGN called him back to the booth. Here, Harry comes to the park, looking forward to baseball on the first 80-degree day of the spring. And here he gets to talking about hockey and enjoying the memories.

"There was just something about this guy. He had all of us glued to him telling this hockey story. So many people know him for baseball. They don't know he was a hockey announcer, too."

Spears had first met Caray after the latter came back from his stroke in 1987. Out on the catwalk behind the old Wrigley Field press box, he greeted Caray, telling him he looked great. "Harry grabs my hand. He had never met me, and said, 'It's good to see you. You look great,'" Spears says. "If anyone in the sport made me feel welcome, it was Harry."

Stuart Shea

A columnist for the Total Sports service on the Internet, Stuart Shea always was on Harry Caray's meet-and-greet list in the Wrigley Field press box.

"He was always willing to joke with you," Shea says. "I came into the press box one day carrying a computer, a bag and my lunch tray, and I hear him call out from behind me, 'Young man, got a match?' That's an old-time joke. That's something you say to someone who has his hands full. He turned around and laughed, and walked back into the booth. He never called me by name. Always 'young man.'

"We were all fools to Falstaff."

Tim McCarver

Tim McCarver, catcher for the St. Louis Cardinals from 1959-69, and now a color analyst for the New York Mets and Fox Sports baseball broadcasts, grew up in Memphis listening to Caray broadcast Cardinal games.

McCarver described the important role Harry played in neighborhood cork ball games.

To McCarver and his friend Louie Trumper, "it wasn't a matter of who won the game, but who could do the best imitation of Harry calling the play by play.

"My imitation was good. It was very good. As a matter of fact, Harry had me on a rain delay one day and Arne Harris said 'McCarver does a good imitation of you.' So Harry had me do it on the air.

"He asked for immediate performance. 'Tim I heard you did a great imitation of me. Let's hear it.' When somebody says it like that it is very difficult. So I told him, what you were doing just then is my imitation of you!"

Another of McCarver's favorite Caray memories involved Harry announcing the White Sox outfield defense one night. "In left field was Carlos May, who had half of his thumb blown off in a grenade or mortar accident in the Army Reserves, Walt 'No Neck' Williams was in center field, and Pat Kelly, who couldn't throw, was in right. Harry giving the outfield defense, said, 'Tonight for the White Sox we have no thumb in left, no neck in center and no arm in right.'"

Recounting another story told to him by Bob Verdi of the *Chicago Tribune*, McCarver described an episode with Butch Wynegar and Dave Boswell in Minnesota doing a game between the Twins and White Sox.

"Wynegar is chewing out Boswell for some reason. They are really animated, and they're going at it. The television is showing them and they are [swearing] at one another and all that sort of stuff and Harry says, 'Well, Boswell is gonna leave the game. We'll try to find out what Wynegar was saying to Boswell. He was really airing him out. We'll be right back after this from Budweiser.' So they come back out of commercial and Harry says, 'We found out what Wynegar was saying to Boswell. He called him a pussy.' He said that on the air. Then he said, 'What do you think, Jimmy?' All Piersall could do was stutter.

"Harry is the only guy in the world who could get away with stuff like that. Anyone else would have been fired on the spot."

"Now the stretch ... Ready ... Everybody standing up ... The pitch! A high pop foul...McCarver's there ... The-e-e Cardinals win the pennant! The Cardinals win the pennant! The Cardinals win the pennant! Everybody out ... Johnny! Everybody congratulating everybody ... I don't know if they'll get here ... I don't know if they'll ever get here ... The Cardinals have just won the pennant! Mayhem on the field!"

— ***Harry Caray, October 4, 1964***
(Photo courtesy of Ted Patterson).

CHAPTER SIX

Entertainers and Sports Figures

Mike Ditka

Yes, Chicago was big enough for Harry Caray and Mike Ditka.

But "Da Coach" has never severed his Chicago ties despite moving to the Big Easy and tackling the task of reviving the New Orleans Saints. He's still passionate about the people he left behind, including Caray.

"Harry? It's hard to describe him without getting into a long description," Ditka says. "He really enjoyed life. He was fun to be around. And he was real. He was genuine. There was no phoniness to Harry Caray around me.

"I loved him for that. He was genuine. And he didn't make it a secret that when he wanted a beer, he had a beer. There was no put-on, no show-up front. He was just real people.

"And I think he took time with people. That's the thing I noticed. Every time I was with him, he always took time with people. He always signed the autographs. He talked to the people. And a lot of it could have been very aggravating, but he did it.

"A lot of celebrities won't do that and I thought that was one of the greatest things about him, the way he did that."

Ditka's famed restaurant on Chicago's West Ontario Street predated Harry Caray's eatery as a trendy place. But Caray's had the staying power. Ditka now is associated with another restaurant in the Streeterville area a few blocks further east. Caray did patronize the original Ditka's.

"He was there a few times," Ditka says. "Actually, the guy who put Harry in business in his restaurant, Ben Stein, was a partner in our business for awhile, the original restaurant."

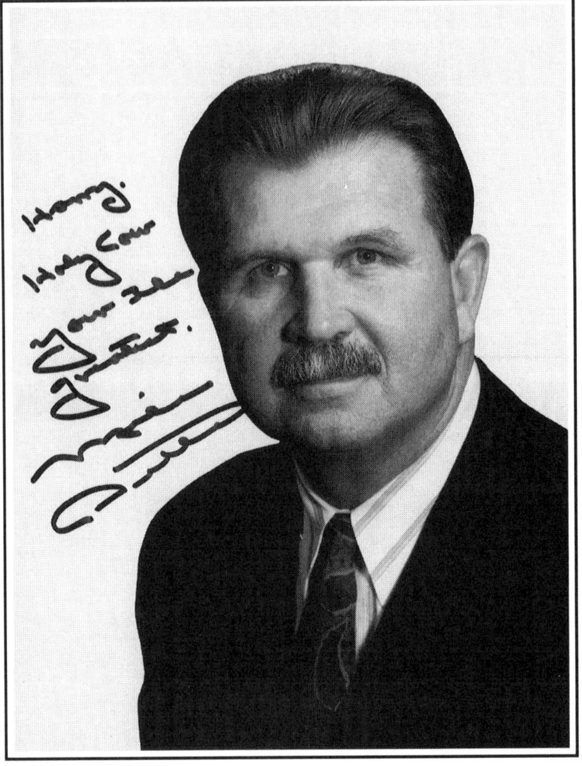

Mike Ditka *(photo courtesy of Harry Caray's Restaurant).*

On the original menu at Harry Caray's Restaurant, after the listing for pork chops, it read, 'Go to Ditka's.'

When asked how that originated, Ditka said, "I think that was Ben. And I think they were just being honest. That wasn't their specialty. Their specialty was steaks. At the original Ditka's, we had the best pork chops in the country."

The two characters once teamed up for a commercial.

"We shot up at Ditka's (restaurant) by the (O'Hare) airport," Ditka says. "At the bar. It was funnier than heck, because it was not very hard to do, but Harry had had a few pops and he was continuing to drink his Budweiser as we were trying to do the shoot. Oh my gosh. It took him about 25 to 30 shoots to get it. And I'll tell you what, after awhile, I was the problem because I was laughing so hard at him. But he was beautiful.

"And he loved the Cubs. You think back to how strong his relationship was with the Cardinals and, of course, he worked for the White Sox. But I don't think anything was as strong as the Cubs. And I think he probably anguished more with that relationship than any of the others. He really just wanted them to win.

"Even I'm pulling for the Cubs now. Believe me."

Jay Leno

One of a parade of celebrity "guest conductors" of the "Take Me Out to the Ball Game" at Wrigley Field in 1998, "Tonight Show" host Leno fondly recalls the several appearances Caray made on the late-night talkfest.

"I met him enough to get a real sense of him and have some fun with it," Leno says. "I don't know if 'entertainer' is

Jay Leno with Harry Caray *(Photo courtesy of Jay Blunk Collection).*

the word to use. It's just 'character,' an interesting character. When you grow up in a neighborhood, he's like a neighborhood guy. He'd be the guy at the end of the bar, one of those sort of people everyone gathers around. He's an interesting, funny character. There's no other way to put it.

"There are people who try to manufacture that kind of personality. You see it in Hollywood all the time. But they really can't. It's really the real thing."

When Leno brought the "Tonight Show" to Chicago in 1995, Caray was scheduled to sing "Take Me Out to the Ball Game" coming out of a commercial break. But when the spotlight focused on Caray in the studio's balcony, the entire crowd rose and began chanting, "Harry! Harry!" The NBC-TV crew had to stop taping due to the commotion, which had drowned out Leno, and wait for the throng to calm down. The Leno staff said they had never seen one of their audiences react that spontaneously.

Tom Dreesen

Frank Sinatra never lied about his age. Harry Caray did. But they were less than two years apart, Harry the older of the pair. Yet both master showmen were a lot closer in plenty of aspects of their personal lives. Oddly enough, both died in 1998, just three months apart, their giant shadows crowding all over Page Ones and the newscasts' lead stories.

The comparisons can be forwarded to you by comedian Tom Dreesen. A native of Chicago's south suburbs, Dreesen has carved out a career as a standup comic, emcee, and opening act for Sinatra.

"It's nice to meet some legends," Dreesen says. The Ernie Bankses, the Gale Sayerses, the Frank Sinatras, the Bob Hopes. As you get to know them, they are people. And some of them you like and some you don't like.

"When you spend time with a guy like Harry, you don't always see the Harry Caray the fans see. Harry Caray the man

Comedian Tom Dreesen (L) talks with Harry Caray at Spring Training in 1985 *(Photo courtesy of Bill Wills).*

is a man. He's a man. I've seen him get impatient. I've seen him get pissed off. I've disagreed with some of the things he has done and said. But you know what? You can't ever forget the fact of what a person has accomplished in their life. You can never take that away from somebody."

Dreesen was witness to the meeting of giants —Sinatra and Caray. Of course, it took place after dark. And, for once, Caray suffered from a momentary loss for words.

"Harry, as you know, could hit Rush Street and stay out all night long," Dreesen says. "But he met his match when he met Sinatra. Because Sinatra stayed out until the sun came up. That was the way Frank did it. So if you hung out with Frank, you had to be a pro at hanging out.

"Let me digress a little bit here. I'm a hang-out guy, in quotations, hang-out. I love to hang out. I think most street guys love to hang out. And when we meet another hang-out person, we recognize him right away. Sinatra was a hang-out guy. Harry was a hang-out guy.

"Now what constitutes a great hang-out person? It's somebody who can hear the same stories over and over and over again and still laugh as if it was the first time they heard them. Hang-out people are great story tellers and they are great story listeners. Harry, of course, was a great story teller and loved to hang out. And when he met Frank, he met his match.

"One particular time I was with Sinatra—we were at the Chicago Theatre performing—and we were hanging out at a Rush Street bar. The guy closed the doors and let us stay in the bar. They do that a lot in Chicago.

"This was around 1984 and I said, 'Name me 11 guys who hit 50 or more home runs in a season.' There were about 15 guys in there drinking. And so Harry started. And he named them and named them and named them. And all of a sudden he got down to 10 and he couldn't remember the 11th guy.

"I knew who it was and Harry said, 'All right, damn it, I can't think of it.' So I said, 'Oh, I don't know. I knew there were 11.' Everybody stood around and said, 'I don't know, uh ...'

"So Harry finally said, 'That's it. This is bulls—. I've got a book back in my room.' And he left the bar at around 4 in the morning. He got in a cab and went back to the Ambassador East. He rummaged through the room, woke up Dutchie and then came back to the bar about a half-hour later. But in the meantime I had told everybody in the bar 'Ralph Kiner.'

"And when Harry walked back into the bar and had the book up over his head, we all shouted at the same time, 'Ralph Kiner!'

"Well, he walked over to me and he said, 'Dreesen, I can forgive you for a lot of things but I will never forgive you for cheating me out of a half an hour of quality drinking time.'"

Another Caray story Dreesen tells in stand-up fashion took place the last time he saw Harry at Wrigley Field.

"I had a girl with me," he says. "Harry loved it when I brought girls into the booth, because he loved to flirt. And the first thing he would do is get me on the air. I'd go up there and plug whatever I was doing, but he also loved to tease me.

So he'd say,'Well, when are you going to marry her?'You know, to put me on the spot, which I would love.

"Anyhow, I saw Harry down on the field before the game and I said, 'Harry, how are you doing?' And he said, 'Tom, I haven't had a drink in two years.' I said, 'Really?' And he said, 'Yeah.'

"He said, 'You know all that stuff, how people tell you that you can have just as much fun not drinking as you can drinking?' I said yeah. He said, 'They're full of s—. I've never been so bored in my entire life.'"

Dreesen feels like he knew Caray his entire life.

"Not only me," he says. "He made everybody feel that way. If a person met Harry in his restaurant, he'd sign an autograph and talk to them for a few minutes. People didn't feel intimidated at all. And people do this to me, too, and I take it as a compliment. They don't feel intimidated at all to walk up in a middle of a meal and say, 'Tom Dreesen, geez ...' And they put their arm around me and sit down and I'm in the middle of a meal with my family.

"Harry was the same way. People would walk up to Harry in a heartbeat. They felt free to walk up to him because they knew he would not say, 'Hey, who are you to come up and interrupt my meal?'

"But Harry was a guy of the people. He really was. To me, Harry's success as a broadcaster was that Harry looked like a bartender behind the bar at a place you wanted to hang out in. Chicago is a neighborhood city. Beyond all cities it's a neighborhood city. When Chicago burned down in the Great Chicago Fire, the way it was rebuilt is that the Germans would first build the tavern on the corner and then they would build the rest of the neighborhood. So when they were working on a building, when they would take a lunch break, they would go to the corner tavern. So every neighborhood had a corner tavern.

"So that's why we are so fond of our neighborhood bartenders. Neighborhood bartenders when I was growing up in Chicago were almost celebrities. In fact, they were. My father used to point and say, 'Tom, see that guy over there? That's Boris. Boy he can pour a draught beer.'

"I was a neighborhood bartender. My mother was a neighborhood bartender. I heard my first jokes behind a bar. The point being that sometimes you went to a certain bar not because of the location, but because you liked that bartender. Being around that bartender made it a comfort zone for you.

"Harry represented to me every neighborhood bartender in Chicago. He looked like the guy you'd like to sit down in a bar and say, 'Hey, Harry, how'd the Cubs do today?'"

Dreesen was one of the headliners when Caray was roasted in Las Vegas in 1989.

"Jack Buck got up and he said something funny, Buck said, 'I don't understand his popularity. He dresses like a flood victim.' I thought that was an hysterical line.

"My joke was the one Pete Vonachen did at his funeral. I said, 'Harry, I hope you live to be 100. But when you die, I hope they don't cremate you. You'll burn forever.'"

John Caponera

Among the legion of Caray mimics is John Caponera, a comedian who does Miller and McDonalds commercials and starred in "The Good Life" sitcom, which aired on NBC for 13 weeks in 1994.

"I started doing Harry before anyone was doing him, because I grew up with Harry on the South Side of Chicago," he says. "I grew up six blocks from Comiskey Park and I used to live at the ballpark. I was a big Sox fan and I'd see Harry all the time. I was just a big fan of Harry's because he was doing the Sox games.

"Then when I started doing stand-up in 1979 and '80, I started doing Harry in my act because I did a lot of impressions. I did a baseball routine and Harry Caray was in it.

"In fact, I remember back in '82, Harry came in. He was out on the town that night and he and Dutchie came into

Zanies. I had already gone on stage, but when I came back off stage, Harry came in. I didn't do the baseball routine that night, so I went back on stage and did the baseball routine. I did it because I knew Harry was in the crowd. It was with him and Jimmy Piersall in it. He got so tickled by it he called 'Kup' and had me in Kup's column the next day. That was my first encounter with Harry, actually meeting him."

Talk about a rising tide lifting all boats. When Caray's fame spread nationwide via WGN-TV, Caponera was able to expand his routine beyond his hometown.

"It was fun to do in Chicago, but he was only a local celebrity at the time," he says, "so I could only do him in Chicago. Then when he went to the Cubs, he became a national figure on WGN, and I was able to start doing him on the road. Then I started being recognized as the guy who did Harry Caray. I started doing him around the country, came back to Chicago and everyone was doing him. So I don't have carte blanche on Harry Caray's personality. But everyone knows I started doing him.

"I heard Jack Buck after dinner speaking once and he said, 'Harry Caray and I were doing a game, the bases were loaded and Harry was doing the play-by-play. 'The wind-up, the pitch, h-eee struck him out ... Wait a minute. It's a smash down to third. He steps on the bag for one, throws to second for two, to first for three. Triple play. Holy Cow!'

"And Jack says, 'No, Harry. He actually did strike him out. They're just throwing it around the infield.' That hit home. It's a funny Harry Caray story and I tell it in my act sometimes."

Ken Sevara

Yet another Harry Caray impersonator is comedian Ken Sevara.

"I was the first guy in Chicago, to my knowledge, to ever do Harry's voice," Sevara says. "I was doing him when he was still with the White Sox. I just started messing around with it.

Ken Sevara *(Photo courtesy of Ken Sevara).*

"One day I was at Wrigley Field and John Caponera, a friend of mine who also does Harry Caray, were sitting there doing (impressions) and had a whole section of the bleachers watching us more than they were watching the Cubs.

"I'm a White Sox fan so I started listening to Harry with the Sox. He and Jimmy Piersall. And one night I was listening to Piersall and Piersall goes 'Harry, you're crazy.' And Harry goes, 'Jimmy, I'm crazy? You're the crazy one and you have the papers to prove it.' I thought that was fantastic. I almost drove off the road, I was laughing so hard.

"I guess that's what attracted me to doing Harry's voice. Because, you know, he used to sit in the bleachers and take his shirt off and he had the butterfly net. And I'm going, 'Man, who is this guy? This guy is insane. And he's hilarious.'

"We've always had great announcers in Chicago, but he was so different. He broke the mold, you know. I'm a hard-core Sox fan. A hard-core Sox fan. And I always felt that Harry actually fit in more with the White Sox crowd, the blue-collar, shot-and-a-beer crowd, you know.

"So I started doing him. And it was funny because I never really had thought about doing him on stage. Then one night I was in a club called The Punchline in Greenville, S.C., and it was very late at night. I decided I was going to do Harry. I didn't care if they liked it or not.

"I started into this bit and it is killing. I mean it is killing. I think Harry had just gone over to WGN at the time. And I thought, Oh my God, if it works here, I might be able to do this thing anywhere.

"I went to California shortly after that and I did a show at the Ice House in Pasadena. I closed my set there and it just blew the doors off the place. And I thought, well, this is incredible. I'm just going to start doing the guy everywhere. And it became a major part of my act.

"The way I started doing him originally is I was in Peoria, Illinois, working a club on Main Street and there was like a sea of blue-haired old ladies in the club that night. It just sucked. Horrible. There were a couple of comics in the back and I just started to do Harry Caray on acid and Harry Caray falling out of the booth singing 'Take Me Out to the Ball Game.' And it was working. These guys were just dying. I figured, well, I made the comics laugh, so I'll bring it out on stage again tomorrow night. It killed and I said, 'Oh my God, I've really got something here.' So that's when I started doing him in Greenville and Pasadena and places like that."

"Harry never did see my act, although I met Harry on a couple of occasions. (Steve) Stone had me do the voice for him one time and he said to me, 'Harry never speaks that clearly.'"

"One night I was working at the Star Plaza Theatre in Merrillville, Indiana, and I was working in this little comedy club that's kind of tucked away there. The Cubs were in town doing their Caravan that night. And Jim Lefebvre, Ron Santo,

Jim Bullinger and Bruce Levine, the sports guy from MVP, were there. Somebody walked up to me and said, 'You're never going to guess in a million years who is here.' I said, 'Who?' He told me, 'Lefebvre and Santo, etc.' and I thought, This is going to be a riot.

"So I'm up on stage and Lefebvre had tears coming out of his eyes, Santo is pounding the table and these guys are going nuts—Bullinger, Levine, all of them. I had a radio show the next morning and I'm very disciplined when I have a radio show and I told my wife before I left I'd be home early.

"Well, after I do my set before the Cubs, Lefebvre grabs me by the arm and he goes, 'Come here.' And he says, 'You have no idea how well you know that son of a b——.' So they take me out and they're buying me drinks and I don't drink. And Lefebvre goes, 'Come on, you want a beer?' And I said, 'I really don't drink that much.' And Lefebvre goes, 'Ah, bulls—. What are you worried about? (Tribune Co. executive) Stanton Cook's paying for it.'

"We start, one drink after the other, talking baseball, and I just have a passion for talking baseball. And I look at my watch and it's five in the morning. I go flying out of there and I go, 'Listen guys, I really appreciate it but ...'

"I get home. I put the key in the keyhole and my wife comes flying down the hall in tears, crying at the top of her lungs. She thought I got killed. She's got the state police in Illinois and Indiana looking for my car, all because I do Harry Caray.

"And the greatest thing was in the middle of the night, Levine looks at me and goes, 'You're a damned White Sox fan, aren't you?' And I said, 'Well, I'm not going to lie to you guys. I am.' And Lefebvre goes, 'I don't give a s—. Have another beer. Stanton Cook's paying for it.'"

Sevara is true to his Chicago roots in his act.

"I have a passion for Chicago sports. I do all kinds of things in my act. I talk about politics. I talk about relationships. I don't like to get pegged into any one area. I like to jump around. But I do a lot of stuff about Chicago sports.

"For instance, I talk a lot about the fact that the White Sox have not won a World Series since 1917 and the Cubs haven't won one since 1908. If you really think about it, Orville and Wilbur (Wright) had recently taken off from Kitty Hawk. Haley's Comet comes around more frequently than a damn Cubs championship.

"I did a satirical look at Caray. I did him falling out of the booth. I talked about his glasses. I said, 'My God, they're getting bigger every year. They're starting to look like Harry staring through an aquarium. Somebody had to be working a triple-shift at Lens Crafters to finish those things. You know your glasses might be a little large when in the fifth inning, guys drop down on scaffolding with squeegees.'

"I said, 'Thank God booze was Harry's only vice. You wouldn't want to see the guy drop acid.' It would have been like, 'Holy Cow, the scoreboard has lips. It's telling me the score, Steve. Heeey, the AstroTurf just ate Mark Grace. The left-field bleachers are melting. Steve, Holy Cow, you have two heads. Why don't you sing a duet? Hey, looks like a double-header.'

"In part of my act, I say, 'It's merciful that God took Harry when he did because one more year of watching the Cubs suck and he was going to snap. It would have been like, "Here's the wind-up and the pitch. There's a ground ball to short. Over to second. The relay ... SON OF A B——! You know, Steve, I'm getting so sick of this s—. Two million dollars a year for that rickety-kneed son of a b——. This damn team couldn't hit a bull in the ass with a banjo. You know the only person to have more trouble with a glove was O.J. Simpson."'

"Sometimes I would break into a Harry Caray-oke bit. You know, Harry would get a little tired of 'Take Me out to the Ball Game' and break into Zepplin. And it ends with Harry falling out of the booth, dangling beneath the press box with just the cord around his neck holding him up.

"It would have been, 'Aw right, eveerybawdayyy, ah one, a two, a threeeeeeeee.... Holy Cow, pull my drunken ass up will you, Steve? I'm a Cub fan. I'm a Bud man. And I'm about to be a very dead man. So long, everybody.'"

Sevara admits that Harry Caray has meant a lot to his success.

"He's been huge for me. I was doing a radio broadcast for the Omaha Royals. They had a rain delay. I was supposed to go up for a couple of minutes during the regular broadcast, but when the rain delay hit, they said, 'Let's get his guy up here and kill some time.'

"I went up there, did Harry dropping acid and all that other stuff and these guys are just going nuts. Because of that, three other radio stations in Omaha call up this comedy club and said we got to get this guy. As a result of that, I go back every year for the College World Series.

"I was in Des Moines for the Iowa Cubs, actually doing play-by-play. I did an inning on the radio and an inning on TV. Harry on acid and all these guys are in the press box are absolutely falling down. And this woman walks up the stairs and actually thinks Harry was in the booth. What the hell would Harry be doing talking about dropping acid on a broadcast? She didn't even put two and two together that this might not actually be Harry."

Sevara was devastated when Harry left the White Sox.

"Very typical of Reinsdorf. And seeing what Reinsdorf has done to the team, you can say that Harry was pretty much correct. Guys like Harry and Bill Veeck were once with the White Sox and then Reinsdorf made it a point to alienate Harry much like he's alienating all of the Bulls and all of the White Sox.

"It made me sick. Harry was White Sox baseball. Announcers of his quality and stature come along maybe once in a lifetime. This is so typical of Reinsdorf to make it a point to alienate him."

Bob Jay

Another comedian who has incorporated Harry Caray in his act is Chicago native Bob Jay.

"I first did Harry when he was with the White Sox, when he used to do the Falstaff commercials and the chicken commercials and he had that Holy Cow with him. Had somebody dress up in a cow outfit.

"I just totally admired him. I thought he was great because he told the game as it is. It wasn't this, 'Oh we can't say anything against Ron Santo.' No. If a White Sox player screwed up, he let everybody know he screwed up. That's what I really admired about him. Like if I was watching a game, I'd think, Why'd he swing at that pitch? And that's the way Harry was.

"His greatness was when he would just get blasted during doubleheaders. Oh, my gosh. You wouldn't even want to watch the first game. It was, 'Oh, good. The Sox are playing a doubleheader. Let's watch Game Two.' Harry would just be all over the place.

Jay was once the P.A. announcer for his nephew's Little League game in suburban Chicago.

"What I was supposed to do was just announce the batters. But I did it as Harry. I screwed up the kids' names and then I started announcing the game. It was like, 'Ahhhlll right, here we go with the bottom of the seventh inning.' And people in the stands would go, 'It's only the fourth inning.' Oh, the kids all loved it. The kids sometimes didn't want to go up to bat. They'd just stop and stare up to the booth.

"As years went by, I went and bought these SCUBA-diving goggles, put them on and now what I do—and people just go totally nuts—I do Harry announcing a game if he could just say anything. Like, 'Sammy Sosa spelled backwards is assos.' Or, 'The bases are loaded and so am I.' I did a thing like, 'Mark Grace is the batter, here's an out. There's a drive. It might be. It could be. It is. A foul ball.' Then Harry would snap. 'Son of a b——. What the hell is he swinging at, for crissakes?'"

"It's gotten where I have started doing a show and when people see me on-stage, they start yelling 'Harry!'"

Dan Devine

Harry Caray's autumn role through many of his St. Louis days was as voice of University of Missouri football. At Mizzou, longtime coach Dan Devine got to know Caray.

"We laughed a lot," Devine says. "But he wasn't a prankster. I was really close to Harry. We spent a lot of time together. Over the years, we've had hundreds of lunches and dinners together. We laughed a lot, but we never did pull anything funny.

"I missed last year when he had invited his grandson, Chip. My wife, who has multiple sclerosis, needed some help here so I couldn't go. I missed meeting his grandson and that really bothers me. I feel bad that I never had a chance to tell his grandson how much I thought of his grandfather and how good his grandfather had been to me.

"In a way, Harry and I were opposites. But I think this outpouring of thanking God for Harry Caray, part of that was he broke down that wide gap that was getting wider between sports people and the general public."

Caray narrated a video of Notre Dame's 1979 Cotton Bowl season, "7 1/2 Minutes to Destiny," after Devine had moved over to the Fighting Irish. Devine always knew when Caray would make an appearance at Notre Dame Stadium.

"I would hear from my pro-Caray fans and a few negative ones, always at a particular time in a game that he sat up high and walked down through the stands to go to the bathroom," Devine says. "And, of course, everybody stood up and yelled 'Harry, Harry, Harry.' And he loved every second of it."

Paul Palian

What was some of the job training for Paul Palian's present gig as assistant commissioner of the Mid-American Conference?

Doing Harry Caray impressions as public address announcer for the minor-league Kane County Cougars baseball team in Geneva, Illinois, of course.

"I tried to use it the way Harry would use it," Palian recalls. "Things like introducing birthdays, singing in the seventh inning. I did something every inning. People would bring up notes and want it read in Harry's voice."

Palian never pretended to be as good as the real Harry, who he met on several occasions.

"The first time was in spring training 1991, when I was in college at Northern Illinois University," he says. "My friend, Eric Maul, and I were working for the student cable-TV station and we had a video camera in the HoHoKam Room. Eric asked Harry a question: 'How long are you going to keep broadcasting?' Harry said, 'How old are you?' Eric said, 'Twenty-one.' And Harry shot back, 'I've been broadcasting major-league baseball for 47 years and if I was to broadcast for 21 more years, you still wouldn't be 47, would you?' Eric said, 'Definitely not.' Harry walks away and says, 'I hate that. I'm going to broadcast as long as I love it!'"

"Cubs win! The Cubs are the champions!"

— Harry Caray calling the NL East clincher in 1984 (Photo courtesy of Steve Green).

CHAPTER SEVEN

Fans

Richard Lindberg

It's safe to say Richard Lindberg is a dyed-in-the-wool White Sox fan. When he was a kid, in 1964, he embarked on laborious, half-a-morning trips on four city buses to reach old Comiskey Park from his home in the Norwood Park neighborhood of Chicago's far Northwest Side.

No wonder budding author Lindberg's first book was titled *Stuck on the Sox*, published in 1978. He went on to pen the *White Sox Encyclopedia* and six other books while serving as the Sox's unofficial historian.

So he has the rights of seniority to comment on Harry Caray's impact —positively and negatively—on his favorite Pale Hose. Harry was both savior and detriment to the Sox, in his view, all in the span of five years in the 1970s.

"In 1971, Harry Caray undoubtedly was the savior of the franchise," Lindberg says. "Caray injected vigor, life and vitality into a moribund team that was headed out of town. Bob Elson had broadcast the Sox for 40 years and concluded his relationship with the team on an unhappy note. Red Rush was enthusiastic as Elson's last partner, but he did not blend well with Elson's laid-back, laconic style. And along comes Harry, who was like a gale force coming from St. Louis, with a one-year detour to Oakland."

Lindberg traced the "good and bad" of Caray for his 11 seasons on the South Side. He was positive in the first couple of years, then "helped drag down what he had built up" as 1974 and '75 proceeded.

Still, Lindberg views Caray's Sox connection as more beneficial than not in the end.

"As a Sox fan, one of the worst mistakes was to let him go," he says. "Veeck apparently had a thicker skin than the current ownership. The departure was mutual. Harry knew he wouldn't be seen on as many TV households as before when the Sox started their pay-TV operation. He had to be seen by the general public. And Jerry Reinsdorf miscalculated what an icon he had become."

Caray's move to the Cubs in 1982 couldn't have been worse timing for the Sox, Lindberg theorizes.

"Harry and WGN were a deadly combination against the Sox," he says. "The Cubs had been a happening in 1969 and '70, but they began sliding (in appeal) in the mid-1970s. They were (by 1981) slipping precipitously back to where they were in the mid-1960s. Harry going to the Cubs made Wrigley Field an event rather than just a game. He made it a happening."

Dan Evans

Even in his job as White Sox assistant general manager, Dan Evans is first and foremost a baseball fan. He grew up learning to love the game, rooting for the Sox from his boyhood home just two miles northwest of . . . Wrigley Field.

What really helped Evans fall in love with the game was the sounds of Harry Caray.

"My family was on vacation in Mountain Home, Arkansas, in 1969, when I was 9," he says. "One day it was hotter than heck, and I was trying to stay out of the heat. I turned on the Cardinals game and heard this exciting announcer. He kept me listening. On the way back home, we stayed one night in St. Louis. My dad and I went to a doubleheader with the Reds. Lee May hit a couple of homers. I remember having a transistor radio with those old earplugs. I really liked hearing Harry. So my father then pointed out you could listen to KMOX at night after we got home to Chicago. Harry was fun."

Evans' interest in baseball really picked up in the early 1970s with Caray at the Sox mike. He remembers them as fun, innocent times, with no awareness of the controversy Caray generated by his criticism of players.

"I really liked the Sox red pinstriped uniforms," Evans says. "I was a huge Bucky Dent and Ken Henderson fan. It was a real fun broadcast. Bart Johnson was one of my favorite pitchers, and he called him Black Bart. I used to take my radio to bed and listen to Harry on those West Coast games."

Evans sat out in the old Comiskey Park's centerfield bleachers on days Caray did his broadcasts from there. "There was no way on other days you'd get me sitting 475 feet away from the plate in centerfield," he says. "I usually sat in the lower deck, left-field grandstands where they displayed all those signs."

Evans finally dealt with Caray one on one when he started with the Sox as an intern in 1981. "He was very cordial to me, as he was in later years when I scouted games at Wrigley Field," he says.

Evans' wife, Susan, produced a TV documentary, "When Harry Met Baseball," marking Caray's 50th season as a baseball announcer in 1994. Bob Costas hosted the show and interviewed Caray.

"It was fun on that show to listen to the broadcasts I heard in my youth," Evans says. "It was great to hear the reminisces. Both Harry Caray and Jack Brickhouse made me gravitate toward baseball. What Harry and Jack did more than anything—even with contrasting styles—was help you develop a real love for the players. They wanted you to know about these guys, and you rooted for them."

Mike Clark

As a 13-year-old White Sox fan growing up in rural Manteno, 40 miles south of Chicago, in 1971, Mike Clark welcomed Harry Caray's arrival as his team's announcer. Like Richard Lindberg, Clark believed Caray's energy was needed, both to enliven the team and the broadcasts after Bob Elson.

"What it meant was a sign the franchise was heading in the right direction," says Clark, now a sportswriter with *The Times*, a daily newspaper circulating in northwest Indiana and the southern Chicago suburbs.

"I already knew Harry was a well known figure in baseball broadcasting. I didn't care much for Elson, who was at the end of his career. It seemed like there wasn't a lot of enthusiasm and energy in the organization until Harry came in."

With the Sox on a UHF station in Chicago and on a network of low power stations in Caray's first two seasons in town, Clark sometimes had to strain to pick up the TV and radio broadcasts in the fringe reception area of Manteno. But listen he did, including to some marathon extra-inning games against the Athletics in Oakland that lasted to the wee hours. On radio only, Caray's riveting play-by-play kept Clark's eyes and ears open after midnight.

"I'd leave a note for my dad for when he left for work in the morning, telling him who won," he says.

In another agreement with Richard Lindberg, Clark believes Caray was too tough on some Sox players.

"He was way too hard on Bill Melton," he says. "Melton was a guy who, like Harry, helped save the franchise for Chicago. He won the American League home run title in 1971, and nobody thought a Sox player could ever do that. He then got hurt with a back injury, and that affected his play. I don't think Harry understood how severe that back injury was. That was Harry's biggest fault—he was too hard on some players. I don't think all fans were as hard on Melton as he was. I think he drove Melton out of town. That was the bad side of him. But he also fell in love with some players. In his last years, Ryne Sandberg wasn't up to his old standards. And Harry didn't get on him."

Bill Motluck

Longtime White Sox fan Bill Motluck is in the insurance business in the south suburbs of Chicago. He had two good views of Harry Caray—as a fan a generation ago and as a local radio talk-show host in the early 1990s.

"The way the White Sox franchise was going 30 years ago was terrible," Motluck says. "The Sox had a near-miss in the pennant race in 1967. Then the games were invisible on TV when they went to a UHF station in 1968, when the majority of fans couldn't get UHF. And they lost 106 games in 1970, their worst season in modern times. Harry was great coming in for 1971, bringing the fans back in. In Bill Veeck's first year back as owner, in 1976, they were terrible again, and Harry bailed them out again. Without Harry, maybe the White Sox might be in Denver, Seattle or Milwaukee.

"Later, when I was in radio, I saw how he treated everyone the same. He treated the guys working for the smaller media outlets the same as the largest. When he'd walk onto Wrigley Field, he was a Pied Piper. You never found anyone who the people were so in love with. Harry just made the ballpark fun.

"Have you ever seen an announcer as the No. 1 marketing tool of two franchises? Everybody wanted to be Harry's friend, to say they went out and had a beer with him. He never forgot where he came from."

Carol Haddon

Harry Caray may have had a nice, long tenure in the Cubs broadcast booth. But a nice lady like Carol Haddon had it way over Caray in seniority around Wrigley Field. Ultimate fan Haddon has been entrenched as a season ticket holder by the visitor's batting circle since 1971, and is well known to both the Cubs and visiting players alike.

Haddon became friends with former Cubs ball girl Marla Collins, who departed her job amid some controversy in the mid-1980s after posing for *Playboy* magazine. Collins, stationed near Haddon's seat, always attracted the flirtatious Caray's on-air attention—and a famous utterance one cold day. "There's Marla Collins without her shorts," Caray said of the ball girl, eschewing her usual briefer uniform for comfort in the wind chill. Of course, with Caray, it was, 'Don't listen to what I say. Listen to what I mean.' Haddon and Collins attended his wake together.

"She did feel a sense of companionship for Harry," Haddon says. "He was so nice to Marla, nice to everybody. My birthday was announced at the ballpark. Harry would make fun of me. He would say, 'Happy 39th birthday to Carol Haddon. Thirty-nine? Who are you kidding? I've known her for 39 years.'"

Haddon's parents, Ruth and Rudy Stern, now live in St. Louis. "Going down there, I learned the people of St. Louis were very forgiving of any illustrious acts Harry may or may not have done," she says. "They were very excited in the seventh inning. They forced Harry to stand up and acknowledge them (at Busch Stadium) by their own cheers."

Bob Beck

Like Haddon, Bob Beck had a big edge in seniority over Caray in their connection to the Cubs. A lifelong fan who attended his first Cubs game in 1929, Beck is well into his third decade as a season ticket holder.

Beck welcomed Caray to the Cubs in 1982. Two years later, after the 1984 National League East title season, Beck joined scores of fans, Caray, Cubs management and players on a cruise. Daily bingo games netted a jackpot, which was to be distributed on the cruise's final day.

"Harry yells, 'Bingo!'" Beck recalls. "He walks up with his card, shakin' like a leaf like we all would be. He wins $2,400.

He buys everyone in the room—a lot of people—a drink. He put the rest in the tip jar for the cruise's crew members. That's the kind of guy he was."

Beck attended two 1989 events: Caray's Hall of Fame induction and his roast in Las Vegas. But another great memory took place in 1993 at Mile High Stadium in Denver, during the first season of the Colorado Rockies.

"In the top of the seventh inning, 70,000 people stood up and chanted, 'Harry, Harry!" Beck says. "He wasn't allowed to sing, but he waved. That was amazing."

Carmela Hartigan

Carmela Hartigan has kept her Cubs loyalty perhaps longer than any other fan. A longtime Wrigley Field bleachers patron, she's 96. Hartigan tells everyone she's 12 years older than the ballpark, and saw Bill Veeck plant the ivy. So she has earned her right to say anything she wants about Harry Caray.

"I heard him 1,000 times," Hartigan says. "I never met the man. The only time I ever got close to him I was about 10 feet away from him, but I couldn't get closer. He was announcing the game from the bleachers and I walked up there, but I couldn't get to him.

"To me, he was one of the best. He really could sing. Well, he thought he could sing anyway. And we sang along with him."

J. B. Hooker

A devoted baseball fan in his spare time working as program director of Chicago radio station WAIT-AM, J.B. Hooker especially treasures a 1995 Cubs scorecard in his possession. It is autographed, 'J.B.—Holy Cow! Harry Caray.'"

Hooker had gone to the strike-delayed Opening Day in '95 at Wrigley Field. Glum because of the strike, his mood changed when he encountered Harry being driven on his cart up the ramp to the press box.

"I'm absolutely going to frame that scorecard," Hooker says. "That whole game, I kept looking at it and Harry's autograph."

Part of Hooker's job is putting the best voices possible on the air. But Caray was the antithesis of that.

"I think it was his trademark," Hooker says of Caray's throat-clearing in his later years. "He could entertain a crowd at a game like no one else could. I don't think you'll see such a person who's not only a lovable guy, but also a character.

"The Cubs being the lovable losers that they were and Harry being the lovable announcer who would mispronounce names and sometimes get the facts wrong, all that became a whole package of great entertainment."

R.C. Baker

R.C. Baker, of Springfield, Missouri, has been a Harry Caray fan for as long as he can remember.

"Harry's the greatest," Baker says. "The best story about him I ever heard was the Cracker Jack tale. Cracker Jack was having its 100-year celebration and they say, 'What better place than Wrigley (Field) and the Cubs? Right? Harry even sings 'Take Me Out to the Ball Game' with Cracker Jack in it. It's part of the song.

"They have the sailor guy throwing out the first pitch as part of it. And then, without warning Harry or telling him, they bring the Cracker Jack board of directors into the broadcast booth. You know, 'Hello, Harry. This is the board of directors for Cracker Jack.'

"And Harry says, 'You know, you guys should be investigated'—and this is all live—'by Congress. You say you put those prizes in those boxes. Well, I know for a fact you don't. You should all go to jail. I think Congress should investigate you.'

"I think what happened is Harry was an orphan, and he saved up his pennies and bought a box of Cracker Jack and there was no prize in it. And it devastated him for life. He just went on and on. Steve Stone, being Mr. Polished Guy, tried getting in there and Steve said something like, 'I think some little boy didn't get his prize in his Cracker Jack.' Then Harry went off on Steve and said, 'I speak my mind. I'm not in any body's pocket.' He felt it was his public duty to warn the fans that there was a box that didn't have a prize. It was his chance to teach the company a lesson for hurting an orphan."

Jim Rygelski

St. Louis journalist Jim Rygelski grew up on the usual diet of Harry Caray baseball on KMOX-Radio. But he never met the man himself until late in the summer of 1997—just outside the Wrigley Field press box washroom, of all places.

Caray, renowned for his encyclopedic memory, told Rygelski, "I've met you somewhere before." Rygelski tugged on his earlobe. "Yes, we have. On the radio, Harry," he told Caray.

"We both laughed," Rygelski says. "The look in his eyes demonstrated to me that he was always on the side of the fans."

Caray's Cardinals calls of a generation and a half ago are still as clear as yesterday to Rygelski.

"I'll never forget when Joe Cunningham was batting one day," he says. "He was trying to sacrifice a runner into scoring position. Here's Harry: 'He bunts. Ohhh, terrible bunt. They're going to throw him out by 15 feet.' Then there was 30 seconds of silence. Either he was so steamed or he let that silence in there for effect."

Another time, in September 1963, Rygelski was sitting down the right-field line in the Busch Stadium grandstands. Stan Musial, then in his last days in the big leagues, hit a ball halfway up the screen attached to the right-field pavilion.

"Someone had a transistor radio nearby, and Harry said it hit the top of the screen. We all started laughing. We didn't mind if it was inaccurate. We all revered Caray. He did baseball on radio the best anyone has ever done it."

Rygelski theorizes that Caray's departure from St. Louis after the 1969 season came at just the right time for him.

"Harry's career went in the right direction when he came to Chicago," he says. "As an entertainer, he found his calling in the bigger city. I couldn't have seen him continuing as Cardinals announcer into the 1970s."

Jerry Pritikin

As the "Bleacher Preacher" and a lifelong Cubs fan growing up near Wrigley Field, Jerry Pritikin never knew he would get into a pickle with Harry Caray.

Living in San Francisco in 1985 before moving back to Chicago, Pritikin sent some kosher pickles up to the broadcast booth.

"Of course, the game was on and they weren't showing Harry eating them," Pritikin recalls, "but throughout the game Harry kept making these almost obscene sounds of 'Mmmmmmm' and going crazy about them. He kept going on and on.

"And after about a minute-and-a-half, Arne (Harris) wrote down on the screen, 'If you tuned in late, there is nothing wrong with your television. The sounds you hear are Harry falling in love with a kosher pickle."

Pritikin has listened to Caray since childhood.

"I'm 61 years old and I used to listen to Harry Caray on the radio at night with my brother, who was a Cardinals fan growing up in Chicago," he says. "We listened to him on KMOX

Jerry Pritikin with Harry Caray (*Photo courtesy of Jerry Pritikin*).

and his announcing was unbelievable. When he said he struck him out, I don't think we needed the microphone to hear him. He really was into the game. So I knew of Harry from 1946 on. I always liked Harry as an announcer. I might have been a subliminal Cardinals fan myself.

"I always was a Harry Caray fan, you might say. I enjoyed the things that he would say between pitches. When he would tell his stories you could tell he was in love with Musial or such. And Harry Caray was one of the first announcers who gave nicknames. Stan the Man. Harry the Hat Walker. And I'm almost certain these names were being given by Harry Caray. I listened because I was getting an education.

"Besides describing the game, he always described the atmosphere that was going on. He painted pictures of what was happening. He never lost interest and he always announced it like you were listening to baseball for the first time. It wasn't boring. Harry always kept you on your toes.

Even when Harry made mistakes you didn't mind it. You almost always knew what he meant to say.

"Years later, when Harry came out to the bleachers at Wrigley Field, it was always well loved. The fans ate it up and it was an experience baseball fans would enjoy, because it was like going to the game with your buddies."

Pritikin's father bought a television in '48. In those early days, three stations used to televise games.

"I almost broke my father's television. The cameras were located in different places. So I would switch stations because a left-handed hitter would look better on one station than the other. And in those days they didn't have those changers they have now.

"I was fortunate because I was able to hear what Rogers Hornsby would say, what Joe Wilson would have to say and what Jack Brickhouse was saying on WGN. And, at night, because the Cubs mostly played day games, I would listen to Harry Caray.

Pritikin also is an actor who had a role in the play "Bleacher Bums."

"Did you ever see the play? There wasn't an intermission. Instead, they had a seventh-inning stretch. And the people in the audience would stand up and sing 'Take Me Out to the Ball Game.'

"This has been said many times. Harry didn't have the greatest singing voice in the world. So that was the beauty of it. You didn't mind singing. And believe me, I don't even sound good in the shower. I sang 'Take Me Out to the Ball Game' every time I was at the ball park, which for a decade averaged 80 times a year."

Pritikin invoked Caray's name when he officially won over fans to the Cubs.

"I used to do conversions," he says. "The funniest thing about the conversions is if you were a Cardinals fan and I see you in a Cardinals hat, I would normally go up to the guy and say 'What other problems do you have?' They would always wind up admitting that, subliminally, they were Cubs fans.

"After a few Buds, I would do these conversions. What I would do is take a Cubs logo in my hand and say repeat after me, 'In the name of the father—Bill Veeck Sr.—and the son — Bill Veeck, Jr.—and the holy soul of Charlie Grimm, Holy Cow, you're now a Cubs fan and that allows you to stand up with Harry and sing "Take Me Out to the Ball Game" in the seventh.'

"People told me they would stand up in their house and sing 'Take Me Out to the Ball Game.' Harry mesmerized a lot of people."

Mark Stangl

Cardinals fan Mark Stangl's best memory of Caray was his call of the pennant-clincher on October 4, 1964 at old Busch Stadium.

"They won the pennant against the Mets when McCarver caught the foul pop," Stangl says. "I just thought that was the neatest thing I ever heard in terms of a call.

"It was a hard-fought game. The Cardinals were nip-and-tuck all the way. They hadn't taken control of the game until after about the sixth inning. It was 11-5. Gibson had just pitched his heart out and was basically drained. They bring in Barney Schultz to get the last out. I think (Ed) Kranepool was the batter. Harry just went nuts.

"One thing to remember is this was their first pennant in 18 years and their first under the brewery's

***Harry Caray with Bob Gibson** (Photo courtesy of Ted Patterson).*

ownership. So he was just unbelievably excited. And just the way he interviewed people afterward was something. I was 8 at the time."

Other Baseball Titles From Sports Publishing

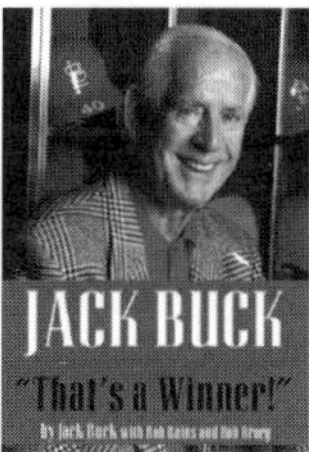

Jack Buck: "That's A Winner!" ($24.95)
by Jack Buck with Rob Rains and Bob Broeg

In his forthright and honest autobiography, Jack Buck will entertain all of his fans once more in a different setting. ***Jack Buck: "That's A Winner!"*** does more than entertain, however. It provides readers with an inside look at a man they have listened to so often they consider him part of the family. ***Jack Buck: "That's a Winner!"*** is the story of a remarkable man's life. A member of 11 Halls of Fame. Jack Buck is indeed a legend.

The Yankee Encyclopedia: Volume 3 ($39.95)
by Mark Gallagher

Who was the first manager of the Yankees? What year did the Yankees win their first World Series? Who pitched the shutout in Game 5 of the 1996 World Series? Who had the key hit in Game 4 of the 1996 World Series? These questions, along with hundreds more, are answered in ***The Yankee Encyclopedia: Volume 3.***

Chicago Cubs: Seasons at the Summit: The 50 Greatest Individual Seasons ($19.95)
by William Hageman and Warren Wilbert

From April 22, 1876 through today, more than 1,750 ballplayers have pulled on Cubs uniforms, and out of that number, coauthors Warren Wilbert and William Hageman have chosen players who have put together individual seasons of such magnificence that they have merited a top-50 billing. From Al Spalding to the Peerless Leader, Frank Chance and on to "Ole Pete" Alexander and Hack Wilson; Gabby Harnett and Billy Herman on to Ron Santo and "Let's Play Two" Ernie Banks; including the more recent past with Ryne Sandberg and Mark Grace, the famous and the not-so-famous are presented in rank order from number one through number 50.

All copies are autographed by authors William Hageman and Warren Wilbert

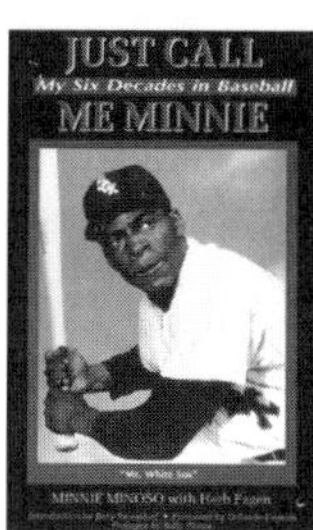

Just Call Me Minnie (19.95)
by Minnie Minoso with Herb Fagen

In ***Just Call Me Minnie***, Saturnino Orestes Arrieta Armas Minoso tells his story. The living drama of this six-decade baseball legend is told with a rare blend of candor, insight and honesty. Minnie says, "I want to finally open my heart. There are lots of things I haven't been able to say until now."

The Perfect Yankee ($22.95)
by Don Larsen with Mark Shaw

By all accounts, the no-hit, perfect game pitched by New York Yankee right-hander Don Larsen in the 1956 World Series qualifies as a true miracle. No one knows why it happened, or why an unlikely baseball player like Don Larsen was chosen to perform it. In ***The Perfect Yankee***, Larsen and coauthor Mark Shaw describe for the first time the facts surrounding one of the most famous games in baseball history.

Autographed copies (Larsen) are available by calling Sports Publishing at 1-800-327-5557.

Lou Boudreau: Covering All the Bases ($24.95)
by Lou Boudreau with Russell Schneider

Lou Boudreau: Covering All the Bases is the personal story of one of the most extraordinary men in baseball history. While leading the Cleveland Indians to a World Series victory in 1948, he invented the "Ted William's shift", and became the only player/manager ever to win the American League Most Valuable Player award. Boudreau tells about winning the 1944 American League Batting Championship with a hit in his final at-bat of the season, and how he became the youngest manager in baseball history at the age of 24. His illustrious playing career culminated in 1970, when he was voted into the Baseball Hall of Fame.

Available at your local bookstore, online at www.SportsPublishingInc.com, or by calling 1-800-327-5557